# BOB DYLAN

# Lyrics, 1962–1985

## Grafton

*An Imprint of* HarperCollins*Publishers*

Grafton
An Imprint of HarperCollins*Publishers*
77–85 Fulham Palace Road,
Hammersmith, London W6 8JB

Published by Grafton 1993
9 8 7 6 5 4 3 2 1

First published in Great Britain by
Jonathan Cape Ltd 1987

P:ublished by Paladin 1988
Reprinted twice

ISBN 0 586 08647 1

Set in Optima

Printed in Great Britain by
HarperCollinsManufacturing Glasgow

Bob Dylan was born in Duluth, Minnesota in 1941. He grew up in nearby Hibbing, a depressed mining town, and briefly attended the University of Minnesota before moving to New York, where he began a career as a songwriter and performer that has lasted more than 25 years. He is also the author of the experimental novel, *Tarantula*, and director/writer of the films *Renaldo and Clara* and *Eat the Document*.

**For Narette**

# Contents

# Bob Dylan

**Talking New York**
**Song to Woody**

early songs . . .

Hard Times in New York Town
Talking Bear Mountain Picnic Massacre Blues
Rambling, Gambling Willie
Standing on the Highway
Poor Boy Blues
Ballad for a Friend
Man on the Street
Talkin' John Birch Paranoid Blues
The Death of Emmett Till
Let Me Die in My Footsteps
Baby, I'm in the Mood for You
Long Ago, Far Away
Ain't Gonna Grieve
Gypsy Lou
Long Time Gone
Walkin' Down the Line
Train A-Travelin'
Ballad of Donald White
Last Thoughts on Woody Guthrie
Quit Your Low Down Ways
I'd Hate to Be You on That Dreadful Day
Mixed Up Confusion
Hero Blues
Tomorrow Is a Long Time
Bob Dylan's New Orleans Rag
All Over You
John Brown
Farewell

# Talking New York

Ramblin' outa the wild West,
Leavin' the towns I love the best.
Thought I'd seen some ups and downs,
'Til I come into New York town.
People goin' down to the ground,
Buildings goin' up to the sky.

Wintertime in New York town,
The wind blowin' snow around.
Walk around with nowhere to go,
Somebody could freeze right to the bone.
I froze right to the bone.
New York Times said it was the coldest winter in seventeen
    years;
I didn't feel so cold then.

I swung on to my old guitar,
Grabbed hold of a subway car,
And after a rocking, reeling, rolling ride,
I landed up on the downtown side;
Greenwich Village.

I walked down there and ended up
In one of them coffee-houses on the block.
Got on the stage to sing and play,
Man there said, 'Come back some other day,
You sound like a hillbilly;
We want folk singers here.'

Well, I got a harmonica job, begun to play,
Blowin' my lungs out for a dollar a day.
I blowed inside out and upside down.
The man there said he loved m' sound.

He was ravin' about how he loved m' sound;
Dollar a day's worth.

And after weeks and weeks of hangin' around,
I finally got a job in New York town,
In a bigger place, bigger money too.
Even joined the union and paid m' dues.

Now, a very great man once said
That some people rob you with a fountain pen.
It didn't take too long to find out
Just what he was talkin' about.
A lot of people don't have much food on their table,
But they got a lot of forks 'n' knives,
And they gotta cut somethin'.

So one mornin' when the sun was warm,
I rambled out of New York town.
Pulled my cap down over my eyes
And headed out for the western skies.
So long, New York.
Howdy, East Orange.

# Song to Woody

I'm out here a thousand miles from my home,
Walkin' a road other men have gone down.
I'm seein' your world of people and things,
Your paupers and peasants and princes and kings.

Hey, hey, Woody Guthrie, I wrote you a song
'Bout a funny ol' world that's a-comin' along.
Seems sick an' it's hungry, it's tired an' it's torn,
It looks like it's a-dyin' an' it's hardly been born.

Hey, Woody Guthrie, but I know that you know
All the things that I'm a-sayin' an' a-many times more.
I'm a-singin' you the song, but I can't sing enough,
'Cause there's not many men that done the things that you've
   done.

Here's to Cisco an' Sonny an' Leadbelly too,
An' to all the good people that traveled with you.
Here's to the hearts and the hands of the men
That come with the dust and are gone with the wind.

I'm a-leavin' tomorrow, but I could leave today,
Somewhere down the road someday.
The very last thing that I'd want to do
Is to say I've been hittin' some hard travelin' too.

# Hard Times in New York Town

Come you ladies and you gentlemen, a-listen to my song.
Sing it to you right, but you might think it's wrong.
Just a little glimpse of a story I'll tell
'Bout an East Coast city that you all know well.
It's hard times in the city,
Livin' down in New York town.

Old New York City is a friendly old town,
From Washington Heights to Harlem on down.
There's a-mighty many people all millin' all around,
They'll kick you when you're up and knock you when you're
    down.
It's hard times in the city,
Livin' down in New York town.

It's a mighty long ways from the Golden Gate
To Rockefeller Plaza 'n' the Empire State.
Mister Rockefeller sets up as high as a bird,
Old Mister Empire never says a word.
It's hard times from the country,
Livin' down in New York town.

Well, it's up in the mornin' tryin' to find a job of work.
Stand in one place till your feet begin to hurt.
If you got a lot o' money you can make yourself merry,
If you only got a nickel, it's the Staten Island Ferry.
And it's hard times in the city,
Livin' down in New York town.

Mister Hudson come a-sailin' down the stream
And old Mister Minuet paid for his dream.
Bought your city on a one-way track,
'F I had my way I'd sell it right back.

And it's hard times in the city,
Livin' down in New York town.

I'll take all the smog in Cal-i-for-ne-ay,
'N' every bit of dust in the Oklahoma plains,
'N' the dirt in the caves of the Rocky Mountain mines.
It's all much cleaner than the New York kind.
And it's hard times in the city,
Livin' down in New York town.

So all you newsy people, spread the news around,
You c'n listen to m' story, listen to m' song.
You c'n step on my name, you c'n try 'n' get me beat,
When I leave New York, I'll be standin' on my feet.
And it's hard times in the city,
Livin' down in New York town.

# Talking Bear Mountain
# Picnic Massacre Blues

I saw it advertised one day,
Bear Mountain picnic was comin' my way.
'Come along 'n' take a trip,
We'll bring you up there on a ship.
Bring the wife and kids.
Bring the whole family.'
Yippee!

Well, I run right down 'n' bought a ticket
To this Bear Mountain Picnic.
But little did I realize
I was in for a picnic surprise.
Had nothin' to do with mountains.
I didn't even come close to a bear.

Took the wife 'n' kids down to the pier,
Six thousand people there,
Everyone had a ticket for the trip.
'Oh well,' I said, 'it's a pretty big ship.
Besides, anyway, the more the merrier.'

Well, we all got on 'n' what d'ya think,
That big old boat started t' sink.
More people kept a-pilin' on,
That old ship was a-slowly goin' down.
Funny way t' start a picnic.

Well, I soon lost track of m' kids 'n' wife,
So many people there I never saw in m' life.
That old ship sinkin' down in the water,
Six thousand people tryin' t' kill each other,
Dogs a-barkin', cats a-meowin',
Women screamin', fists a-flyin', babies cryin',

17

Cops a-comin', me a-runnin'.
Maybe we just better call off the picnic.

I got shoved down 'n' pushed around,
All I could hear there was a screamin' sound.
Don't remember one thing more,
Just remember wakin' up on a little shore,
Head busted, stomach cracked,
Feet splintered, I was bald, naked . . .
Quite lucky to be alive though.

Feelin' like I climbed outa m' casket,
I grabbed back hold of m' picnic basket.
Took the wife 'n' kids 'n' started home,
Wishin' I'd never got up that morn.

Now, I don't care just what you do,
If you wanta have a picnic, that's up t' you.
But don't tell me about it, I don't wanta hear it,
'Cause, see, I just lost all m' picnic spirit.
Stay in m' kitchen, have m' own picnic . . .
In the bathroom.

Now, it don't seem to me quite so funny
What some people are gonna do f'r money.
There's a bran' new gimmick every day
Just t' take somebody's money away.
I think we oughta take some o' these people
And put 'em on a boat, send 'em up to Bear Mountain . . .
For a picnic.

18

# Rambling, Gambling Willie

Come around you rovin' gamblers and a story I will tell
About the greatest gambler, you all should know him well.
His name was Will O'Conley and he gambled all his life,
He had twenty-seven children, yet he never had a wife.
And it's ride, Willie, ride,
Roll, Willie, roll,
Wherever you are a-gamblin' now, nobody really knows.

He gambled in the White House and in the railroad yards,
Wherever there was people, there was Willie and his cards.
He had the reputation as the gamblin'est man around,
Wives would keep their husbands home when Willie came to
    town.
And it's ride, Willie, ride,
Roll, Willie, roll,
Wherever you are a-gamblin' now, nobody really knows.

Sailin' down the Mississippi to a town called New Orleans,
They're still talkin' about their card game on that Jackson River
    Queen.
'I've come to win some money,' Gamblin' Willie says,
When the game finally ended up, the whole damn boat was
    his.
And it's ride, Willie, ride,
Roll, Willie, roll,
Wherever you are a-gamblin' now, nobody really knows.

Up in the Rocky Mountains in a town called Cripple Creek,
There was an all-night poker game, lasted about a week.
Nine hundred miners had laid their money down,
When Willie finally left the room, he owned the whole damn
    town.
And it's ride, Willie, ride,
Roll, Willie, roll,
Wherever you are a-gamblin' now, nobody really knows.

But Willie had a heart of gold and this I know is true,
He supported all his children, and all their mothers too.
He wore no rings or fancy things, like other gamblers wore,
He spread his money far and wide, to help the sick and the poor.
And it's ride, Willie, ride,
Roll, Willie, roll,
Wherever you are a-gamblin' now, nobody really knows.

When you played your cards with Willie, you never really knew
Whether he was bluffin' or whether he was true.
He won a fortune from a man who folded in his chair.
The man, he left a diamond flush, Willie didn't even have a
    pair.
And it's ride, Willie, ride,
Roll, Willie, roll,
Wherever you are a-gamblin' now, nobody really knows.

It was late one evenin' during a poker game,
A man lost all his money, he said Willie was to blame.
He shot poor Willie through the head, which was a tragic fate,
When Willie's cards fell on the floor, they were aces backed
    with eights.
And it's ride, Willie, ride,
Roll, Willie, roll,
Wherever you are a-gamblin' now, nobody really knows.

So all you rovin' gamblers, wherever you might be,
The moral of the story is very plain to see.
Make your money while you can, before you have to stop.
For when you pull that dead man's hand, your gamblin' days
    are up.
And it's ride, Willie, ride,
Roll, Willie, roll,
Wherever you are a-gamblin' now, nobody really knows.

# Standing on the Highway

Well, I'm standin' on the highway
Tryin' to bum a ride, tryin' to bum a ride,
Tryin' to bum a ride.
Well, I'm standin' on the highway
Tryin' to bum a ride, tryin' to bum a ride,
Tryin' to bum a ride.
Nobody seem to know me'
Everybody pass me by.

Well, I'm standin' on the highway
Tryin' to hold up, tryin' to hold up,
Tryin' to hold up and be brave.
Well, I'm standin' on the highway
Tryin' to hold up, tryin' to hold up and be brave.
One road's goin' to the bright lights,
The other's goin' down to my grave.

Well, I'm lookin' down at two cards,
They seem to be handmade.
Well, I'm lookin' down at two cards,
They seem to be handmade.
One looks like it's the ace of diamonds,
The other looks like it is the ace of spades.

Well, I'm standin' on the highway
Watchin' my life roll by.
Well, I'm standin' on the highway
Watchin' my life roll by.
Well, I'm standin' on the highway
Tryin' to bum a ride.

Well, I'm standin' on the highway
Wonderin' where everybody went, wonderin' where
   everybody went,

Wonderin' where everybody went.
Well, I'm standin' on the highway
Wonderin' where everybody went, wonderin' where
    everybody went,
Wonderin' where everybody went.
Please mister, pick me up,
I swear I ain't gonna kill nobody's kids.

I wonder if my good gal,
I wonder if she knows I'm here,
Nobody else seems to know I'm here.
I wonder if my good gal,
I wonder if she knows I'm here,
Nobody else seems to know I'm here.
If she knows I'm here, Lawd,
I wonder if she said a prayer.

# Poor Boy Blues

Mm, tell mama,
Where'd ya sleep last night?
Cain't ya hear me cryin'?
Hm, hm, hm.

Hey, tell me baby,
What's the matter here?
Cain't ya hear me cryin'?
Hm, hm, hm.

Hey, stop you ol' train,
Let a poor boy ride.
Cain't ya hear me cryin'?
Hm, hm, hm.

Hey, Mister Bartender,
I swear I'm not too young.
Cain't ya hear me cryin'?
Hm, hm, hm.

Blow your whistle, policeman,
My poor feet are trained to run.
Cain't ya hear me cryin'?
Hm, hm, hm.

Long-distance operator,
I hear this phone call is on the house.
Cain't ya hear me cryin'?
Hm, hm, hm.

Ashes and diamonds,
The diff'rence I cain't see.
Cain't ya hear me cryin'?
Hm, hm, hm.

Mister Judge and Jury,
Cain't you see the shape I'm in?
Don't ya hear me cryin'?
Hm, hm, hm.

Mississippi River,
You a-runnin' too fast for me.
Cain't ya hear me cryin'?
Hm, hm, hm.

# Ballad for a Friend

Sad I'm a-sittin' on the railroad track,
Watchin' that old smokestack.
Train is a-leavin' but it won't be back.

Years ago we hung around,
Watchin' trains roll through the town.
Now that train is a-graveyard bound.

Where we go up in that North Country,
Lakes and streams and mines so free.
I had no better friend than he.

Something happened to him that day,
I thought I heard a stranger say.
I hung my head and stole away.

A diesel truck was rollin' slow,
Pullin' down a heavy load.
It left him on a Utah road.

They carried him back to his home town.
His mother cried, his sister moaned,
Listenin' to them church bells tone.

# Man on the Street

I'll sing you a song, ain't very long,
'Bout an old man who never done wrong.
How he died nobody can say,
They found him dead in the street one day.

Well, the crowd, they gathered one fine morn,
At the man whose clothes 'n' shoes were torn.
There on the sidewalk he did lay,
They stopped 'n' stared 'n' walked their way.

Well, the p'liceman come and he looked around,
'Get up, old man, or I'm a-takin' you down.'
He jabbed him once with his billy club
And the old man then rolled off the curb.

Well, he jabbed him again and loudly said,
'Call the wagon; this man is dead.'
The wagon come, they loaded him in,
I never saw the man again.

I've sung you my song, it ain't very long,
'Bout an old man who never done wrong.
How he died no one can say,
They found him dead in the street one day.

# Talkin' John Birch Paranoid Blues

Well, I was feelin' sad and feelin' blue,
I didn't know what in the world I wus gonna do.
Them Communists they wus comin' around,
They wus in the air,
They wus on the ground.
They wouldn't gimme no peace . . .

So I run down most hurriedly
And joined up with the John Birch Society.
I got me a secret membership card
And started off a-walkin' down the road.
Yee-hoo, I'm a real John Bircher now!
Look out you Commies!

Now we all agree with Hitler's views,
Although he killed six million Jews.
It don't matter too much that he was a Fascist,
At least you can't say he was a Communist!
That's to say like if you got a cold you take a shot of malaria.

Well, I wus lookin' everywhere for them gol-darned Reds.
I got up in the mornin' 'n' looked under my bed,
Looked in the sink, behind the door,
Looked in the glove compartment of my car.
Couldn't find 'em . . .

I wus lookin' high an' low for them Reds everywhere,
I wus lookin' in the sink an' underneath the chair.
I looked way up my chimney hole,
I even looked deep down inside my toilet bowl.
They got away . . .

Well, I wus sittin' home alone an' started to sweat,
Figured they wus in my TV set.

Peeked behind the picture frame,
Got a shock from my feet, hittin' right up in the brain.
Them Reds caused it!
I know they did . . . them hard-core ones.

Well, I quit my job so I could work all alone,
Then I changed my name to Sherlock Holmes.
Followed some clues from my detective bag
And discovered they wus red stripes on the American flag!
That ol' Betsy Ross . . .

Well, I investigated all the books in the library,
Ninety percent of 'em gotta be burned away.
I investigated all the people that I knowed,
Ninety-eight percent of them gotta go.
The other two percent are fellow Birchers . . . just like me.

Now Eisenhower, he's a Russian spy,
Lincoln, Jefferson and that Roosevelt guy.
To my knowledge there's just one man
That's really a true American: George Lincoln Rockwell.
I know for a fact he hates Commies cus he picketed the movie
    Exodus.

Well, I fin'ly started thinkin' straight
When I run outa things to investigate.
Couldn't imagine doin' anything else,
So now I'm sittin' home investigatin' myself!
Hope I don't find out anything . . . hmm, great God!

# The Death of Emmett Till

'Twas down in Mississippi not so long ago,
When a young boy from Chicago town stepped through a
    Southern door.
This boy's dreadful tragedy I can still remember well,
The color of his skin was black and his name was Emmett Till.

Some men they dragged him to a barn and there they beat him
    up.
They said they had a reason, but I can't remember what.
They tortured him and did some things too evil to repeat.
There were screaming sounds inside the barn, there was
    laughing sounds out on the street.

They they rolled his body down a gulf amidst a bloody red rain
And they threw him in the waters wide to cease his screaming
    pain.
The reason that they killed him there, and I'm sure it ain't no lie,
Was just for the fun of killin' him and to watch him slowly die.

And then to stop the United States of yelling for a trial,
Two brothers they confessed that they had killed poor Emmett
    Till.
But on the jury there were men who helped the brothers
    commit this awful crime,
And so this trial was a mockery, but nobody seemed to mind.

I saw the morning papers but I could not bear to see
The smiling brothers walkin' down the courthouse stairs.
For the jury found them innocent and the brothers they went
    free,
While Emmett's body floats the foam of a Jim Crow southern
    sea.

If you can't speak out against this kind of thing, a crime that's so
    unjust,
Your eyes are filled with dead men's dirt, your mind is filled
    with dust.
Your arms and legs they must be in shackles and chains, and
    your blood it must refuse to flow,
For you let this human race fall down so God-awful low!

This song is just a reminder to remind your fellow man
That this kind of thing still lives today in that ghost-robed Ku
    Klux Klan.
But if all of us folks that thinks alike, if we gave all we could
    give,
We could make this great land of ours a greater place to live.

# Let Me Die in My Footsteps

I will not go down under the ground
'Cause somebody tells me that death's comin' 'round
An' I will not carry myself down to die
When I go to my grave my head will be high.
Let me die in my footsteps
Before I go down under the ground.

There's been rumors of war and wars that have been
The meaning of life has been lost in the wind
And some people thinkin' that the end is close by
'Stead of learnin' to live they are learning to die.
Let me die in my footsteps
Before I go down under the ground.

I don't know if I'm smart but I think I can see
When someone is pullin' the wool over me
And if this war comes and death's all around
Let me die on this land 'fore I die underground.
Let me die in my footsteps
Before I go down under the ground.

There's always been people that have to cause fear
They've been talking of the war now for many long years
I have read all their statements and I've not said a word
But now Lawd God, let my poor voice be heard.
Let me die in my footsteps
Before I go down under the ground.

If I had rubies and riches and crowns
I'd buy the whole world and change things around
I'd throw all the guns and the tanks in the sea
For they are mistakes of a past history.
Let me die in my footsteps
Before I go down under the ground.

Let me drink from the waters where the mountain streams flood
Let the smell of wildflowers flow free through my blood
Let me sleep in your meadows with the green grassy leaves
Let me walk down the highway with my brother in peace.
Let me die in my footsteps
Before I go down under the ground.

Go out in your country where the land meets the sun
See the craters and the canyons where the waterfalls run
Nevada, New Mexico, Arizona, Idaho
Let every state in this union seep down deep in your souls.
And you'll die in your footsteps
Before you go down under the ground.

# Baby, I'm in the Mood for You

Sometimes I'm in the mood, I wanna leave my lonesome home
And sometimes I'm in the mood, I wanna hear my milk cow
  moan
And sometimes I'm in the mood, I wanna hit that highway road
But then again, but then again, I said oh, I said oh, I said
Oh babe, I'm in the mood for you.

Sometimes I'm in the mood, Lord, I had my overflowin' fill
Sometimes I'm in the mood, I'm gonna make out my final will
Sometimes I'm in the mood, I'm gonna head for the walkin' hill
But then again, but then again, I said oh, I said oh, I said
Oh babe, I'm in the mood for you.

Sometimes I'm in the mood, I wanna lay right down and die
Sometimes I'm in the mood, I wanna climb up to the sky
Sometimes I'm in the mood, I'm gonna laugh until I cry
But then again, I said again, I said again, I said
Oh babe, I'm in the mood for you.

Sometimes I'm in the mood, I'm gonna sleep in my pony's stall
Sometimes I'm in the mood, I ain't gonna do nothin' at all
Sometimes I'm in the mood, I wanna fly like a cannon ball
But then again, but then again, I said oh, I said oh, I said
Oh babe, I'm in the mood for you.

Sometimes I'm in the mood, I wanna back up against the wall
Sometimes I'm in the mood, I wanna run till I have to crawl
Sometimes I'm in the mood, I ain't gonna do nothin' at all
But then again, but then again, I said oh, I said oh, I said
Oh babe, I'm in the mood for you.

Sometimes I'm in the mood, I wanna change my house around
Sometimes I'm in the mood, I'm gonna make a change in this
  here town

Sometimes I'm in the mood, I'm gonna change the world
  around
But then again, but then again, I said oh, I said oh, I said
Oh babe, I'm in the mood for you.

# Long Ago, Far Away

To preach of peace and brotherhood,
Oh, what might be the cost!
A man he did it long ago
And they hung him on a cross.
Long ago, far away;
These things don't happen
No more, nowadays.

The chains of slaves
They dragged the ground
With heads and hearts hung low.
But it was during Lincoln's time
And it was long ago.
Long ago, far away;
Things like that don't happen
No more, nowadays.

The war guns they went off wild,
The whole world bled its blood.
Men's bodies floated on the edge
Of oceans made of mud.
Long ago, far away;
Those kind of things don't happen
No more, nowadays.

One man had much money,
One man had not enough to eat,
One man he lived just like a king,
The other man begged on the street.
Long ago, far away;
Things like that don't happen
No more, nowadays.

One man died of a knife so sharp,
One man died from the bullet of a gun,
One man died of a broken heart
To see the lynchin' of his son.
Long ago, far away;
Things like that don't happen
No more, nowadays.

Gladiators killed themselves,
It was during the Roman times.
People cheered with bloodshot grins
As eyes and minds went blind.
Long ago, far away;
Things like that don't happen
No more, nowadays.

And to talk of peace and brotherhood,
Oh, what might be the cost!
A man he did it long ago
And they hung him on a cross.
Long ago, far away;
Things like that don't happen
No more, nowadays, do they?

# Ain't Gonna Grieve

Well, I ain't a-gonna grieve no more, no more
Ain't a-gonna grieve no more, no more
Ain't a-gonna grieve no more, no more
And ain't a-gonna grieve no more.

Come on brothers, join the band,
Come on sisters, clap your hands.
Tell everybody that's in the land,
You ain't a-gonna grieve no more.

Well, I ain't a-gonna grieve no more, no more
Ain't a-gonna grieve no more, no more
Ain't a-gonna grieve no more, no more
And ain't a-gonna grieve no more.

Brown and blue and white and black,
All one color on the one-way track.
We got this far and ain't·a-goin' back
And I ain't a-gonna grieve no more.

Well, I ain't a-gonna grieve no more, no more
Ain't a-gonna grieve no more, no more
Ain't a-gonna grieve no more, no more
I ain't a-gonna grieve no more.

We're gonna notify your next of kin,
You're gonna raise the roof until the house falls in.
If you get knocked down get up again,
We ain't a-gonna grieve no more.

Well, I ain't a-gonna grieve no more, no more
Ain't a-gonna grieve no more, no more
Ain't a-gonna grieve no more, no more
I ain't a-gonna grieve no more.

We'll sing this song all night long,
Sing it to my baby from midnight on.
She'll sing it to you when I'm dead and gone,
Ain't a-gonna grieve no more.

Well, I ain't a-gonna grieve no more, no more
Ain't a-gonna grieve no more, no more
Ain't a-gonna grieve no more, no more
I ain't a-gonna grieve no more.

# Gypsy Lou

If you getcha one girl, better get two
Case you run into Gypsy Lou
She's a-ramblin' woman with a ramblin' mind
Always leavin' somebody behind.
Hey, 'round the bend
Gypsy Lou's gone again
Gypsy Lou's gone again.

Well, I seen the whole country through
Just to find Gypsy Lou
Seen it up, seen it down
Followin' Gypsy Lou around.
Hey, 'round the bend
Gypsy Lou's gone again
Gypsy Lou's gone again.

Well, I gotta stop and take some rest
My poor feet are second best
My poor feet are wearin' thin
Gypsy Lou's gone again.
Hey, gone again
Gypsy Lou's 'round the bend
Gypsy Lou's 'round the bend.

Well, seen her up in old Cheyenne
Turned my head and away she ran
From Denver Town to Wichita
Last I heard she's in Arkansas.
Hey, 'round the bend
Gypsy Lou's gone again
Gypsy Lou's gone again.

Well, I tell you what if you want to do
Tell you what, you'll wear out your shoes

If you want to wear out your shoes
Try and follow Gypsy Lou.
Hey, gone again
Gypsy Lou's 'round the bend
Gypsy Lou's 'round the bend.

Well, Gypsy Lou, I been told
Livin' down on Gallus Road
Gallus Road, Arlington
Moved away to Washington.
Hey, 'round the bend
Gypsy Lou's gone again
Gypsy Lou's gone again.

Well, I went down to Washington
Then she went to Oregon
I skipped the ground and hopped a train
She's back in Gallus Road again.
Hey, I can't win
Gypsy Lou's gone again
Gypsy Lou's gone again.

Well, the last I heard of Gypsy Lou
She's in a Memphis calaboose
She left one too many a boy behind
He committed suicide.
Hey, you can't win
Gypsy Lou's gone again
Gypsy Lou's gone again.

# Long Time Gone

My parents raised me tenderly,
I was their only son.
My mind got mixed with ramblin'
When I was all so young,
And I left my home the first time
When I was twelve and one.
I'm a long time a-comin', Maw,
An' I'll be a long time gone.

On the western side of Texas,
On the Texas plains,
I tried to find a job o' work
But they said I's young of age.
My eyes they burned when I heard,
'Go home where you belong!'
I'm a long time a-comin'
An' I'll be a long time gone.

I remember when I's ramblin'
Around with the carnival trains,
Different towns, different people,
Somehow they're all the same.
I remember children's faces best,
I remember travelin' on.
I'm a long time a-comin',
I'll be a long time gone.

I once loved a fair young maid
An' I ain't too big to tell,
If she broke my heart a single time,
She broke it ten or twelve.
I walked and talked all by myself,
I did not tell no one.

I'm a long time a-comin', babe,
An' I'll be a long time gone.

Many times by the highwayside,
I tried to flag a ride.
With bloodshot eyes and gritting teeth,
I'd watch the cars roll by.
The empty air hung in my head
I's thinkin' all day long.
I'm a long time a-comin',
I'll be a long time gone.

You might see me on your crossroads
When I'm a-passin' through.
Remember me how you wished to
As I'm a-driftin' from your view.
I ain't got the time to think about it,
I got too much to get done.
Well, I'm a long time comin'
An' I'll be a long time gone.

If I can't help somebody
With a word or song,
If I can't show somebody
They are travelin' wrong.
But I know I ain't no prophet
An' I ain't no prophet's son.
I'm just a long time a-comin'
An' I'll be a long time gone.

So you can have your beauty,
It's skin deep and it only lies.
And you can have your youth,
It'll rot before your eyes.

Just give to me my gravestone
With it clearly carved upon:
'I's a long time a-comin'
An' I'll be a long time gone.'

# Walkin' Down the Line

Well, I'm walkin' down the line,
I'm walkin' down the line
An' I'm walkin' down the line.
My feet'll be a-flyin'
To tell about my troubled mind.

I got a heavy-headed gal
I got a heavy-headed gal
I got a heavy-headed gal
She ain't a-feelin' well
When she's better only time will tell

Well, I'm walkin' down the line,
I'm walkin' down the line
An' I'm walkin' down the line.
My feet'll be a-flyin'
To tell about my troubled mind.

My money comes and goes
My money comes and goes
My money comes and goes
And rolls and flows and rolls and flows
Through the holes in the pockets in my clothes

Well, I'm walkin' down the line,
I'm walkin' down the line
An' I'm walkin' down the line.
My feet'll be a-flyin'
To tell about my troubled mind.

I see the morning light
I see the morning light
Well, it's not because

I'm an early riser
I didn't go to sleep last night

Well, I'm walkin' down the line,
I'm walkin' down the line
An' I'm walkin' down the line.
My feet'll be a-flyin'
To tell about my troubled mind.

I got my walkin' shoes
I got my walkin' shoes
I got my walkin' shoes
An' I ain't a-gonna lose
I believe I got the walkin' blues

Well, I'm walkin' down the line,
I'm walkin' down the line
An' I'm walkin' down the line.
My feet'll be a-flyin'
To tell about my troubled mind.

# Train A-Travelin'

There's an iron train a-travelin' that's been a-rollin' through the
  years,
With a firebox of hatred and a furnace full of fears.
If you ever heard its sound or seen its blood-red broken frame,
Then you heard my voice a-singin' and you know my name.

Did you ever stop to wonder 'bout the hatred that it holds?
Did you ever see its passengers, its crazy mixed-up souls?
Did you ever start a-thinkin' that you gotta stop that train?
Then you heard my voice a-singin' and you know my name.

Do you ever get tired of the preachin' sounds of fear
When they're hammered at your head and pounded in your
  ear?
Have you ever asked about it and not been answered plain?
Then you heard my voice a-singin' and you know my name.

I'm a-wonderin' if the leaders of the nations understand
This murder-minded world that they're leavin' in my hands.
Have you ever laid awake at night and wondered 'bout the
  same?
Then you've heard my voice a-singin' and you know my name.

Have you ever had it on your lips or said it in your head
That the person standin' next to you just might be misled?
Does the raving of the maniacs make your insides go insane?
Then you've heard my voice a-singin' and you know my name.

Do the kill-crazy bandits and the haters get you down?
Does the preachin' and the politics spin your head around?
Does the burning of the buses give your heart a pain?
Then you've heard my voice a-singin' and you know my name.

# Ballad of Donald White

My name is Donald White, you see,
I stand before you all.
I was judged by you a murderer
And the hangman's knot must fall.
I will die upon the gallows pole
When the moon is shining clear,
And these are my final words
That you will ever hear.

I left my home in Kansas
When I was very young.
I landed in the old Northwest,
Seattle, Washington.
Although I'd a-traveled many miles,
I never made a friend,
For I could never get along in life
With people that I met.

If I had some education
To give me a decent start,
I might have been a doctor or
A master in the arts.
But I used my hands for stealing
When I was very young,
And they locked me down in jailhouse cells,
That's how my life begun.

Oh, the inmates and the prisoners,
I found they were my kind,
And it was there inside the bars
I found my peace of mind.
But the jails they were too crowded,
Institutions overflowed,

So they turned me loose to walk upon
Life's hurried tangled road.

And there's danger on the ocean
Where the salt sea waves split high,
And there's danger on the battlefield
Where the shells of bullets fly,
And there's danger in this open world
Where men strive to be free,
And for me the greatest danger
Was in society.

So I asked them to send me back
To the institution home.
But they said they were too crowded,
For me they had no room.
I got down on my knees and begged,
'Oh, please put me away,'
But they would not listen to my plea
Or nothing I would say.

And so it was on Christmas eve
In the year of '59,
It was on that night I killed a man,
I did not try to hide.
The jury found me guilty
And I won't disagree,
For I knew that it would happen
If I wasn't put away.

And I'm glad I've had no parents
To care for me or cry,
For now they will never know
The horrible death I die.

And I'm also glad I've had no friends
To see me in disgrace,
For they'll never see that hangman's hood
Wrap around my face.

Farewell unto the old north woods
Of which I used to roam,
Farewell unto the crowded bars
Of which've been my home,
Farewell to all you people
Who think the worst of me,
I guess you'll feel much better when
I'm on that hanging tree.

But there's just one question
Before they kill me dead,
I'm wondering just how much
To you I really said
Concerning all the boys that come
Down a road like me,
Are they enemies or victims
Of your society?

# Last Thoughts on Woody Guthrie

When yer head gets twisted and yer mind grows numb
When you think you're too old, too young, too smart or too
    dumb
When yer laggin' behind an' losin' yer pace
In a slow-motion crawl or life's busy race
No matter what yer doing if you start givin' up
If the wine don't come to the top of yer cup
If the wind's got you sideways with one hand holdin' on
And the other starts slipping and the feeling is gone
And yer train engine fire needs a new spark to catch it
And the wood's easy findin' but yer lazy to fetch it
And yer sidewalk starts curlin' and the street gets too long
And you start walkin' backwards though you know that it's
    wrong
And lonesome comes up as down goes the day
And tomorrow's mornin' seems so far away
And you feel the reins from yer pony are slippin'
And yer rope is a-slidin' 'cause yer hands are a-drippin'
And yer sun-decked desert and evergreen valleys
Turn to broken down slums and trash-can alleys
And yer sky cries water and yer drain pipe's a-pourin'
And the lightnin's a-flashing and the thunder's a-crashin'
And the windows are rattlin' and breakin' and the roof tops a-
    shakin'
And yer whole world's a-slammin' and bangin'
And yer minutes of sun turn to hours of storm
And to yourself you sometimes say
'I never knew it was gonna be this way
Why didn't they tell me the day I was born'
And you start gettin' chills and yer jumping from sweat
And you're lookin' for somethin' you ain't quite found yet
And yer knee-deep in dark water with yer hands in the air
And the whole world's a-watchin' with a window-peek stare
And yer good gal leaves and she's long gone a-flying
And yer heart feels sick like fish when they're fryin'

And yer jackhammer falls from yer hands to yer feet
And you need it badly but it lays on the street
And yer bell's bangin' loudly but you can't hear its beat
And you think yer ears might a been hurt
Or yer eyes've turned filthy from the sight-blindin' dirt
And you figured you failed in yesterday's rush
When you were faked out an' fooled while facing a four flush
And all the time you were holdin' three queens
And it's makin' you mad, it's makin' you mean
Like in the middle of Life magazine
Bouncin' around a pinball machine
And there's something on yer mind that you wanna be saying
that somebody someplace oughta be hearin'
But it's trapped on yer tongue and sealed in yer head
And it bothers you badly when you're layin' in bed
And no matter how you try you just can't say it
And yer scared to yer soul you just might forget it
And yer eyes get swimmy from the tears in yer head
And yer pillows of feathers turn to blankets of lead
And the lion's mouth opens and yer staring at his teeth
And his jaws start closin' with you underneath
And yer flat on yer belly with yer hands tied behind
And you wish you'd never taken that last detour sign
And you say to yerself just what am I doin'
On this road I'm walkin', on this trail I'm turnin'
On this curve I'm hanging
On this pathway I'm strolling, in the space I'm taking
In this air I'm inhaling
Am I mixed up too much, am I mixed up too hard
Why am I walking, where am I running
What am I saying, what am I knowing
On this guitar I'm playing, on this banjo I'm frailin'
On this mandolin I'm strummin', in the song I'm singin'
In the tune I'm hummin', in the words that I'm writin'

In the words that I'm thinkin'
In this ocean of hours I'm all the time drinkin'
Who am I helping, what am I breaking
What am I giving, what am I taking
But you try with yer whole soul best
Never to think these thoughts and never to let
Them kind of thoughts gain ground
Or make yer heart pound
But then again you know why they're around
Just waiting for a chance to slip and drop down
'Cause sometime you hear 'em when the night time comes
    creeping
And you fear that they might catch you a-sleeping
And you jump from yer bed, from yer last chapter of dreamin'
And you can't remember for the best of yer thinking
If that was you in the dream that was screaming
And you know that it's somethin' special you're needin'
And you know that there's no drug that'll do for the healin'
And no liquor in the land to stop yer brain from bleeding
And you need something special
Yeah, you need something special all right
You need a fast flyin' train on a tornado track
To shoot you someplace and shoot you back
You need a cyclone wind on a steam engine howler
That's been banging and booming and blowing forever
That knows yer troubles a hundred times over
You need a Greyhound bus that don't bar no race
That won't laugh at yer looks
Your voice or your face
And by any number of bets in the book
Will be rollin' long after the bubblegum craze
You need something to open up a new door
To show you something you seen before
But overlooked a hundred times or more

53

You need something to open yer eyes
You need something to make it known
That it's you and no one else that owns
That spot that yer standing, that space that you're sitting
That the world ain't got you beat
That it ain't got you licked
It can't get you crazy no matter how many
Times you might get kicked
You need something special all right
You need something special to give you hope
But hope's just a word
That maybe you said or maybe you heard
On some windy corner 'round a wide-angled curve

But that's what you need man, and you need it bad
And yer trouble is you know it too good
'Cause you look an' you start getting the chills

'Cause you can't find it on a dollar bill
And it ain't on Macy's window sill
And it ain't on no rich kid's road map
And it ain't no fat kid's fraternity house
And it ain't made in no Hollywood wheat germ
And it ain't on that dimlit stage
With that half-wit comedian on it
Ranting and raving and taking yer money
And you think it's funny
No you can't find it in no night club or no yacht club
And it ain't in the seats of a supper club
And sure as hell you're bound to tell
That no matter how hard you rub
You just ain't a-gonna find it on yer ticket stub
No, and it ain't in the rumors people're tellin' you
And it ain't in the pimple-lotion people are sellin' you

And it ain't in no cardboard-box house
Or down any movie star's blouse
And you can't find it on the golf course
And Uncle Remus can't tell you and neither can Santa Claus
And it ain't in the cream puff hair-do or cotton candy clothes
And it ain't in the dime store dummies or bubblegum goons
And it ain't in the marshmallow noises of the chocolate cake
    voices
That come knockin' and tappin' in Christmas wrappin'
Sayin' ain't I pretty and ain't I cute and look at my skin
Look at my skin shine, look at my skin glow
Look at my skin laugh, look at my skin cry
When you can't even sense if they got any insides
These people so pretty in their ribbons and bows
No you'll not now or no other day
Find it on the doorsteps made out-a paper maché
And inside it the people made of molasses
That every other day buy a new pair of sunglasses
And it ain't in the fifty-star generals and flipped-out phonies
Who'd turn yuh in for a tenth of a penny
Who breathe and burp and bend and crack
And before you can count from one to ten
Do it all over again but this time behind yer back
My friend
The ones that wheel and deal and whirl and twirl
And play games with each other in their sand-box world
And you can't find it either in the no-talent fools
That run around gallant
And make all rules for the ones that got talent
And it ain't in the ones that ain't got any talent but think they do
And think they're foolin' you
The ones who jump on the wagon
Just for a while' cause they know it's in style
To get their kicks, get out of it quick

And make all kinds of money and chicks
And you yell to yourself and you throw down yer hat
Sayin', 'Christ do I gotta be like that
Ain't there no one here that knows where I'm at
Ain't there no one here that knows how I feel
Good God Almighty
                    THAT STUFF AIN'T REAL'

No but that ain't yer game, it ain't even yer race
You can't hear yer name, you can't see yer face
You gotta look some other place
And where do you look for this hope that yer seekin'
Where do you look for this lamp that's a-burnin'
Where do you look for this oil well gushin'
Where do you look for this candle that's glowin'
Where do you look for this hope that you know is there
And out there somewhere
And your feet can only walk down two kinds of roads
Your eyes can only look through two kinds of windows
Your nose can only smell two kinds of hallways
You can touch and twist
And turn two kinds of doorknobs
You can either go to the church of your choice
Or you can go to Brooklyn State Hospital
You'll find God in the church of your choice
You'll find Woody Guthrie in Brooklyn State Hospital

And though it's only my opinion
I may be right or wrong
You'll find them both
In the Grand Canyon
At sundown

# Quit Your Low Down Ways

Oh, you can read out your Bible,
You can fall down on your knees, pretty mama,
And pray to the Lord
But it ain't gonna do no good.

You're gonna need
You're gonna need my help someday
Well, if you can't quit your sinnin'
Please quit your low down ways.

Well, you can run down to the White House,
You can gaze at the Capitol Dome, pretty mama,
You can pound on the President's gate
But you oughta know by now it's gonna be too late.

You're gonna need
You're gonna need my help someday
Well, if you can't quit your sinnin'
Please quit your low down ways.

Well, you can run down to the desert,
Throw yourself on the burning sand.
You can raise up your right hand, pretty mama,
But you better understand you done lost your one good man.

You're gonna need
You're gonna need my help someday
Well, if you can't quit your sinnin'
Please quit your low down ways.

And you can hitchhike on the highway,
You can stand all alone by the side of the road.
You can try to flag a ride back home, pretty mama,
But you can't ride in my car no more.

You're gonna need
You're gonna need my help someday
Well, if you can't quit your sinnin'
Please quit your low down ways.

Oh, you can read out your Bible,
You can fall down on your knees, pretty mama,
And pray to the Lord
But it ain't gonna do no good.

You're gonna need
You're gonna need my help someday
Well, if you can't quit your sinnin'
Please quit your low down ways.

# I'd Hate to Be You
# on That Dreadful Day

Well, your clock is gonna stop
At Saint Peter's gate.
Ya gonna ask him what time it is,
He's gonna say, 'It's too late.'
Hey, hey!
I'd sure hate to be you
On that dreadful day.

You're gonna start to sweat
And you ain't gonna stop.
You're gonna have a nightmare
And never wake up.
Hey, hey, hey!
I'd sure hate to be you
On that dreadful day.

You're gonna cry for pills
And your head's gonna be in a knot,
But the pills are gonna cost more
Than what you've got.
Hey, hey!
I'd sure hate to be you
On that dreadful day.

You're gonna have to walk naked,
Can't ride in no car.
You're gonna let ev'rybody see
Just what you are.
Hey, hey!
I'd sure hate to be you
On that dreadful day.

Well, the good wine's a-flowin'
For five cents a quart.

You're gonna look in your moneybags
And find you're one cent short.
Hey, hey, hey!
I'd sure hate to be you
On that dreadful day.

You're gonna yell and scream,
'Don't anybody care?'
You're gonna hear out a voice say,
'Shoulda listened when you heard
   the word down there.'
Hey, hey!
I'd sure hate to be you
On that dreadful day.

# Mixed Up Confusion

I got mixed up confusion
Man, it's a-killin' me

Well, there's too many people
And they're all too hard to please

Well, my hat's in my hand
Babe, I'm walkin' down the line

An' I'm lookin' for a woman
Whose head's mixed up like mine

Well, my head's full of questions
My temp'rature's risin' fast

Well, I'm lookin' for some answers
But I don't know who to ask

But I'm walkin' and wonderin'
And my poor feet don't ever stop

Seein' my reflection
I'm hung over, hung down, hung up!

# Hero Blues

Yes, the gal I got
I swear she's the screaming end
She wants me to be a hero
So she can tell all her friends

Well, she begged, she cried
She pleaded with me all last night
Well, she begged, she cried
She pleaded with me all last night
She wants me to go out
And find somebody to fight

She reads too many books
She got new movies inside her head
She reads too many books
She got movies inside her head
She wants me to walk out running
She wants me to crawl back dead

You need a different kinda man, babe
One that can grab and hold your heart
Need a different kind of man, babe
One that can hold and grab your heart
You need a different kind of man, babe
You need Napoleon Boneeparte

Well, when I'm dead
No more good times will I crave
When I'm dead
No more good times will I crave
You can stand and shout hero
All over my lonesome grave

# Tomorrow Is a Long Time

If today was not an endless highway,
If tonight was not a crooked trail,
If tomorrow wasn't such a long time,
Then lonesome would mean nothing to you at all.
Yes, and only if my own true love was waitin',
Yes, and if I could hear her heart a-softly poundin',
Only if she was lyin' by me,
Then I'd lie in my bed once again.

I can't see my reflection in the waters,
I can't speak the sounds that show no pain,
I can't hear the echo of my footsteps,
Or can't remember the sound of my own name.
Yes, and only if my own true love was waitin',
Yes, and if I could hear her heart a-softly poundin',
Only if she was lyin' by me,
Then I'd lie in my bed once again.

There's beauty in the silver, singin' river,
There's beauty in the sunrise in the sky,
But none of these and nothing else can touch the beauty
That I remember in my true love's eyes.
Yes, and only if my own true love was waitin',
Yes, and if I could hear her heart a-softly poundin',
Only if she was lyin' by me,
Then I'd lie in my bed once again.

# Bob Dylan's New Orleans Rag

I was sittin' on a stump
Down in New Orleans,
I was feelin' kinda low down,
Dirty and mean.
Along came a fella
And he didn't even ask.
He says, 'I know of a woman
That can fix you up fast.'
I didn't think twice,
I said like I should,
'Let's go find this lady
That can do me some good.'
We walked across the river
On a sailin' spree
And we came to a door
Called one-oh-three.

I was just about ready
To give it a little knock
When out comes a fella
Who couldn't even walk.
He's linkin' and a-slinkin',
Couldn't stand on his feet,
And he moaned and he groaned
And he shuffled down the street.
Well, out of the door
There comes another man.
He wiggled and he wobbled,
He couldn't hardly stand.
He had this frightened
Look in his eyes,
Like he just fought a bear,
He was ready to die.

Well, I peeked through the key crack,
Comin' down the hall
Was a long-legged man
Who couldn't hardly crawl.
He muttered and he uttered
In broken French,
And he looked like he'd been through
A monkey wrench.

Well, by this time
I was a-scared to knock,
I was a-scared to move,
I's in a state of shock.
I hummed a little tune
And I shuffled my feet
And I started walkin' backwards
Down that broad street.
Well, I got to the corner,
I tried my best to smile.
I turned around the corner
And I ran a bloody mile.
Man, I wasn't runnin'
'Cause I was sick,
I was just a-runnin'
To get out of there quick.

Well, I tripped right along
And I'm a-wheezin' in my chest.
I musta run a mile
In a minute or less.
I walked on a log
And I tripped on a stump,
I caught a fast freight
With a one-arm jump.

So, if you're travelin' down
Louisiana way,
And you feel kinda lonesome
And you need a place to stay,
Man, you're better off
In your misery
Than to tackle that lady
At one-oh-three.

# All Over You

Well, if I had to do it all over again,
Babe, I'd do it all over you.
And if I had to wait for ten thousand years,
Babe, I'd even do that too.
Well, a dog's got his bone in the alley,
A cat, she's got nine lives,
A millionaire's got a million dollars,
King Saud's got four hundred wives.
Well, ev'rybody's got somethin'
That they're lookin' forward to.
I'm lookin' forward to when I can do it all again
And babe, I'll do it all over you.

Well, if I had my way tomorrow or today,
Babe, I'd run circles all around.
I'd jump up in the wind, do a somersault and spin,
I'd even dance a jig on the ground.
Well, everybody gets their hour,
Everybody gets their time,
Little David when he picked up his pebbles,
Even Sampson after he went blind.
Well, everybody gets their chance
To do what they want to do.
When my time arrives you better run for your life
'Cause babe, I'll do it all over you.

Well, I don't need no money, I just need a day that's sunny,
Baby, and my days are gonna come.
And I grab me a pint, you know that I'm a giant
When you hear me yellin', 'Fee-fi-fo-fum.'
Well, you cut me like a jigsaw puzzle,
You made me to a walkin' wreck,
Then you pushed my heart through my backbone,
Then you knocked off my head from my neck.

Well, if I'm ever standin' steady
A-doin' what I want to do,
Well, I tell you little lover that you better run for cover
'Cause babe, I'll do it all over you.

I'm just restin' at your gate so that I won't be late
And, momma, I'm a-just sittin' on the shelf.
Look out your window fair and you'll see me squattin' there
Just a-fumblin' and a-mumblin' to myself.
Well, after my cigarette's been smoked up,
After all my liquor's been drunk,
After my dreams are dreamed out,
After all my thoughts have been thunk,
Well, after I do some of these things,
I'm gonna do what I have to do.
And I tell you on the side, that you better run and hide
'Cause babe, I'll do it all over you.

# John Brown

John Brown went off to war to fight on a foreign shore.
His mama sure was proud of him!
He stood straight and tall in his uniform and all.
His mama's face broke out all in a grin.

'Oh son, you look so fine, I'm glad you're a son of mine,
You make me proud to know you hold a gun.
Do what the captain says, lots of medals you will get,
And we'll put them on the wall when you come home.'

As that old train pulled out, John's ma began to shout,
Tellin' ev'ryone in the neighborhood:
'That's my son that's about to go, he's a soldier now, you
    know.'
She made well sure her neighbors understood.

She got a letter once in a while and her face broke into a smile
As she showed them to the people from next door.
And she bragged about her son with his uniform and gun,
And these things you called a good old-fashioned war.

Oh! Good old-fashioned war!

Then the letters ceased to come, for a long time they did not
    come.
They ceased to come for about ten months or more.
Then a letter finally came saying, 'Go down and meet the train.
Your son's a-coming home from the war.'

She smiled and went right down, she looked everywhere
    around
But she could not see her soldier son in sight.
But as all the people passed, she saw her son at last,
When she did she could hardly believe her eyes.

Oh his face was all shot up and his hand was all blown off
And he wore a metal brace around his waist.
He whispered kind of slow, in a voice she did not know,
While she couldn't even recognize his face!

Oh! Lord! Not even recognize his face.

'Oh tell me, my darling son, pray tell me what they done.
How is it you come to be this way?'
He tried his best to talk but his mouth could hardly move
And the mother had to turn her face away.

'Don't you remember, Ma, when I went off to war
You thought it was the best thing I could do?
I was on the battleground, you were home . . . acting proud.
You wasn't there standing in my shoes.

'Oh, and I thought when I was there, God, what am I doing
     here?
I'm a-tryin' to kill somebody or die tryin'.
But the thing that scared me most was when my enemy came
     close
And I saw that his face looked just like mine.'

Oh! Lord! Just like mine!

'And I couldn't help but think, through the thunder rolling and
     stink,
That I was just a puppet in a play.
And through the roar and smoke, this string is finally broke,
And a cannon ball blew my eyes away.'

As he turned away to walk, his Ma was still in shock
At seein' the metal brace that helped him stand.

But as he turned to go, he called his mother close
And he dropped his medals down into her hand.

# Farewell

Oh it's fare thee well my darlin' true,
I'm leavin' in the first hour of the morn.
I'm bound off for the bay of Mexico
Or maybe the coast of Californ.
So it's fare thee well my own true love,
We'll meet another day, another time.
It ain't the leavin'
That's a-grievin' me
But my true love who's bound to stay behind.

Oh the weather is against me and the wind blows hard
And the rain she's a-turnin' into hail.
I still might strike it lucky on a highway goin' west,
Though I'm travelin' on a path beaten trail.
So it's fare thee well my own true love,
We'll meet another day, another time.
It ain't the leavin'
That's a-grievin' me
But my true love who's bound to stay behind.

I will write you a letter from time to time,
As I'm ramblin' you can travel with me too.
With my head, my heart and my hands, my love,
I will send what I learn back home to you.
So it's fare thee well my own true love,
We'll meet another day, another time.
It ain't the leavin'
That's a-grievin' me
But my true love who's bound to stay behind.

I will tell you of the laughter and of troubles,
Be them somebody else's or my own.
With my hands in my pockets and my coat collar high,
I will travel unnoticed and unknown.

So it's fare thee well my own true love,
We'll meet another day, another time.
It ain't the leavin'
That's a-grievin' me
But my true love who's bound to stay behind.

I've heard tell of a town where I might as well be bound,
It's down around the old Mexican plains.
They say that the people are all friendly there
And all they ask of you is your name.
So it's fare thee well my own true love,
We'll meet another day, another time.
It ain't the leavin'
That's a-grievin' me
But my true love who's bound to stay behind.

# The Freewheelin' Bob Dylan

**Blowin' in the Wind**
**Girl of the North Country**
**Down the Highway**
**Masters of War**
**Bob Dylan's Blues**
**A Hard Rain's A-Gonna Fall**
**Don't Think Twice, It's All Right**
**Bob Dylan's Dream**
**Oxford Town**
**Talkin' World War III Blues**
**Corrina, Corrina**
**Honey, Just Allow Me One More Chance**
**I Shall Be Free**

My Life in a Stolen Moment
Whatcha Gonna Do
Walls of Red Wing
Who Killed Davey Moore?
Seven Curses
Joan Baez in Concert, Part 2 (jacket notes)
Dusty Old Fairgrounds

# Blowin' in the Wind

How many roads must a man walk down
Before you call him a man?
Yes, 'n' how many seas must a white dove sail
Before she sleeps in the sand?
Yes, 'n' how many times must the cannon balls fly
Before they're forever banned?
The answer, my friend, is blowin' in the wind,
The answer is blowin' in the wind.

How many times must a man look up
Before he can see the sky?
Yes, 'n' how many ears must one man have
Before he can hear people cry?
Yes, 'n' how many deaths will it take till he knows
That too many people have died?
The answer, my friend, is blowin' in the wind,
The answer is blowin' in the wind.

How many years can a mountain exist
Before it's washed to the sea?
Yes, 'n' how many years can some people exist
Before they're allowed to be free?
Yes, 'n' how many times can a man turn his head,
Pretending he just doesn't see?
The answer, my friend, is blowin' in the wind,
The answer is blowin' in the wind.

# Girl of the North Country

Well, if you're travelin' in the north country fair,
Where the winds hit heavy on the borderline,
Remember me to one who lives there.
She once was a true love of mine.

Well, if you go when the snowflakes storm,
When the rivers freeze and summer ends,
Please see if she's wearing a coat so warm,
To keep her from the howlin' winds.

Please see for me if her hair hangs long,
If it rolls and flows all down her breast.
Please see for me if her hair hangs long,
That's the way I remember her best.

I'm a-wonderin' if she remembers me at all.
Many times I've often prayed
In the darkness of my night,
In the brightness of my day.

So if you're travelin' in the north country fair,
Where the winds hit heavy on the borderline,
Remember me to one who lives there.
She once was a true love of mine.

# Down the Highway

Well, I'm walkin' down the highway
With my suitcase in my hand.
Yes, I'm walkin' down the highway
With my suitcase in my hand.
Lord, I really miss my baby,
She's in some far-off land.

Well, your streets are gettin' empty,
Lord, your highway's gettin' filled.
And your streets are gettin' empty
And your highway's gettin' filled.
Well, the way I love that woman,
I swear it's bound to get me killed.

Well, I been gamblin' so long,
Lord, I ain't got much more to lose.
Yes, I been gamblin' so long,
Lord, I ain't got much more to lose.
Right now I'm havin' trouble,
Please don't take away my highway shoes.

Well, I'm bound to get lucky, baby,
Or I'm bound to die tryin'.
Yes, I'm a-bound to get lucky, baby,
Lord, Lord I'm a-bound to die tryin'.
Well, meet me in the middle of the ocean
And we'll leave this ol' highway behind.

Well, the ocean took my baby,
My baby stole my heart from me.
Yes, the ocean took my baby,
My baby took my heart from me.
She packed it all up in a suitcase,
Lord, she took it away to Italy, Italy.

So, I'm a-walkin' down your highway
Just as far as my poor eyes can see.
Yes, I'm a-walkin' down your highway
Just as far as my eyes can see.
From the Golden Gate Bridge
All the way to the Statue of Liberty.

# Masters of War

Come you masters of war
You that build all the guns
You that build the death planes
You that build the big bombs
You that hide behind walls
You that hide behind desks
I just want you to know
I can see through your masks

You that never done nothin'
But build to destroy
You play with my world
Like it's your little toy
You put a gun in my hand
And you hide from my eyes
And you turn and run farther
When the fast bullets fly

Like Judas of old
You lie and deceive
A world war can be won
You want me to believe
But I see through your eyes
And I see through your brain
Like I see through the water
That runs down my drain

You fasten the triggers
For the others to fire
Then you set back and watch
When the death count gets higher
You hide in your mansion
As young people's blood

Flows out of their bodies
And is buried in the mud

You've thrown the worst fear
That can ever be hurled
Fear to bring children
Into the world
For threatening my baby
Unborn and unnamed
You ain't worth the blood
That runs in your veins

How much do I know
To talk out of turn
You might say that I'm young
You might say I'm unlearned
But there's one thing I know
Though I'm younger than you
Even Jesus would never
Forgive what you do

Let me ask you one question
Is your money that good
Will it buy you forgiveness
Do you think that it could
I think you will find
When your death takes its toll
All the money you made
Will never buy back your soul

And I hope that you die
And your death'll come soon
I will follow your casket
In the pale afternoon

And I'll watch while you're lowered
Down to your deathbed
And I'll stand o'er your grave
'Til I'm sure that you're dead

# Bob Dylan's Blues

Well, the Lone Ranger and Tonto
They are ridin' down the line
Fixin' ev'rybody's troubles
Ev'rybody's 'cept mine
Somebody musta tol' 'em
That I was doin' fine

Oh you five and ten cent women
With nothin' in your heads
I got a real gal I'm lovin'
And Lord I'll love her till I'm dead
Go away from my door and my window too
Right now

Lord, I ain't goin' down to no race track
See no sports car run
I don't have no sports car
And I don't even care to have one
I can walk anytime around the block

Well, the wind keeps a-blowin' me
Up and down the street
With my hat in my hand
And my boots on my feet
Watch out so you don't step on me

Well, lookit here buddy
You want to be like me
Pull out your six-shooter
And rob every bank you can see
Tell the judge I said it was all right
Yes!

# A Hard Rain's A-Gonna Fall

Oh, where have you been, my blue-eyed son?
Oh, where have you been, my darling young one?
I've stumbled on the side of twelve misty mountains,
I've walked and I've crawled on six crooked highways,
I've stepped in the middle of seven sad forests,
I've been out in front of a dozen dead oceans,
I've been ten thousand miles in the mouth of a graveyard,
And it's a hard, and it's a hard, it's a hard, and it's a hard,
And it's a hard rain's a-gonna fall.

Oh, what did you see, my blue-eyed son?
Oh, what did you see, my darling young one?
I saw a newborn baby with wild wolves all around it,
I saw a highway of diamonds with nobody on it,
I saw a black branch with blood that kept drippin',
I saw a room full of men with their hammers a-bleedin',
I saw a white ladder all covered with water,
I saw ten thousand talkers whose tongues were all broken,
I saw guns and sharp swords in the hands of young children,
And it's a hard, and it's a hard, it's a hard, it's a hard,
And it's a hard rain's a-gonna fall.

And what did you hear, my blue-eyed son?
And what did you hear, my darling young one?
I heard the sound of a thunder, it roared out a warnin',
Heard the roar of a wave that could drown the whole world,
Heard one hundred drummers whose hands were a-blazin',
Heard ten thousand whisperin' and nobody listenin',
Heard one person starve, I heard many people laughin',
Heard the song of a poet who died in the gutter,
Heard the sound of a clown who cried in the alley,
And it's a hard, and it's a hard, it's a hard, it's a hard,
And it's a hard rain's a-gonna fall.

Oh, who did you meet, my blue-eyed son?
Who did you meet, my darling young one?

I met a young child beside a dead pony,
I met a white man who walked a black dog,
I met a young woman whose body was burning,
I met a young girl, she gave me a rainbow,
I met one man who was wounded in love,
I met another man who was wounded with hatred,
And it's a hard, it's a hard, it's a hard, it's a hard,
It's a hard rain's a-gonna fall.

Oh, what'll you do now, my blue-eyed son?
Oh, what'll you do now, my darling young one?
I'm a-goin' back out 'fore the rain starts a-fallin',
I'll walk to the depths of the deepest black forest,
Where the people are many and their hands are all empty,
Where the pellets of poison are flooding their waters,
Where the home in the valley meets the damp dirty prison,
Where the executioner's face is always well hidden,
Where hunger is ugly, where souls are forgotten,
Where black is the color, where none is the number,
And I'll tell it and think it and speak it and breathe it,
And reflect it from the mountain so all souls can see it,
Then I'll stand on the ocean until I start sinkin',
But I'll know my song well before I start singin',
And it's a hard, it's a hard, it's a hard, it's a hard,
It's a hard rain's a-gonna fall.

# Don't Think Twice, It's All Right

It ain't no use to sit and wonder why, babe
It don't matter, anyhow
An' it ain't no use to sit and wonder why, babe
If you don't know by now
When your rooster crows at the break of dawn
Look out your window and I'll be gone
You're the reason I'm trav'lin' on
Don't think twice, it's all right

It ain't no use in turnin' on your light, babe
That light I never knowed
An' it ain't no use in turnin' on your light, babe
I'm on the dark side of the road
Still I wish there was somethin' you would do or say
To try and make me change my mind and stay
We never did too much talkin' anyway
So don't think twice, it's all right

It ain't no use in callin' out my name, gal
Like you never did before
It ain't no use in callin' out my name, gal
I can't hear you any more
I'm a-thinkin' and a-wond'rin' all the way down the road
I once loved a woman, a child I'm told
I give her my heart but she wanted my soul
But don't think twice, it's all right

I'm walkin' down that long, lonesome road, babe
Where I'm bound, I can't tell
But goodbye's too good a word, gal
So I'll just say fare thee well
I ain't sayin' you treated me unkind
You could have done better but I don't mind
You just kinda wasted my precious time

# But don't think twice, it's all right

# Bob Dylan's Dream

While riding on a train goin' west,
I fell asleep for to take my rest.
I dreamed a dream that make me sad,
Concerning myself and the first few friends I had.

With half-damp eyes I stared to the room
Where my friends and I spent many an afternoon,
Where we together weathered many a storm,
Laughin' and singin' till the early hours of the morn.

By the old wooden stove where our hats was hung,
Our words were told, our songs were sung,
Where we longed for nothin' and were quite satisfied
Talkin' and a-jokin' about the world outside.

With haunted hearts through the heat and cold,
We never thought we could ever get old.
We thought we could sit forever in fun
But our chances really was a million to one.

As easy it was to tell black from white,
It was all that easy to tell wrong from right.
And our choices were few and the thought never hit
That the one road we traveled would ever shatter and split.

How many a year has passed and gone,
And many a gamble has been lost and won,
And many a road taken by many a friend,
And each one I've never seen again.

I wish, I wish, I wish in vain,
That we could sit simply in that room again,
Ten thousand dollars at the drop of a hat,
I'd give it all gladly if our lives could be like that.

# Oxford Town

Oxford Town, Oxford Town
Ev'rybody's got their heads bowed down
The sun don't shine above the ground
Ain't a-goin' down to Oxford Town

He went down to Oxford Town
Guns and clubs followed him down
All because his face was brown
Better get away from Oxford Town

Oxford Town around the bend
He come in to the door, he couldn't get in
All because of the color of his skin
What do you think about that, my frien'?

Me and my gal, my gal's son
We got met with a tear gas bomb
I don't even know why we come
Goin' back where we come from

Oxford Town in the afternoon
Ev'rybody singin' a sorrowful tune
Two men died 'neath the Mississippi moon
Somebody better investigate soon

Oxford Town, Oxford Town
Ev'rybody's got their heads bowed down
The sun don't shine above the ground
Ain't a-goin' down to Oxford Town

# Talkin' World War III Blues

Some time ago a crazy dream came to me,
I dreamt I was walkin' into World War Three.
I went to the doctor the very next day
To see what kinda words he could say.
He said it was a bad dream.
I wouldn't worry 'bout it none, though,
They were my own dreams and they're only in my head.

I said, 'Hold it, Doc, a World War passed through my brain.'
He said, 'Nurse, get your pad, this boy's insane.'
He grabbed my arm, I said, 'Ouch!'
As I landed on the psychiatric couch,
He said, 'Tell me about it.'

Well, the whole thing started at 3 o'clock fast,
It was all over by quarter past.
I was down in the sewer with some little lover
When I peeked out from a manhole cover
Wondering who turned the lights on.

Well, I got up and walked around
And up and down the lonesome town.
I stood a-wondering which way to go,
I lit a cigarette on a parking meter
And walked on down the road.
It was a normal day.

Well, I rung the fallout shelter bell
And I leaned my head and I gave a yell,
'Give me a string bean, I'm a hungry man.'
A shotgun fired and away I ran.
I don't blame them too much though,
I know I look funny.

Down at the corner by a hot-dog stand
I seen a man, I said, 'Howdy friend,
I guess there's just us two.'
He screamed a bit and away he flew.
Thought I was a Communist.

Well, I spied a girl and before she could leave,
'Let's go and play Adam and Eve.'
I took her by the hand and my heart it was thumpin'
When she said, 'Hey man, you crazy or sumpin',
You see what happened last time they started.'

Well, I seen a Cadillac window uptown
And there was nobody aroun'.
I got into the driver's seat
And I drove down 42nd Street
In my Cadillac.
Good car to drive after a war.

Well, I remember seein' some ad,
So I turned on my Conelrad.
But I didn't pay my Con Ed bill,
So the radio didn't work so well.
Turned on my record player —
It was Rock-A-Day, Johnny singin',
'Tell Your Ma, Tell Your Pa,
Our Loves Are Gonna Grow Ooh-wah, Ooh-wah.'

I was feelin' kinda lonesome and blue,
I needed somebody to talk to.
So I called up the operator of time
Just to hear a voice of some kind.
'When you hear the beep
It will be three o'clock.'

She said that for over an hour
And I hung up.

Well, the doctor interrupted me just about then,
Sayin', 'Hey I've been havin' the same old dreams,
But mine was a little different you see.
I dreamt that the only person left after the war was me.
I didn't see you around.'

Well, now time passed and now it seems
Everybody's having them dreams.
Everybody sees themselves walkin' around with no one else.
Half of the people can be part right all of the time,
Some of the people can be all right part of the time,
But all of the people can't be right all of the time.
I think Abraham Lincoln said that.
'I'll let you be in my dreams if I can be in yours.'
I said that.

# Corrina, Corrina

Corrina, Corrina,
Gal, where you been so long?
Corrina, Corrina,
Gal, where you been so long?
I been worr'in' 'bout you, baby,
Baby, please come home.

I got a bird that whistles,
I got a bird that sings.
I got a bird that whistles,
I got a bird that sings.
But I ain't a-got Corrina,
Life don't mean a thing.

Corrina, Corrina,
Gal, you're on my mind.
Corrina, Corrina,
Gal, you're on my mind.
I'm a-thinkin' 'bout you, baby,
I just can't keep from crying.

# Honey, Just Allow Me One More Chance

Honey, just allow me one more chance
To get along with you.
Honey, just allow me one more chance,
Ah'll do anything with you.
Well, I'm a-walkin' down the road
With my head in my hand,
I'm lookin' for a woman
Needs a worried man.
Just-a one kind favor I ask you,
'Low me just-a one more chance.

Honey, just allow me one more chance
To ride your aeroplane.
Honey, just allow me one more chance
To ride your passenger train.
Well, I've been lookin' all over
For a gal like you,
I can't find nobody
So you'll have to do.
Just-a one kind favor I ask you,
'Low me just-a one more chance.

Honey, just allow me one more chance
To get along with you.
Honey, just allow me one more chance,
Ah'll do anything with you.
Well, lookin' for a woman
That ain't got no man,
Is just lookin' for a needle
That is lost in the sand.
Just-a one kind favor I ask you,
'Low me just-a one more chance.

# I Shall Be Free

Well, I took me a woman late last night,
I's three-fourths drunk, she looked uptight.
She took off her wheel, took off her bell,
Took off her wig, said, 'How do I smell?'
I hot-footed it . . . bare-naked . . .
Out the window!

Well, sometimes I might get drunk,
Walk like a duck and stomp like a skunk.
Don't hurt me none, don't hurt my pride
'Cause I got my little lady right by my side.
(Right there
Proud as can be)

I's out there paintin' on the old woodshed
When a can a black paint it fell on my head.
I went down to scrub and rub
But I had to sit in back of the tub.
(Cost a quarter
And I had to get out quick . . .
Someone wanted to come in and take a sauna)

Well, my telephone rang it would not stop,
It's President Kennedy callin' me up.
He said, 'My friend, Bob, what do we need to make the
    country grow?'
I said, 'My friend, John, Brigitte Bardot,
Anita Ekberg,
Sophia Loren.'
(Put 'em all in the same room with Ernest Borgnine!)

Well, I got a woman sleeps on a cot,
She yells and hollers and squeals a lot.
Licks my face and tickles my ear,

Bends me over and buys me beer.
(She's a honeymooner
A June crooner
A spoon feeder
And a natural leader)


Oh, there ain't no use in me workin' so heavy,
I got a woman who works on the levee.
Pumping that water up to her neck,
Every week she sends me a monthly check.
(She's a humdinger
Folk singer
Dead ringer
For a thing-a-muh jigger)


Late one day in the middle of the week,
Eyes were closed I was half asleep.
I chased me a woman up the hill,
Right in the middle of an air raid drill.
It was Little Bo Peep!
(I jumped a fallout shelter
I jumped a bean stalk
I jumped a ferris wheel)


Now, the man on the stand he wants my vote,
He's a-runnin' for office on the ballot note.
He's out there preachin' in front of the steeple,
Tellin' me he loves all kinds-a people.
(He's eatin' bagels
He's eatin' pizza
He's eatin' chitlins
He's eatin' bullshit!)

Oh, set me down on a television floor,
I'll flip the channel to number four.
Out of the shower comes a grown-up man
With a bottle of hair oil in his hand.
(It's that greasy kid stuff.
What I want to know, Mr Football Man, is
What do you do about Willy Mays and Yul Brynner,
Charles de Gaulle
And Robert Louis Stevenson?)

Well, the funniest woman I ever seen
Was the great-granddaughter of Mr Clean.
She takes about fifteen baths a day,
Wants me to grow a cigar on my face.
(She's a little bit heavy!)

Well, ask me why I'm drunk alla time,
It levels my head and eases my mind.
I just walk along and stroll and sing,
I see better days and I do better things.
(I catch dinosaurs
I make love to Elizabeth Taylor . . .
Catch hell from Richard Burton!)

# My Life in a Stolen Moment

Duluth's an iron ore shipping town in Minnesota
It's built up on a rocky cliff that runs into Lake Superior
I was born there – my father was born there –
My mother's from the Iron Range Country up north
The Iron Range is a long line a mining towns
   that begin at Grand Rapids and end at Eveleth
We moved up there to live with my mother's folks
   in Hibbing when I was young –
Hibbing's got the biggest open pit ore mine in the world
Hibbing's got schools, churches, grocery stores an' a jail
It's got high school football games an' a movie house
Hibbing's got souped-up cars runnin' full blast
   on a Friday night
Hibbing's got corner bars with polka bands
You can stand at one end of Hibbing on the main drag
   an' see clear past the city limits on the other end
Hibbing's a good ol' town
I ran away from it when I was 10, 12, 13, 15, 15½, 17 an' 18
I been caught an' brought back all but once
I wrote my first song to my mother an' titled it 'To Mother'
I wrote that in 5th grade an' the teacher gave me a B+
I started smoking at 11 years old an' only stopped once
   to catch my breath
I don't remember my parents singing too much
At least I don't remember swapping any songs with them
Later I sat in college at the University of Minnesota
   on a phony scholarship that I never had
I sat in science class an' flunked out for refusin' to watch
   a rabbit die
I got expelled from English class for using four-letter words
   in a paper describing the English teacher
I also failed out of communication class for callin' up
   every day and sayin' I couldn't come
I did OK in Spanish though but I knew it beforehand

I's kept around for kicks at a fraternity house
They let me live there an' I did until they wanted me to join
I moved in with two girls from South Dakota
    in a two-room apartment for two nights
I crossed the bridge to 14th Street an' moved in above
    a bookstore that also sold bad hamburgers
    basketball sweatshirts an' bulldog statues
I fell hard for an actress girl who kneed me in the guts
    an' I ended up on the East Side a the Mississippi River
    with about ten friends in a condemned house underneath
    the Washington Avenue Bridge just south a Seven Corners
That's pretty well my college life
After that I thumbed my way to Galveston, Texas in four days
    tryin' to find an ol' friend whose ma met me
    at the screen door and said he's in the Army —
    By the time the kitchen door closed
    I was passin' California — almost in Oregon —
    I met a waitress in the woods who picked me up
    an' dropped me off in Washington someplace
I danced my way from the Indian festivals in Gallup, New
    Mexico
To the Mardi Gras in New Orleans, Louisiana
With my thumb out, my eyes asleep, my hat turned up
    an' my head turned on
I's driftin' an' learnin' new lessons
I was making my own depression
I rode freight trains for kicks
An' got beat up for laughs
Cut grass for quarters
An' sang for dimes
Hitchhiked on 61 – 51 – 75 – 169 – 37 – 66 – 22
Gopher Road – Route 40 an' Howard Johnson Turnpike
Got jailed for suspicion of armed robbery
Got held four hours on a murder rap

Got busted for looking like I do
An' I never done none a them things
Somewheres back I took the time to start playin' the guitar
Somewheres back I took time to start singin'
Somewheres back I took the time to start writin'
But I never ever did take the time to find out why
I took the time to do these things – when they ask
Me why an' where I got started, I gotta shake my head
    an' weave my eyes an' walk away dumbfounded
From Shreveport I landed in Madison, Wisconsin
From Madison we filled up a four-door Pontiac with five people
An' shot straight south an' sharp to the East an'
    in 24 hours was still hanging on through the Hudson Tunnel –
Gettin' out in a snowstorm an' wavin' goodbye
    to the three others, we swept on to MacDougal Street
    with five dollars between us – but we weren't poor
I had my guitar an' harmonica to play
An' he had his brother's clothes to pawn
In a week, he went back to Madison while I stayed behind an'
Walked a winter's line from the Lower East Side
    to Gerde's Folk City
In May, I thumbed west an' took the wrong highway to Florida
Mad as hell an' tired as well, I scrambled my way back to
South Dakota by keepin' a truck driver up all day an' singin'
One night in Cincinnati
I looked up a long time friend in Sioux Falls an' was let down,
    worried blind, and hit hard by seein' how little we had to say
I rolled back to Kansas, Iowa, Minnesota, lookin' up
    ol' time pals an' first-run gals an' I was beginnin'
    to find out that my road an' their road
    is two different kinds a roads
I found myself back in New York City in the middle part
    a summer staying on 28th Street with kind, honest
    hard-working people who were good to me

I got wrote up in the Times after playin' in the fall
   at Gerde's Folk City
I got recorded at Columbia after being wrote up in the Times
An' I still can't find the time to go back an' see why an' where
I started doing what I'm doing
I can't tell you the influences 'cause there's too many
   to mention an' I might leave one out
An' that wouldn't be fair
Woody Guthrie, sure
Big Joe Williams, yeah
It's easy to remember those names
But what about the faces you can't find again
What about the curves an' corners an' cut-offs
   that drop out a sight an' fall behind
What about the records you hear but one time
What about the coyote's call an' the bulldog's bark
What about the tomcat's meow an' milk cow's moo
An' the train whistle's moan
Open up yer eyes an' ears an' yer influenced
   an' there's nothing you can do about it
Hibbing's a good ol' town
I ran away from it when I was 10, 12, 13, 15, 15½, 17 an' 18
I been caught an' brought back all at once

# Whatcha Gonna Do

Tell me what you're gonna do
When the shadow comes under your door.
Tell me what you're gonna do
When the shadow comes under your door.
Tell me what you're gonna do
When the shadow comes under your door.
O Lord, O Lord,
What shall you do?

Tell me what you're gonna do
When the devil calls your cards.
Tell me what you're gonna do
When the devil calls your cards.
Tell me what you're gonna do
When the devil calls your cards.
O Lord, O Lord,
What shall you do?

Tell me what you're gonna do
When your water turns to wine.
Tell me what you're gonna do
When your water turns to wine.
Tell me what you're gonna do
When your water turns to wine.
O Lord, O Lord,
What shall you do?

Tell me what you're gonna do
When you can't play God no more.
Tell me what you're gonna do
When you can't play God no more.
Tell me what you're gonna do
When you can't play God no more.

O Lord, O Lord,
What shall you do?

Tell me what you're gonna do
When the shadow comes creepin' in your room.
Tell me what you're gonna do
When the shadow comes creepin' in your room.
Tell me what you're gonna do
When the shadow comes creepin' in your room.
O Lord, O Lord,
What should you do?

# Walls of Red Wing

Oh, the age of the inmates
I remember quite freely:
No younger than twelve,
No older 'n seventeen.
Thrown in like bandits
And cast off like criminals,
Inside the walls,
The walls of Red Wing.

From the dirty old mess hall
You march to the brick wall,
Too weary to talk
And too tired to sing.
Oh, it's all afternoon
You remember your home town,
Inside the walls,
The walls of Red Wing.

Oh, the gates are cast iron
And the walls are barbed wire.
Stay far from the fence
With the 'lectricity sting.
And it's keep down your head
And stay in your number,
Inside the walls,
The walls of Red Wing.

Oh, it's fare thee well
To the deep hollow dungeon,
Farewell to the boardwalk
That takes you to the screen.
And farewell to the minutes
They threaten you with it,

Inside the walls,
The walls of Red Wing.

Its many a guard
That stands around smilin',
Holdin' his club
Like he was a king.
Hopin' to get you
Behind a wood pilin',
Inside the walls,
The walls of Red Wing.

The night aimed shadows
Through the crossbar windows,
And the wind punched hard
To make the wall-siding sing.
It's many a night
I pretended to be a-sleepin',
Inside the walls,
The walls of Red Wing.

As the rain rattled heavy
On the bunk-house shingles,
And the sounds in the night,
They made my ears ring.
'Til the keys of the guards
Clicked the tune of the morning,
Inside the walls,
The walls of Red Wing.

Oh, some of us'll end up
In St Cloud Prison,
And some of us'll wind up
To be lawyers and things,

And some of us'll stand up
To meet you on your crossroads,
From inside the walls,
The walls of Red Wing.

# Who Killed Davey Moore?

Who killed Davey Moore,
Why an' what's the reason for?

'Not I,' says the referee,
'Don't point your finger at me.
I could've stopped it in the eighth
An' maybe kept him from his fate,
But the crowd would've booed, I'm sure,
At not gettin' their money's worth.
It's too bad he had to go,
But there was a pressure on me too, you know.
It wasn't me that made him fall.
No, you can't blame me at all.'

Who killed Davey Moore,
Why an' what's the reason for?

'Not us,' says the angry crowd,
Whose screams filled the arena loud.
'It's too bad he died that night
But we just like to see a fight.
We didn't mean for him t' meet his death,
We just meant to see some sweat,
There ain't nothing wrong in that.
It wasn't us that made him fall.
No, you can't blame us at all.'

Who killed Davey Moore,
Why an' what's the reason for?

'Not me,' says his manager,
Puffing on a big cigar.
'It's hard to say, it's hard to tell,
I always thought that he was well.

It's too bad for his wife an' kids he's dead,
But if he was sick, he should've said.
It wasn't me that made him fall.
No, you can't blame me at all.'

Who killed Davey Moore,
Why an' what's the reason for?

'Not me,' says the gambling man,
With his ticket stub still in his hand.
'It wasn't me that knocked him down,
My hands never touched him none.
I didn't commit no ugly sin,
Anyway, I put money on him to win.
It wasn't me that made him fall.
No, you can't blame me at all.'

Who killed Davey Moore,
Why an' what's the reason for?

'Not me,' says the boxing writer,
Pounding print on his old typewriter,
Sayin', 'Boxing ain't to blame,
There's just as much danger in a football game.'
Sayin', 'Fist fighting is here to stay,
It's just the old American way.
It wasn't me that made him fall.
No, you can't blame me at all.'

Who killed Davey Moore,
Why an' what's the reason for?

'Not me,' says the man whose fists
Laid him low in a cloud of mist,
Who came here from Cuba's door
Where boxing ain't allowed no more.
'I hit him, yes, it's true,
But that's what I am paid to do.
Don't say "murder," don't say "kill."
It was destiny, it was God's will.'

Who killed Davey Moore,
Why an' what's the reason for?

# Seven Curses

Old Reilly stole a stallion
But they caught him and they brought him back
And they laid him down on the jailhouse ground
With an iron chain around his neck.

Old Reilly's daughter got a message
That her father was goin' to hang.
She rode by night and came by morning
With gold and silver in her hand.

When the judge he saw Reilly's daughter
His old eyes deepened in his head,
Sayin', 'Gold will never free your father,
The price, my dear, is you instead.'

'Oh I'm as good as dead,' cried Reilly,
'It's only you that he does crave
And my skin will surely crawl if he touches you at all.
Get on your horse and ride away.'

'Oh father you will surely die
If I don't take the chance to try
And pay the price and not take your advice.
For that reason I will have to stay.'

The gallows shadows shook the evening,
In the night a hound dog bayed,
In the night the grounds were groanin',
In the night the price was paid.

The next mornin' she had awoken
To know that the judge had never spoken.
She saw that hangin' branch a-bendin',
She saw her father's body broken.

These be seven curses on a judge so cruel:
That one doctor will not save him,
That two healers will not heal him,
That three eyes will not see him.

That four ears will not hear him,
That five walls will not hide him,
That six diggers will not bury him
And that seven deaths shall never kill him.

# Joan Baez in Concert, Part 2 (jacket notes)

In my youngest years I used t' kneel
By my aunt's house on a railroad field
An' yank the grass outa the ground
An' rip savagely at its roots
An' pass the hours countin' strands
An' stains a green grew on my hands
As I waited till I heard the sound
A the iron ore cars rollin' down
The tracks'd hum an' I'd bite my lip
An' hold my grip as the whistle whined
Crouchin' low as the engine growled
I'd shyly wave t' the throttle man
An' count the cars as they rolled past
But when the echo faded in the day
An' I understood the train was gone
It's then that my eyes'd turn
Back t' my hands with stains a green
That lined my palms like blood that tells
I'd taken an' not given in return
But glancin' back t' the empty patch
Where the ground was turned upside down
An' the roots lay dead beside the tree
I'd say 'how can this bother me'
Or 'I'm sure the grass don' give a damn
Anyway it'll grow again an'
What's a patch a grass anyhow'
An' I'd wipe my hand t' wash the stain
An' fling a rock across the track
With the echo a the railroad train
Hangin' heavy like a thunder cloud
In the dawn a t'morrow's rain
An' I asked myself t' be my friend
An' I walked my road like a frightened fox
An' I sung my song like a demon child

With a kick an' a curse
From inside my mother's womb —

In later years although still young
My head swung heavy with windin' curves
An' a mixed-up path revolved an' strung
Within the boundaries a my youth
'Til at last I backed so far away
From the world's walls an' friendless games
That I did not have a word t' say
T' anyone who'd meet my eyes
An' I locked myself an' lost the key
An' let the symbols take their shape
An' form a foe for me t' fight
T' lash my tongue an' rebel against
An' spit at strong with vomit words
But I learned t' choose my idols well
T' be my voice an' tell my tale
An' help me fight my phantom brawl
An' my first idol was Hank Williams
For he sang about the railroad lines
An' the iron bars an' rattlin' wheels
Left no doubt that they were real
An' my first symbol was the word 'beautiful'
For the railroad lines were not beautiful
They were smoky black an' gutter-colored
An' filled with stink an' soot an' dust
An' I'd judge beauty with these rules
An' accept it only 'f it was ugly
An' 'f I could touch it with my hand
For it's only then I'd understand
An' say 'yeah this's real'
An' I walked my road an' sung my song
Like a saddened clown
In the circus a my own world —

In later times my idols fell
For I learned that they were only men
An' had reasons for their deeds
'F which weren't mine not mine at all
An' no more on them could I depend
But what I learned from each forgotten god
Was that the battlefield was mine alone
An' only I could cast me stone
An' the symbols which by now had grown
Outa shape but strong in sight
Were seen by me in a sharper light
An' the symbol 'beauty' still struck my guts
But now with more a shameful sound
An' I rebelled twice as hard an' ten times as proud
An' I walked my road an' sung my song
Like an arch criminal who'd done no wrong
An' committed no crime but was screamin' through the bars
A someone else's prison —

Later yet in New York town
On my own terms I said with age
'The only beauty's in the cracks an' curbs
Clothed in robes a dust an' grime'
An' I searched for it in every hole
An' jumped head-on t' meet its breast
An' whispered tunes into its ear
An' kissed its mouth an' held its waist
An' in its body swum around
An' on its belly passed out cold
An' like a blind lover bold in flight
I shouted from inside my wounds
'The voice t' speak for me an' mine
Is the hard filthy gutter sound
For it's only this that I can touch

An' the only beauty I can feel'
An' I dove back in by my own choice
T' feed my skin a hungry holes
An' rejected every other voice
An' I walked my road an' sung my song
Like a lonesome king
Standin' in the fury a the queen's garden
Starin' into
A shallow grave —

Time traveled an' faces passed
An' many thoughts t' me were taught
By names an' heads too many t' count
That touched my path an' soon were gone
But some stayed on t' remain as friends
An' though each is first an' none is best
It is at this time I speak 'f one
An' it is at this time I speak 'f one
Who proved t' me that boys still grow
A girl I met on common ground
Who like me strummed lonesome tunes
With a 'lovely voice' so I first heard
'A thing a beauty' people said
'Wondrous sounds' writers wrote
'I hate that kind a sound' said I
'The only beauty's ugly, man
The crackin' shakin' breakin' sounds're
The only beauty I understand'
So between our tongues there was a bar
An' though we talked a the world's fears
An' at the same jokes loudly laughed
An' held our eyes at the same aim
When I saw she was set t' sing
A fence a deafness with a bullet's speed

117

Sprang up like a protectin' glass
Outside the linin' a my ears
An' I talked loud inside my head
As a double shield against the sounds
'Ain't no voice but an ugly voice
A the rest I don' give a damn
'F I can't feel it with my hand
Then don' wish me t' understand
But I'll wait though 'til yer song is done
'Cause there's something about yuh
But I don' know what'
An' I walked my road an' sung my song
Like a scared poet
Walkin' on the shore
Kickin' driftwood with my shadow
Afraid a the sea —

In a cruisin' car I heard her tell
About the childhood hours she spent
As a little girl in an Arab land
An' she told me 'f the dogs she saw
Slaughtered wholly on the street
An' I learned 'f how the people'd laugh
As they beat the gentle dogs t' death
Through a child's eyes who tried an' failed
T' hide one dog inside her house
An' I turned my head without a word
An' coldly stared out t' the road
An' with the wind hittin' half my face
My memory creeped as the highway rolled
Back if not but for a flash
T' an empty patch a grass that died
About the same time a dog was hid
An' that guilty feelin' sprang again

Not over the roots I'd pulled
But over she who saw the dogs get killed
An' I said it softly underneath my breath
'Yuh oughta listen t' her voice . . .
Maybe somethin's in the sound . . .
Ah but what could she care anyway
Kill them thoughts – they ain't no good
Only ugly's understood'
An' I stuck my head out in the wind
An' let the breeze blow the words
Outa my breath as a truck roared by
An' almost blew us off the road
An' at that time I had no song t' sing –

In Woodstock at a painter's house
With friends scattered 'round the room
An' she talkin' from a chair
An' me crosslegged on the rug
I lit a cigarette an' laughed
An' gulped light red wine an' lost
Every shakin' vein that dwelled
Within the roots a my dancin' heart
An' the room it whirled an' twirled an' sailed
Without one fence standin' guard
When all at once the silent air
Split open from her soundin' voice
Without no warnin' from her lips
An' by instinct my blood reversed
An' I shook an' started reachin' for
That wall that was supposed t' fall
But my restin' nerves weren't restless now
An' this time they wouldn't jump
'Let her voice ring out,' they cried
'We're too tired t' stop 'er sing

Which shattered all the rules I owned
An' left me puzzled without no choice
'Cept t' listen t' her voice
An' when I leaned upon my elbows bare
That limply held my body up
I felt my face freeze t' the bone
An' my mouth like ice or solid stone
Could not've moved 'f called upon
An' the time like velvet floated by
Until with hunger pains it cried
'Don' stop singing . . . sing again'
An' like others who have taught me well
Not about themselves but me
She laughed out loud as 'f t' know
That the bars between us busted down
An' I laughed almost an insane laugh
An' aimed it at the ceiling walls
When I realized the command I called
An' my elbows folded under me
An' my head lay back upon the floor
An' my shaky nerves went floatin' free
But I memorized the words t' write
For another time in t'morrow's dawn
An' held close unchallenged dreams
As I passed out somewheres in the night –

    I did not begin t' touch
    'Til I finally felt what wasn't there
    Oh how feeble foolish small an' sad
    'F me t' think that beauty was
    Only ugliness an' muck
    When it's really jus' a magic wand
    That waves an' teases at my mind
    An' knows that only it can feel
    An' knows that I ain't got a chance

An' fools me into thinking things
Like it's my hands that understand
Ha ha how it must laugh
At crippled ones like me who try
T' pick apart the sounds a streams
An' pluck apart the rage 'f waves
Ah but yuh won't fool me any more
For the breeze I heard in a young girl's breath
Proved true as sex an' womanhood
An' deep as the lowest depths a death
An' as strong as the weakest winds that blow
An' as long as fate an' fatherhood
An' like gypsy drums
An' Chinese gongs
An' cathedral bells
An' tones 'f chimes
It jus' held hymns 'f mystery
An' mystery's all too involved
It can't be understood or solved
By hands an' feet an' fingertips
An' it shouldn't be called by a shameful name
By those who look for answers plain
In every book 'cept themselves
Go ahead lightnin' laugh at me
Flash yer teeth
Slap yer knee
It's yer joke I agree
I'm even pointin' at myself
But it's a shame it's taken so much time

So, once more it's winter again
An' that means I'll wait 'til spring
T' ramble back t' where I kneeled
When I first heard the ore train sing

An' pulled the ground up by its roots
But this time I won't use my strength
T' pass the time yankin' grass
While I'm waitin' for the train t' sound
No next time'll be a different day
For the train might be there when I come
An' I might wait hours for the cars t' pass
An' then as the echo fades
I'll bend down an' count the strands a grass
But one thing that's bound t' be
Is that instead a pullin' at the earth
I'll jus' pet it as a friend
An' when that train engine comes near
I'll nod my head t' the big brass wheels
An' say 'howdy' t' the engineer
An' yell that Joanie says hello
An' watch the train man scratch his head
An' wonder what I meant by that
An' I'll stand up an' remember when
A rock was flung by a devil child
An' I'll walk my road somewhere between
The unseen green an' the jet-black train
An' I'll sing my song like a rebel wild
For it's that I am an' can't deny
But at least I'll know now not t' hurt
Not t' push
Not t' ache
An' God know . . . not t' try —

# Dusty Old Fairgrounds

Well, it's all up from Florida at the start of the spring,
The trucks and the trailers will be winding
Like a bullet we'll shoot for the carnival route.
We're following them dusty old fairgrounds a-calling.

From the Michigan mud past the Wisconsin sun
'Cross that Minnesota border, keep 'em scrambling
Through the clear county lakes and the lumberjack lands,
We're following them dusty old fairgrounds a-calling.

Hit Fargo on the jump and down to Aberdeen
'Cross them old Black Hills, keep 'em rolling
Through the cow country towns and the sands of old Montana.
We're following them fairgrounds a-calling.

As the white line on the highway sails under your wheels,
I've gazed from the trailer window laughing.
Oh, our clothes they was torn but the colors they was bright.
Following them dusty old fairgrounds a-calling.

It's a-many a friend that follows the bend,
The jugglers, the hustlers, the gamblers.
Well, I've spent my time with the fortune-telling kind
Following them fairgrounds a-calling.

Oh, it's pound down the rails and it's tie down the tents,
Get that canvas flag a-flying.
Well, let the caterpillars spin, let the ferris wheel wind
Following them fairgrounds a-calling.

Well, it's roll into town straight to the fairgrounds
Just behind the posters that are hanging
And it's fill up every space with a different kind of face
Following them fairgrounds a-calling.

Get the dancing girls in front, get the gambling show behind,
Hear that old music box a-banging.
Hear them kids, faces, smiles, up and down the midway aisles
We're following them fairgrounds a-calling.

It's a-drag it on down by the deadline in the town,
Hit the old highway by the morning
And it's ride yourself blind for the next town on time
Following them fairgrounds a-calling.

As the harmonicas whined in the lonesome nighttime
Drinking red wine as we're rolling,
Many a turnin' I turn, many a lesson I learn
From following them fairgrounds a-calling.

And it's roll back down to St. Petersburg
Tie down the trailers and camp 'em
And the money that we made will pay for the space
From following them dusty old fairgrounds a-calling.

# The Times They Are A-Changin'

**The Times They Are A-Changin'**
**Ballad of Hollis Brown**
**With God on Our Side**
**One Too Many Mornings**
**North Country Blues**
**Only a Pawn in Their Game**
**Boots of Spanish Leather**
**When the Ship Comes In**
**The Lonesome Death of Hattie Carroll**
**Restless Farewell**

11 Outlined Epitaphs (liner notes)
Eternal Circle
Paths of Victory
Only a Hobo
Lay Down Your Weary Tune
Percy's Song
Guess I'm Doin' Fine
Advice for Geraldine on Her Miscellaneous Birthday

# The Times They Are A-Changin'

Come gather 'round people
Wherever you roam
And admit that the waters
Around you have grown
And accept it that soon
You'll be drenched to the bone.
If your time to you
Is worth savin'
Then you better start swimmin'
Or you'll sink like a stone
For the times they are a-changin'.

Come writers and critics
Who prophesize with your pen
And keep your eyes wide
The chance won't come again
And don't speak too soon
For the wheel's still in spin
And there's no tellin' who
That it's namin'.
For the loser now
Will be later to win
For the times they are a-changin'.

Come senators, congressmen
Please heed the call
Don't stand in the doorway
Don't block up the hall
For he that gets hurt
Will be he who has stalled
There's a battle outside
And it is ragin'.
It'll soon shake your windows

And rattle your walls
For the times they are a-changin'.

Come mothers and fathers
Throughout the land
And don't criticize
What you can't understand
Your sons and your daughters
Are beyond your command
Your old road is
Rapidly agin'.
Please get out of the new one
If you can't lend your hand
For the times they are a-changin'.

The line it is drawn
The curse it is cast
The slow one now
Will later be fast
As the present now
Will later be past
The order is
Rapidly fadin'.
And the first one now
Will later be last
For the times they are a-changin'.

# Ballad of Hollis Brown

Hollis Brown
He lived on the outside of town
Hollis Brown
He lived on the outside of town
With his wife and five children
And his cabin fallin' down

You looked for work and money
And you walked a rugged mile
You looked for work and money
And you walked a rugged mile
Your children are so hungry
That they don't know how to smile

Your baby's eyes look crazy
They're a-tuggin' at your sleeve
Your baby's eyes look crazy
They're a-tuggin' at your sleeve
You walk the floor and wonder why
With every breath you breathe

The rats have got your flour
Bad blood it got your mare
The rats have got your flour
Bad blood it got your mare
If there's anyone that knows
Is there anyone that cares?

You prayed to the Lord above
Oh please send you a friend
You prayed to the Lord above
Oh please send you a friend
Your empty pocket tell yuh
That you ain't-a-got no friend

Your babies are crying louder
It's pounding on your brain
Your babies are crying louder
It's pounding on your brain
Your wife's screams are stabbin' you
Like the dirty drivin' rain

Your grass it is turning black
There's no water in your well
Your grass it is turning black
There's no water in your well
You spent your last lone dollar
On seven shotgun shells

Way out in the wilderness
A cold coyote calls
Way out in the wilderness
A cold coyote calls
Your eyes fix on the shotgun
That's hangin' on the wall

Your brain is a-bleedin'
And your legs can't seem to stand
Your brain is a-bleedin'
And your legs can't seem to stand
Your eyes fix on the shotgun
That you're holdin' in your hand

There's seven breezes a-blowin'
All around the cabin door
There's seven breezes a-blowin'
All around the cabin door
Seven shots ring out
Like the ocean's pounding roar

There's seven people dead
On a South Dakota farm
There's seven people dead
On a South Dakota farm
Somewhere in the distance
There's seven new people born

# With God on Our Side

Oh my name it is nothin'
My age it means less
The country I come from
Is called the Midwest
I's taught and brought up there
The laws to abide
And that land that I live in
Has God on its side.

Oh the history books tell it
They tell it so well
The cavalries charged
The Indians fell
The cavalries charged
The Indians died
Oh the country was young
With God on its side.

Oh the Spanish-American
War had its day
And the Civil War too
Was soon laid away
And the names of the heroes
I's made to memorize
With guns in their hands
And God on their side.

Oh the First World War, boys
It closed out its fate
The reason for fighting
I never got straight
But I learned to accept it
Accept it with pride
For you don't count the dead
When God's on your side.

132

When the Second World War
Came to an end
We forgave the Germans
And we were friends
Though they murdered six million
In the ovens they fried
The Germans now too
Have God on their side.

I've learned to hate Russians
All through my whole life
If another war starts
It's them we must fight
To hate them and fear them
To run and to hide
And accept it all bravely
With God on my side.

But now we got weapons
Of the chemical dust
If fire them we're forced to
Then fire them we must
One push of the button
And a shot the world wide
And you never ask questions
When God's on your side.

In a many dark hour
I've been thinkin' about this
That Jesus Christ
Was betrayed by a kiss
But I can't think for you
You'll have to decide

Whether Judas Iscariot
Had God on his side.

So now as I'm leavin'
I'm weary as Hell
The confusion I'm feelin'
Ain't no tongue can tell
The words fill my head
And fall to the floor
If God's on our side
He'll stop the next war.

# One Too Many Mornings

Down the street the dogs are barkin'
And the day is a-gettin' dark.
As the night comes in a-fallin',
The dogs'll lose their bark.
An' the silent night will shatter
From the sounds inside my mind,
For I'm one too many mornings
And a thousand miles behind.

From the crossroads of my doorstep,
My eyes they start to fade,
As I turn my head back to the room
Where my love and I have laid.
An' I gaze back to the street,
The sidewalk and the sign,
And I'm one too many mornings
An' a thousand miles behind.

It's a restless hungry feeling
That don't mean no one no good,
When ev'rything I'm a-sayin'
You can say it just as good.
You're right from your side,
I'm right from mine.
We're both just too many mornings
An' a thousand miles behind.

# North Country Blues

Come gather 'round friends
And I'll tell you a tale
Of when the red iron pits ran plenty.
But the cardboard filled windows
And old men on the benches
Tell you now that the whole town is empty.

In the north end of town,
My own children are grown
But I was raised on the other.
In the wee hours of youth,
My mother took sick
And I was brought up by my brother.

The iron ore poured
As the years passed the door,
The drag lines an' the shovels they was a-humming.
'Til one day my brother
Failed to come home
The same as my father before him.

Well a long winter's wait,
From the window I watched.
My friends they couldn't have been kinder.
And my schooling was cut
As I quit in the spring
To marry John Thomas, a miner.

Oh the years passed again
And the givin' was good,
With the lunch bucket filled every season.
What with three babies born,
The work was cut down
To a half a day's shift with no reason.

Then the shaft was soon shut
And more work was cut,
And the fire in the air, it felt frozen.
'Til a man come to speak
And he said in one week
That number eleven was closin'.

They complained in the East,
They are paying too high.
They say that your ore ain't worth digging.
That it's much cheaper down
In the South American towns
Where the miners work almost for nothing.

So the mining gates locked
And the red iron rotted
And the room smelled heavy from drinking.
Where the sad, silent song
Made the hour twice as long
As I waited for the sun to go sinking.

I lived by the window
As he talked to himself,
This silence of tongues it was building.
Then one morning's wake,
The bed it was bare,
And I's left alone with three children.

The summer is gone,
The ground's turning cold,
The stores one by one they're a-foldin'.
My children will go
As soon as they grow.
Well, there ain't nothing here now to hold them.

# Only a Pawn in Their Game

A bullet from the back of a bush took Medgar Evers' blood.
A finger fired the trigger to his name.
A handle hid out in the dark
A hand set the spark
Two eyes took the aim
Behind a man's brain
But he can't be blamed
He's only a pawn in their game.

A South politician preaches to the poor white man,
'You got more than the blacks, don't complain.
You're better than them, you been born with white skin,' they
    explain.
And the Negro's name
Is used it is plain
For the politician's gain
As he rises to fame
And the poor white remains
On the caboose of the train
But it ain't him to blame
He's only a pawn in their game.

The deputy sheriffs, the soldiers, the governors get paid,
And the marshals and cops get the same,
But the poor white man's used in the hands of them all like a
    tool.
He's taught in his school
From the start by the rule
That the laws are with him
To protect his white skin
To keep up his hate
So he never thinks straight
'Bout the shape that he's in

But it ain't him to blame
He's only a pawn in their game.

From the poverty shacks, he looks from the cracks to the tracks,
And the hoof beats pound in his brain.
And he's taught how to walk in a pack
Shoot in the back
With his fist in a clinch
To hang and to lynch
To hide 'neath the hood
To kill with no pain
Like a dog on a chain
He ain't got no name
But it ain't him to blame
He's only a pawn in their game.

Today, Medgar Evers was buried from the bullet he caught.
They lowered him down as a king.
But when the shadowy sun sets on the one
That fired the gun
He'll see by his grave
On the stone that remains
Carved next to his name
His epitaph plain:
Only a pawn in their game.

# Boots of Spanish Leather

Oh, I'm sailin' away my own true love,
I'm sailin' away in the morning.
Is there something I can send you from across the sea,
From the place that I'll be landing?

No, there's nothin' you can send me, my own true love,
There's nothin' I wish to be ownin'.
Just carry yourself back to me unspoiled,
From across that lonesome ocean.

Oh, but I just thought you might want something fine
Made of silver or of golden,
Either from the mountains of Madrid
Or from the coast of Barcelona.

Oh, but if I had the stars from the darkest night
And the diamonds from the deepest ocean,
I'd forsake them all for your sweet kiss,
For that's all I'm wishin' to be ownin'.

That I might be gone a long time
And it's only that I'm askin',
Is there something I can send you to remember me by,
To make your time more easy passin'.

Oh, how can, how can you ask me again,
It only brings me sorrow.
The same thing I want from you today,
I would want again tomorrow.

I got a letter on a lonesome day,
It was from her ship a-sailin',
Saying I don't know when I'll be comin' back again,
It depends on how I'm a-feelin'.

Well, if you, my love, must think that-a-way,
I'm sure your mind is roamin'.
I'm sure your heart is not with me,
But with the country to where you're goin'.

So take heed, take heed of the western wind,
Take heed of the stormy weather.
And yes, there's something you can send back to me,
Spanish boots of Spanish leather.

# When the Ship Comes In

Oh the time will come up
When the winds will stop
And the breeze will cease to be breathin'.
Like the stillness in the wind
'Fore the hurricane begins,
The hour when the ship comes in.

Oh the seas will split
And the ship will hit
And the sands on the shoreline will be shaking.
Then the tide will sound
And the wind will pound
And the morning will be breaking.

Oh the fishes will laugh
As they swim out of the path
And the seagulls they'll be smiling.
And the rocks on the sand
Will proudly stand,
The hour that the ship comes in.

And the words that are used
For to get the ship confused
Will not be understood as they're spoken.
For the chains of the sea
Will have busted in the night
And will be buried at the bottom of the ocean.

A song will lift
As the mainsail shifts
And the boat drifts on to the shoreline.
And the sun will respect
Every face on the deck,
The hour that the ship comes in.

Then the sands will roll
Out a carpet of gold
For your weary toes to be a-touchin'.
And the ship's wise men
Will remind you once again
That the whole wide world is watchin'.

Oh the foes will rise
With the sleep still in their eyes
And they'll jerk from their beds and think they're dreamin'.
But they'll pinch themselves and squeal
And know that it's for real,
The hour when the ship comes in.

Then they'll raise their hands,
Sayin' we'll meet all your demands,
But we'll shout from the bow your days are numbered.
And like Pharaoh's tribe,
They'll be drownded in the tide,
And like Goliath, they'll be conquered.

# The Lonesome Death
# of Hattie Carroll

William Zanzinger killed poor Hattie Carroll
With a cane that he twirled around his diamond ring finger
At a Baltimore hotel society gath'rin'.
And the cops were called in and his weapon took from him
As they rode him in custody down to the station
And booked William Zanzinger for first-degree murder.
But you who philosophize disgrace and criticize all fears,
Take the rag away from your face.
Now ain't the time for your tears.

William Zanzinger, who at twenty-four years
Owns a tobacco farm of six hundred acres
With rich wealthy parents who provide and protect him
And high office relations in the politics of Maryland,
Reacted to his deed with a shrug of his shoulders
And swear words and sneering, and his tongue it was snarling,
In a matter of minutes on bail was out walking.
But you who philosophize disgrace and criticize all fears,
Take the rag away from your face.
Now ain't the time for your tears.

Hattie Carroll was a maid of the kitchen.
She was fifty-one years old and gave birth to ten children
Who carried the dishes and took out the garbage
And never sat once at the head of the table
And didn't even talk to the people at the table
Who just cleaned up all the food from the table
And emptied the ashtrays on a whole other level,
Got killed by a blow, lay slain by a cane
That sailed through the air and came down through the room,
Doomed and determined to destroy all the gentle.
And she never done nothing to William Zanzinger.
But you who philosophize disgrace and criticize all fears,

Take the rag away from your face.
Now ain't the time for your tears.

In the courtroom of honor, the judge pounded his gavel
To show that all's equal and that the courts are on the level
And that the strings in the books ain't pulled and persuaded
And that even the nobles get properly handled
Once that the cops have chased after and caught 'em
And that the ladder of law has no top and no bottom,
Stared at the person who killed for no reason
Who just happened to be feelin' that way without warnin'.
And he spoke through his cloak, most deep and distinguished,
And handed out strongly, for penalty and repentance,
William Zanzinger with a six-month sentence.
Oh, but you who philosophize disgrace and criticize all fears,
Bury the rag deep in your face
For now's the time for your tears.

# Restless Farewell

Oh all the money that in my whole life I did spend,
Be it mine right or wrongfully,
I let it slip gladly past the hands of my friends
To tie up the time most forcefully.
But the bottles are done,
We've killed each one
And the table's full and overflowed.
And the corner sign
Says it's closing time,
So I'll bid farewell and be down the road.

Oh ev'ry girl that ever I've touched,
I did not do it harmfully.
And ev'ry girl that ever I've hurt,
I did not do it knowin'ly.
But to remain as friends and make amends
You need the time and stay behind.
And since my feet are now fast
And point away from the past,
I'll bid farewell and be down the line.

Oh ev'ry foe that ever I faced,
The cause was there before we came.
And ev'ry cause that ever I fought,
I fought it full without regret or shame.
But the dark does die
As the curtain is drawn and somebody's eyes
Must meet the dawn.
And if I see the day
I'd only have to stay,
So I'll bid farewell in the night and be gone.

Oh, ev'ry thought that's strung a knot in my mind,
I might go insane if it couldn't be sprung.

But it's not to stand naked under unknowin' eyes,
It's for myself and my friends my stories are sung.
But the time ain't tall,
Yet on time you depend and no word is possessed
By no special friend.
And though the line is cut,
It ain't quite the end,
I'll just bid farewell till we meet again.

Oh a false clock tries to tick out my time
To disgrace, distract, and bother me.
And the dirt of gossip blows into my face,
And the dust of rumors covers me.
But if the arrow is straight
And the point is slick,
It can pierce through dust no matter how thick.
So I'll make my stand
And remain as I am
And bid farewell and not give a damn.

# 11 Outlined Epitaphs (liner notes)

I end up then
in the early evenin'
blindly punchin' at the blind
breathin' heavy
stutterin'
an' blowin' up
where t' go?
what is it that's exactly wrong?
who t' picket?
who t' fight?
behind what windows
will I at least
hear someone from the supper table
get up t' ask
'did I hear someone outside just now?'
yesterday
an hour ago
it came t' me in
a second's flash
an' was all so clear
it still is now
yes it is
it's maybe hidin'
it must be hidin'
the shot has shook
me up . . . for I've never
heard that sound before
bringing wild thoughts at first
ragged wild
numb wild
now though they've leveled out
an' been wrung out
leavin' nothin' but the strangeness
the roots within a washed-out cloth

drippin' from the clothesline pole
strange thoughts
doubtin' thoughts
useless an' unnecessary
the blast it's true
startled me back but for a spell
content with
all pictures, posters an' the like
that're painted for me
ah but I turned
an' the nex' time I looked
the gloves of garbage
had clobbered the canvas
leavin' truckloads of trash
clutterin' the colors
with a blindin' sting
forcin' me t' once again
slam the shutters of my eyes
but also me to wonderin'
when they'll open
much much stronger
than anyone whose own eyes're
aimed over here at mine
'when will he open up his eyes?'
'who him? doncha know? he's a crazy man
he never opens up his eyes'
'but he'll surely miss the world go by'
'nah! he lives in his own world'
'my my then he really must be a crazy man'
'yeah he's a crazy man'

an' so on spangled streets
an' country roads
I hear sleigh bells

jingle jangle
virgin girls
far into the field
sing an' laugh
with flickerin' voices
softly fadin'
I stop an' smile
an' rest awhile
watchin' the candles
of sundown dim
unnoticed
unnoticed for my eyes're closed

————

The town I was born in holds no memories
but for the honkin' foghorns
the rainy mist
an' the rocky cliffs
I have carried no feelings
up past the Lake Superior hills
the town I grew up in is the one
that has left me with my legacy visions
it was not a rich town
my parents were not rich
it was not a poor town
an' my parents were not poor
it was a dyin' town
(it was a dyin' town)
a train line cuts the ground
showin' where the fathers an' mothers
of me an' my friends had picked
up an' moved from
north Hibbing

t' south Hibbing.
old north Hibbing . . .
deserted
already dead
with its old stone courthouse
decayin' in the wind
long abandoned
windows crashed out
the breath of its broken walls
being smothered in clingin' moss
the old school
where my mother went to
rottin' shiverin' but still livin'
standin' cold an' lonesome
arms cut off
with even the moon bypassin' its jagged body
pretendin' not t'see
an' givin' it its final dignity
dogs howled over the graveyard
where even the markin' stones were dead
an' there was no sound except for the wind
blowin' through the high grass
an' the bricks that fell back
t' the dirt from a slight stab
of the breeze . . . it was as though
the rains of wartime had
left the land bombed-out an' shattered

south Hibbing
is where everybody came t' start their
town again. but the winds of the
north came followin' an' grew fiercer
an' the years went by
but I was young

an' so I ran
an' kept runnin' . . .

I am still runnin' I guess
but my road has seen many changes
for I've served my time as a refugee
in mental terms an' in physical terms
an' many a fear has vanished
an' many an attitude has fallen
an' many a dream has faded
an' I know I shall meet the snowy North
again – but with changed eyes nex' time 'round
t' walk lazily down its streets
an' linger by the edge of town
find old friends if they're still around
talk t' the old people
an' the young people
running yes . . .
but stoppin' for a while
embracin' what I left
an' lovin' it – for I learned by now
never t' expect
what it cannot give me

————

In times behind, I too
wished I'd lived
in the hungry thirties
an' blew in like Woody
t' New York City
an' sang for dimes
on subway trains
satisfied at a nickel fare

an' passin' the hat
an' hittin' the bars
on eighth avenue
an' makin' the rounds
t' the union halls
but when I came in
the fares were higher
up t' fifteen cents an' climbin'
an' those bars that Woody's guitar
rattled . . . they've changed
they've been remodeled
an' those union halls
like the cio
an' the nmu
come now! can you see 'em
needin' me
for a song
or two

ah where are those forces of yesteryear?
why didn't they meet me here
an' greet me here?

the underground's gone deeper
says the old chimney sweeper
the underground's outa work
sing the bells of New York
the underground's more dangerous
ring the bells of Los Angeles
the underground's gone
cry the bells of San Juan
but where has it gone to
ring the bells of Toronto

153

strength now shines through my window
regainin' me an' rousin' me
day by day
from the weariness
of walkin' with ghosts
that rose an' had risen
from the ruins an' remains
of the model T past
even though I clutched t' its sheet
I was still refused
an' left confused
for there was nobody there
t' let me in

a wasteland wind whistled
from behind the billboard
'there's nobody home
all has moved out'
flatly denied
I turned indeed
flinched at first
but said 'ok
I get the message'
feelin' unwanted? no
unloved? no
I felt nothin'
for there was nobody there
I didn't see no one
t' want or unwant
to love or not love
maybe they're there
but won't let me in
not takin' chances
on the ones that come knockin'
should I then be angry?

I feel that the grittin' of my teeth
for only a second
would mean
my mind has just been
swallowed whole
an' so I step back t' the street
an' then turn further down the road
poundin' on doors
lost?
not really
just out lookin'
a stranger?
no not a stranger but rather someone
who just doesn't live here
never pretendin' t' be knowin'
what's worth seekin'
but at least
without ghosts by my side
t' betray my childishness
t' leadeth me down false trails
an' maketh me drink from muddy waters
yes it is I
who is poundin' at your door
if it is you inside
who hears the noise

———

Jim Jim
where is our party?
where is the party that's one
where all members're held equal
an' vow t' infiltrate that thought
among the people it hopes t' serve

an' sets a respected road
for all of those like me
who cry
'I am ragin'ly against absolutely
everything that wants t' force nature
t' be unnatural (be it human or otherwise)
an' I am violently for absolutely
everything that will fight those
forces (be them human or otherwise)'
oh what is the name of this gallant group?
lead me t' the ballot box
what man do we run?
how many votes will it take
for a new set of teeth
in the congress mouths?
how many hands have t' be raised
before hair will grow back
on the white house head?
a Boston tea party don't mean the
same thing . . . as it did in the newborn
years before. even the
meanin' of the word
has changed. ha
ha . . . t' say the least
yes that party is truly gone
but where is the party t' dump the feelings
of the fiery cross burners
an' flamin' match carriers?
if there was such a party
they would've been dumped
long before this . . . who is supposed
t' dump 'em now?
when all can see their threads hang weak
but still hold strong

loyal but dyin'
fightin' for breath
who then will kill its misery?
what sea shall we pollute?

when told t' learn
what others know
in order for a soothin' life
an' t' conquer many a brainwashed dream
I was set forth on records an' books
from the forces that were sold t' me
an' could be found in hung-up style
wanderin' through crowded valleys
searchin' for what others knew
with the eagles' shadows
silent
hungry
watchin' waitin'
from high mountains
an' me just walkin'
butterflies in my head
an' bitter by now
(here! take this kid, an' learn it well
but why sir? my arms're so heavy
I said take it. it'll do yuh good
but I ain't learned last night's lesson yet.
am I gonna have t' get mad with you?
no no gimme gimme just stick it on top
a the rest a the stuff
here! if yuh learn it well yuh'll
get an A . . . an' don't do anything
I wouldn't do)
and with each new brightnin' phrase
more messy

157

till I found myself almost swallowed
deep in burden
spinnin'
walkin' slower
heavier heavier
glassy-eyed
but at last I heard
the eagle drool
as I zombie strolled
up past the foothills
thunderstruck
an' I stopped cold
an' bellowed
'I don't wanna learn no more
I had enough'
an' I took a deep breath
turned around
an' ran for my life
shoutin' shoutin'
back t' the highway
away from the mountain
not carin' no more
what people knew about things
but rather how they felt about things
runnin' down another road
an older road
through time an' dignity
an' I have never taken off my boots
no matter how the miles have burnt
my feet . . .
an' I'm still on that road, Jim
I'm still sleepin' at night by its side
an' eatin' where it'll lead me t' food
where state lines don't stand

an' knowledge don't count
when feelings are hurt
an' I am on the side a them hurt feelings
plunged on by unsensitive hammers
an' made t' bleed by rusty nails
an' I look t' you, Jim
where is the party for those kind of feelings?
how're the gamblers that wheel an' deal an'
shuffle 'em around gonna be got outa the game?
from here in
beyond this
an' from now on

———————

Al's wife claimed I can't be happy
as the New Jersey night ran backwards
an' vanished behind our rollin' ear
'I dig the colors outside, an' I'm happy'
'but you sing such depressin' songs'
'but you say so on your terms'
'but my terms aren't so unreal'
'yes but they're still your terms'
'but what about others that think
in those terms'
'Lenny Bruce says there're no dirty
words . . . just dirty minds an' I say there're
no depressed words just depressed minds'
'but how're you happy an' when're you happy'
'I'm happy enough now'
'why?'
'cause I'm calmly lookin' outside an' watchin'
the night unwind'
'what'd yuh mean "unwind"?'

'I mean somethin' like there's no end t' it
an' it's so big
that every time I see it it's like seein'
for the first time'
'so what?'
'so anything that ain't got no end's
just gotta be poetry in one
way or another'
'yeah but . . .'
'an' poetry makes me feel good'
'but . . .'
'an' it makes me feel happy'
'ok but . . .'
'for lack of a better word'
'but what about the songs you sing on stage?'
'they're nothin' but the unwindin' of my happiness'

_____

Woody Guthrie was my last idol
he was the last idol
because he was the first idol
I'd ever met
that taught me
face t' face
that men are men
shatterin' even himself
as an idol
an' that men have reasons
for what they do
an' what they say
an' every action can be questioned
leavin' no command
untouched an' took for granted
obeyed an' bowed down to

160

forgettin' your own natural instincts
(for there're a million reasons
in the world
an' a million instincts
runnin' wild
an' it's none too many times
the two shall meet)
the unseen idols create the fear
an' trample hopes when busted
Woody never made me fear
and he didn't trample any hopes
for he just carried a book of Man
an' gave it t' me t' read awhile
an' from it I learned my greatest lesson

you ask 'how does it feel t' be an idol?'
it'd be silly of me t' answer, wouldn't it . . .?

———————

A Russian has three an' a half red eyes
five flamin' antennas
drags a beet-colored ball an' chain
an' wants t' slip germs
into my Coke machine
'burn the tree stumps at the border'
shout the sex-hungry lunatics
out warmongerin' in the early mornin'
'poison the sky so the planes won't come'
yell the birch colored knights with
patriotic shields
'an' murder all the un-Americans'
say the card-carryin' American
book burners

161

(yes we burned five books last week)
as my friend, Bobby Lee,
walks back an' forth
free now from his native Harlem
where his ma still sleeps at night
hearin' rats inside the sink
an' underneath her hardwood bed
an' walls of holes
where the cold comes in
scared
wrapped in blankets
an' she, God knows,
is kind
an' gentle
ain't there no closer villains
than the baby-eatin' Russians
rats eat babies too

I talked with one
of the sons of Germany
while walkin' once on foreign ground
an' I learned that
he regards
Adolf Hitler
as we here in the states
regards
Robert E. Lee

fasten up your
holster
mr gunslinger
an' buy new bolts
for your neck
there is no right wing
or left wing . . .

162

there is only up wing
an' down wing

last night I dreamt
that while healin' ceilings
up in Harlem
I saw Canada ablaze
an' nobody knowin'
nothin' about it
except of course
who held the match

———————

Yes, I am a thief of thoughts
not, I pray, a stealer of souls
I have built an' rebuilt
upon what is waitin'
for the sand on the beaches
carves many castles
on what has been opened
before my time
a word, a tune, a story, a line
keys in the wind t' unlock my mind
an' t' grant my closet thoughts backyard air
it is not of me t' sit an' ponder
wonderin' an' wastin' time
thinkin' of thoughts that haven't been thunk
thinkin' of dreams that haven't been dreamt
an' new ideas that haven't been wrote
an' new words t' fit into rhyme
(if it rhymes, it rhymes
if it don't, it don't

if it comes, it comes
if it won't, it won't)

no I must react an' spit fast
with weapons of words
wrapped in tunes
that've rolled through the simple years
teasin' me t' treat them right
t' reshape them an' restring them
t' protect my own world
from the mouths of all those
who'd eat it
an' hold it back from eatin' its own food
(influences?
hundreds thousands
perhaps millions
for all songs lead back t' the sea
an' at one time, there was
no singin' tongue t' imitate it)
t' make new sounds out of old sounds
an' new words out of old words
an' not t' worry about the new rules
for they ain't been made yet
an' t' shout my singin' mind
knowin' that it is me an' my kind
that will make those rules . . .
if the people of tomorrow
really need the rules of today
rally 'round all you prosecutin' attorneys
the world is but a courtroom
yes
but I know the defendants better 'n you
and while you're busy prosecutin'
we're busy whistlin'

164

cleanin' up the courthouse
sweepin' sweepin'
listenin' listenin'
winkin' t' one another
careful
         careful
your spot is comin' up soon

————

Oh where were these magazines
when I was bummin' up an' down
up an' down the street?
is it that they too just sleep
in their high thrones . . . openin'
their eyes when people pass
expectin' each t' bow as they go by
an' say 'thank you Mr Magazine.
did I answer all my questions right?'
ah but mine is of another story
for I do not care t' be made an oddball
bouncin' past reporters' pens
cooperatin' with questions
aimed at eyes that want t' see
'there's nothin' here
go back t' sleep
or look at the ads
on page 33'
I don't like t' be stuck in print
starin' out at cavity minds
who gobble chocolate candy bars
quite content an' satisfied
their day complete
at seein' what I eat for breakfast

165

the kinds of clothes I like t' wear
an' the hobbies that I like t' do

I never eat
   I run naked when I can
      my hobby's collectin' airplane glue

'come come now Mr Dylan our readers want
t' know the truth'
'that is the bare hungry sniffin' truth'
'Mr Dylan, you're very funny, but really now'
'that's all I have t' say today'
'but you'd better answer'
'that sounds like some kind of threat'
'it just could be ha ha ha ha '
'what will be my punishment'
'a rumor tale on you ha ha'
'a what kind of tale ha ha ha ha'
'yes well you'll see, Mr Dylan, you'll see'

an' I seen
or rather I have saw
your questions're ridiculous
an' most of your magazines're also ridiculous
caterin' t' people
who want t' see
the boy nex' door
no I shall not cooperate with reporters' whims
there're other kinds of boys nex' door.
even though they've slanted me
they cannot take what I do away from me
they can disguise it

166

make it out t' be a joke
an' make me seem
the ridiculous one
in the eyes of their readers
they can build me up
accordin' t' their own terms
so that they are able
t' bust me down
an' 'expose' me
in their own terms
givin' blind advice
t' unknown eyes
who have no way of knowin'
that I 'expose' myself
every time I step out
on the stage

———

The night passes fast for me now
an' after dancin' out its dance
undresses
leavin' nothin' but its naked dawn
proudly standin'
smilin' smilin'
turnin' turnin'
gently gently
I have seen it sneak up countless
times . . . leavin' me conscious
with a thousand sleepy thoughts
untamed
an' tryin' t' run
I think at these times
of many things an' many people

I think of Sue most times
beautiful Sue
with the lines of a swan
frightened easy
as a fawn in the forest
by this time deep in dreams
with her long hair spread out
the color of the sun
soakin' the dark
an' scatterin' light
t' the dungeons of my constant night
I think love poems
as a poor lonesome invalid
knowin' of my power
t' destroy
the good souls of the road
that know no sickness
except that of kindness
(you ask of love?
there is no love
except in silence
an' silence doesn't say a word)
ah but Sue
she knows me well
perhaps too well
an' is above all
the true fortuneteller of my soul
I think perhaps the only one
(you ask of truth?
there is no truth
what fool can claim t' carry the truth
for it is but a drunken matter
romantic? yes
tragic? no I think not)

the door still knocks
an' the wind still blows
bringin' me my memories
of friends an' sounds an' colors
that can't escape
trapped in keyholes
Eric . . . bearded Eric
far in Boston
buried beneath my window
yes I feel t' dig the ground up
but I'm so tired
an' know not where t' look for tools
rap tap tap
the rattlin' wind
blows Geno in
tellin' me of Philistines
that he'd run into durin' the night
he stomps across my floor
I laugh
an' drink cold coffee an' old wine
light of feelin'
as I listen t' one of my own tongues
take the reins
guide the path
an' drop me off . . . headin' back again
t' take care of his end of the night
slam an' Geno
then too is gone
outside a siren whines
leadin' me down another line
I jump but get sidetracked
by clunkin' footsteps
down the street
(it is as though my mind

ain't mine t' make up
any more)
I wonder if the cockroaches
still crawl in Dave an' Terri's
fifteenth street kitchen
I wonder if they're the same cockroaches
ah yes the times've changed
Dave still scorns me for not readin' books
an' Terri still laughs at my rakish ways
but fifteenth street has been abandoned
we have moved . . .
the cats across the roof
mad in love
scream into the drainpipes
bringin' in the sounds of music
the only music
an' it is I who is ready
ready t' listen
restin' restin'
a silver peace
reigns an'
becomes the nerves of mornin'
an' I stand up an' yawn
hot with jumpin' pulse
never tired
never sad
never guilty
for I am runnin' in a fair race
with no racetrack but the night
an' no competition but the dawn

———

So at last at least
the sky for me

is a pleasant gray
meanin' rain
or meanin' snow
constantly meanin' change
but a change forewarned
either t' the clearin' of the clouds
or t' the pourin' of the storms
an' after it's desire
returnin'
returnin' with me underneath
returnin' with it
never fearful
finally faithful
it will guide me well
across all bridges
inside all tunnels
never failin' . . .

with the sounds of François Villon
echoin' through my mad streets
as I stumble on lost cigars
of Bertolt Brecht
an' empty bottles
of Brendan Behan
the hypnotic words
of A. L. Lloyd
each one bendin' like its own song
an' the woven spell of Paul Clayton
entrancin' me like China's plague
unescapable
drownin' in the lungs of Edith Piaf
an' in the mystery of Marlene Dietrich
the dead poems of Eddie Freeman
love songs of Allen Ginsberg

an' jail songs of Ray Bremser
the narrow tunes of Modigliani
an' the singin' plains of Harry Jackson
the cries of Charles Aznavour
with melodies of Yevtushenko
through the quiet fire of Miles Davis
above the bells of William Blake
an' beat visions of Johnny Cash
an' the saintliness of Pete Seeger

strokin' my senses
down down
drownin' drownin'
when I need t' drown
for my road is blessed
with many flowers
an' the sounds of flowers
liftin' lost voices of the ground's people
up up
higher higher
all people
no matter what creed
no matter what color skin
no matter what language an' no matter what land
for all people laugh
in the same tongue
an' cry
in the same tongue
endless endless
it's all endless
an' it's all songs
it's just one big world of songs
an' they're all on loan
if they're only turned loose t' sing

lonely? ah yes
but it is the flowers an' the mirrors
of flowers that now meet my
loneliness
an' mine shall be a strong loneliness
dissolvin' deep
t' the depths of my freedom
an' that, then, shall
remain my song

there's a movie called
<u>Shoot the Piano Player</u>
the last line proclaimin'
'music, man, that's where it's at'
it is a religious line
outside, the chimes rung
an' they
    are still ringin'

# Eternal Circle

I sang the song slowly
As she stood in the shadows
She stepped to the light
As my silver strings spun
She called with her eyes
To the tune I's a-playin'
But the song it was long
And I'd only begun

Through a bullet of light
Her face was reflectin'
The fast fading words
That rolled from my tongue
With a long-distance look
Her eyes was on fire
But the song it was long
And there was more to be sung

My eyes danced a circle
Across her clear outline
With her head tilted sideways
She called me again
As the tune drifted out
She breathed hard through the echo
But the song it was long
And it was far to the end

I glanced at my guitar
And played it pretendin'
That of all the eyes out there
I could see none
As her thoughts pounded hard
Like the pierce of an arrow

But the song it was long
And it had to get done

As the tune finally folded
I laid down the guitar
Then looked for the girl
Who'd stayed for so long
But her shadow was missin'
For all of my searchin'
So I picked up my guitar
And began the next song

# Paths of Victory

Trails of troubles,
Roads of battles,
Paths of victory,
I shall walk.

The trail is dusty
And my road it might be rough,
But the better roads are waiting
And boys it ain't far off.

Trails of troubles,
Roads of battles,
Paths of victory,
We shall walk.

I walked down by the river,
I turned my head up high.
I saw that silver linin'
That was hangin' in the sky.

Trails of troubles,
Roads of battles,
Paths of victory,
We shall walk.

The evenin' dusk was rollin',
I was walking down the track.
There was a one-way wind a-blowin'
And it was blowin' at my back.

Trails of troubles,
Roads of battles,
Paths of victory,
We shall walk.

The gravel road is bumpy,
It's a hard road to ride,
But there's a clearer road a-waitin'
With the cinders on the side.

Trails of troubles,
Roads of battles,
Paths of victory,
We shall walk.

That evening train was rollin',
The hummin' of its wheels,
My eyes they saw a better day
As I looked across the fields.

Trails of troubles,
Roads of battles,
Paths of victory,
We shall walk.

The trail is dusty,
The road it might be rough,
But the good road is a-waitin'
And boys it ain't far off.

Trails of troubles,
Roads of battles,
Paths of victory,
We shall walk.

# Only a Hobo

As I was out walking on a corner one day,
I spied an old hobo, in a doorway he lay.
His face was all grounded in the cold sidewalk floor
And I guess he'd been there for the whole night or more.

Only a hobo, but one more is gone
Leavin' nobody to sing his sad song
Leavin' nobody to carry him home
Only a hobo, but one more is gone

A blanket of newspaper covered his head,
As the curb was his pillow, the street was his bed.
One look at his face showed the hard road he'd come
And a fistful of coins showed the money he bummed.

Only a hobo, but one more is gone
Leavin' nobody to sing his sad song
Leavin' nobody to carry him home
Only a hobo, but one more is gone

Does it take much of a man to see his whole life go down,
To look up on the world from a hole in the ground,
To wait for your future like a horse that's gone lame,
To lie in the gutter and die with no name?

Only a hobo, but one more is gone
Leavin' nobody to sing his sad song
Leavin' nobody to carry him home
Only a hobo, but one more is gone

# Lay Down Your Weary Tune

Lay down your weary tune, lay down,
Lay down the song you strum,
And rest yourself 'neath the strength of strings
No voice can hope to hum.

Struck by the sounds before the sun,
I knew the night had gone.
The morning breeze like a bugle blew
Against the drums of dawn.
Lay down your weary tune, lay down,
Lay down the song you strum,
And rest yourself 'neath the strength of strings
No voice can hope to hum.

The ocean wild like an organ played,
The seaweed's wove its strands.
The crashin' waves like cymbals clashed
Against the rocks and sands.
Lay down your weary tune, lay down,
Lay down the song you strum,
And rest yourself 'neath the strength of strings
No voice can hope to hum.

I stood unwound beneath the skies
And clouds unbound by laws.
The cryin' rain like a trumpet sang
And asked for no applause.
Lay down your weary tune, lay down,
Lay down the song you strum,
And rest yourself 'neath the strength of strings
No voice can hope to hum.

The last of leaves fell from the trees
And clung to a new love's breast.

The branches bare like a banjo played
To the winds that listened best.

I gazed down in the river's mirror
And watched its winding strum.
The water smooth ran like a hymn
And like a harp did hum.
Lay down your weary tune, lay down,
Lay down the song you strum,
And rest yourself 'neath the strength of strings
No voice can hope to hum.

# Percy's Song

Bad news, bad news,
Come to me where I sleep,
Turn, turn, turn again.
Sayin' one of your friends
Is in trouble deep,
Turn, turn to the rain
And the wind.

Tell me the trouble,
Tell once to my ear,
Turn, turn, turn again.
Joliet prison
And ninety-nine years,
Turn, turn to the rain
And the wind.

Oh what's the charge
Of how this came to be,
Turn, turn, turn again.
Manslaughter
In the highest of degree,
Turn, turn to the rain
And the wind.

I sat down and wrote
The best words I could write,
Turn, turn, turn again.
Explaining to the judge
I'd be there on Wednesday night,
Turn, turn to the rain
And the wind.

Without a reply,
I left by the moon,

Turn, turn, turn again.
And was in his chambers
By the next afternoon,
Turn, turn to the rain
And the wind.

Could ya tell me the facts?
I said without fear,
Turn, turn, turn again.
That a friend of mine
Would get ninety-nine years,
Turn, turn to the rain
And the wind.

A crash on the highway
Flew the car to a field,
Turn, turn, turn again.
There was four persons killed
And he was at the wheel,
Turn, turn to the rain
And the wind.

But I knew him as good
As I'm knowin' myself,
Turn, turn, turn again.
And he wouldn't harm a life
That belonged to someone else,
Turn, turn to the rain
And the wind.

The judge spoke
Out of the side of his mouth,
Turn, turn, turn again.
Sayin', 'The witness who saw,

He left little doubt,'
Turn, turn to the rain
And the wind.

That may be true,
He's got a sentence to serve,
Turn, turn, turn again.
But ninety-nine years,
He just don't deserve,
Turn, turn to the rain
And the wind.

Too late, too late,
For his case it is sealed,
Turn, turn, turn again.
His sentence is passed
And it cannot be repealed,
Turn, turn to the rain
And the wind.

But he ain't no criminal
And his crime it is none,
Turn, turn, turn again.
What happened to him
Could happen to anyone,
Turn, turn to the rain
And the wind.

And at that the judge jerked forward
And his face it did freeze,
Turn, turn, turn again.
Sayin', 'Could you kindly leave
My office now, please,'

Turn, turn to the rain
And the wind.

Well his eyes looked funny
And I stood up so slow,
Turn, turn, turn again.
With no other choice
Except for to go,
Turn, turn to the rain
And the wind.

I walked down the hallway
And I heard his door slam,
Turn, turn, turn again.
I walked down the courthouse stairs
And I did not understand,
Turn, turn to the rain
And the wind.

And I played my guitar
Through the night to the day,
Turn, turn, turn again.
And the only tune
My guitar could play
Was, 'Oh the Cruel Rain
And the Wind.'

# Guess I'm Doin' Fine

Well, I ain't got my childhood
Or friends I once did know.
No, I ain't got my childhood
Or friends I once did know.
But I still got my voice left,
I can take it anywhere I go.
Hey, hey, so I guess I'm doin' fine.

And I've never had much money
But I'm still around somehow.
No, I've never had much money
But I'm still around somehow.
Many times I've bended
But I ain't never yet bowed.
Hey, hey, so I guess I'm doin' fine.

Trouble, oh trouble,
I've trouble on my mind.
Trouble, oh trouble,
Trouble on my mind.
But the trouble in the world, Lord,
Is much more bigger than mine.
Hey, hey, so I guess I'm doin' fine.

And I never had no armies
To jump at my command.
No, I ain't got no armies
To jump at my command.
But I don't need no armies,
I got me one good friend.
Hey, hey, so I guess I'm doin' fine.

I been kicked and whipped and trampled on,
I been shot at just like you.

I been kicked and whipped and trampled on,
I been shot at just like you.
But as long as the world keeps a-turnin',
I just keep a-turnin' too.
Hey, hey, so I guess I'm doin' fine.

Well, my road might be rocky,
The stones might cut my face.
My road it might be rocky,
The stones might cut my face.
But as some folks ain't got no road at all,
They gotta stand in the same old place.
Hey, hey, so I guess I'm doin' fine.

# Advice for Geraldine
# on Her Miscellaneous Birthday

stay in line. stay in step. people
are afraid of someone who is not
in step with them. it makes them
look foolish t' themselves for
being in step. it might even
cross their mind that they themselves
are in the wrong step. do not run
nor cross the red line. if you go
too far out in any direction, they
will lose sight of you. they'll feel
threatened. thinking that they are
not a part of something that they
saw go past them, they'll feel
something's going on up there that
they don't know about. revenge
will set in. they will start thinking
of how t' get rid of you. act
mannerly towards them. if you don't,
they will take it personal. as you
come directly in contact face t' face
do not make it a secret of how
much you need them. if they sense
that you have no need for them,
the first thing they will do is
try t' make you need them. if
this doesn't work, they will tell
you of how much they don't need
you. if you do not show any sadness
at a remark such as this, they
will immediately tell other people
of how much they don't need you.
your name will begin t' come up
in circles where people gather
to tell about all the people they

don't need. you will begin t' get
famous this way. this, though, will
only get the people who you don't need
in the first place
all the more madder.
you will become
a whole topic of conversation.
needless t' say, these people
who don't need you will start
hating themselves for needing t' talk
about you. then you yourself will
start hating yourself for causing so
much hate. as you can see, it will
all end in one great gunburst.
never trust a cop in a raincoat.
when asked t' define yourself exactly,
say you are an exact mathematician.
do not say or do anything that
he who standing in front of you
watching cannot understand. he will
feel you know something he
doesn't. he will take it as a serious
blow. he will react with blinding
speed and write your name down.
talk on his terms. if his terms
are old-fashioned an' you've
passed that stage all the more easier
t' get back there. say what he
can understand clearly. say it simple
t' keep your tongue out of your
cheek. after he hears you, he can
label you good or bad. anyone will
do. t' some people, there is only
good an' bad. in any case, it will
make him feel somewhat important.

it is better t' stay away from
these people. be careful of
enthusiasm . . . it is all temporary
an' don't let it sway you. when asked
if you go t' church, always answer
yes, never look at your shoes. when
asked what you think of gene autry
singing of hard rains gonna fall say
that nobody can sing it as good as
peter, paul and mary. at the mention
of the president's name, eat a pint of
yogurt an' go t' sleep early . . . when
asked if you're a communist, sing
america the beautiful in an
italian accent. beat up nearest
street cleaner. if by any
chance you're caught naked in a
parked car, quick turn the radio on
full blast an' pretend
that you're driving. never leave
the house without a jar of peanut
butter. do not wear
matched socks. when asked to do 100
pushups always smoke a pound
of deodorant beforehand.
when asked if you're a capitalist, rip
open your shirt, sing buddy can
you spare a dime with your
right foot forward an' proceed t'
chew up a dollar bill.
do not sign any dotted line. do not
fall in trap of criticizing people
who do nothing else but criticize.
do Not create anything, it will be

misinterpreted. it will not change.
it will follow you the
rest of your life. when asked what you
do for a living say you laugh for
a living. be suspicious of people
who say that if you are not nice
t' them, they will commit suicide.
when asked if you care about
the world's problems, look deeply
into the eyes of he that asks
you, he will not ask you again. when
asked if you've spent time in jail,
announce proudly that some of your
best friends've asked you that.
beware of bathroom walls that've not
been written on. when told t' look at
yourself . . . never look. when asked
t' give your real name . . . never give it.

# Another Side of Bob Dylan

**All I Really Want to Do**
**Black Crow Blues**
**Spanish Harlem Incident**
**Chimes of Freedom**
**I Shall Be Free No. 10**
**To Ramona**
**Motorpsycho Nightmare**
**My Back Pages**
**I Don't Believe You**
 **(She Acts Like We Never Have Met)**
**Ballad in Plain D**
**It Ain't Me, Babe**

Some Other Kinds of Songs . . . *(jacket notes)*
Denise
If You Gotta Go, Go Now
Mama, You Been on My Mind
Playboys and Playgirls

# All I Really Want to Do

I ain't lookin' to compete with you,
Beat or cheat or mistreat you,
Simplify you, classify you,
Deny, defy or crucify you.
All I really want to do
Is, baby, be friends with you.

No, and I ain't lookin' to fight with you,
Frighten you or tighten you,
Drag you down or drain you down,
Chain you down or bring you down.
All I really want to do
Is, baby, be friends with you.

I ain't lookin' to block you up,
Shock or knock or lock you up,
Analyze you, categorize you,
Finalize you or advertise you.
All I really want to do
Is, baby, be friends with you.

I don't want to straight-face you,
Race or chase you, track or trace you,
Or disgrace you or displace you,
Or define you or confine you.
All I really want to do
Is, baby, be friends with you.

I don't want to meet your kin,
Make you spin or do you in,
Or select you or dissect you,
Or inspect you or reject you.
All I really want to do
Is, baby, be friends with you.

I don't want to fake you out,
Take or shake or forsake you out,
I ain't lookin' for you to feel like me,
See like me or be like me.
All I really want to do
Is, baby, be friends with you.

# Black Crow Blues

I woke in the mornin', wand'rin',
Wasted and worn out.
I woke in the mornin', wand'rin',
Wasted and worn out.
Wishin' my long-lost lover
Will walk to me, talk to me,
Tell me what it's all about.

I was standin' at the side road
Listenin' to the billboard knock.
Standin' at the side road
Listenin' to the billboard knock.
Well, my wrist was empty
But my nerves were kickin',
Tickin' like a clock.

If I got anything you need, babe,
Let me tell you in front.
If I got anything you need, babe,
Let me tell you in front.
You can come to me sometime,
Night time, day time,
Any time you want.

Sometimes I'm thinkin' I'm
Too high to fall.
Sometimes I'm thinkin' I'm
Too high to fall.
Other times I'm thinkin' I'm
So low I don't know
If I can come up at all.

Black crows in the meadow
Across a broad highway.

Black crows in the meadow
Across a broad highway.
Though it's funny, honey,
I just don't feel much like a
Scarecrow today.

# Spanish Harlem Incident

Gypsy gal, the hands of Harlem
Cannot hold you to its heat.
Your temperature's too hot for taming,
Your flaming feet burn up the street.
I am homeless, come and take me
Into reach of your rattling drums.
Let me know, babe, about my fortune
Down along my restless palms.

Gypsy gal, you got me swallowed.
I have fallen far beneath
Your pearly eyes, so fast an' slashing,
An' your flashing diamond teeth.
The night is pitch black, come an' make my
Pale face fit into place, ah, please!
Let me know, babe, I got to know, babe,
If it's you my lifelines trace.

I been wond'rin' all about me
Ever since I seen you there.
On the cliffs of your wildcat charms I'm riding,
I know I'm 'round you but I don't know where.
You have slayed me, you have made me,
I got to laugh halfways off my heels.
I got to know, babe, will I be touching you
So I can tell if I'm really real.

# Chimes of Freedom

Far between sundown's finish an' midnight's broken toll
We ducked inside the doorway, thunder crashing
As majestic bells of bolts struck shadows in the sounds
Seeming to be the chimes of freedom flashing
Flashing for the warriors whose strength is not to fight
Flashing for the refugees on the unarmed road of flight
An' for each an' ev'ry underdog soldier in the night
An' we gazed upon the chimes of freedom flashing.

In the city's melted furnace, unexpectedly we watched
With faces hidden while the walls were tightening
As the echo of the wedding bells before the blowin' rain
Dissolved into the bells of the lightning
Tolling for the rebel, tolling for the rake
Tolling for the luckless, the abandoned an' forsaked
Tolling for the outcast, burnin' constantly at stake
An' we gazed upon the chimes of freedom flashing.

Through the mad mystic hammering of the wild ripping hail
The sky cracked its poems in naked wonder
That the clinging of the church bells blew far into the breeze
Leaving only bells of lightning and its thunder
Striking for the gentle, striking for the kind
Striking for the guardians and protectors of the mind
An' the unpawned painter behind beyond his rightful time
An' we gazed upon the chimes of freedom flashing.

Through the wild cathedral evening the rain unraveled tales
For the disrobed faceless forms of no position
Tolling for the tongues with no place to bring their thoughts
All down in taken-for granted situations
Tolling for the deaf an' blind, tolling for the mute
Tolling for the mistreated, mateless mother, the mistitled
  prostitute

For the misdemeanor outlaw, chased an' cheated by pursuit
An' we gazed upon the chimes of freedom flashing.

Even though a cloud's white curtain in a far-off corner flashed
An' the hypnotic splattered mist was slowly lifting
Electric light still struck like arrows, fired but for the ones
Condemned to drift or else be kept from drifting
Tolling for the searching ones, on their speechless, seeking trail
For the lonesome-hearted lovers with too personal a tale
An' for each unharmful, gentle soul misplaced inside a jail
An' we gazed upon the chimes of freedom flashing.

Starry-eyed an' laughing as I recall when we were caught
Trapped by no track of hours for they hanged suspended
As we listened one last time an' we watched with one last look
Spellbound an' swallowed 'til the tolling ended
Tolling for the aching ones whose wounds cannot be nursed
For the countless confused, accused, misused, strung-out ones
   an' worse
An' for every hung-up person in the whole wide universe
An' we gazed upon the chimes of freedom flashing.

# I Shall Be Free No. 10

I'm just average, common too
I'm just like him, the same as you
I'm everybody's brother and son
I ain't different from anyone
It ain't no use a-talking to me
It's just the same as talking to you.

I was shadow-boxing earlier in the day
I figured I was ready for Cassius Clay
I said 'Fee, fie, fo, fum, Cassius Clay, here I come
26, 27, 28, 29, I'm gonna make your face look just like mine
Five, four, three, two, one, Cassius Clay you'd better run
99, 100, 101, 102, your ma won't even recognize you
14, 15, 16, 17, 18, 19, gonna knock him clean right out of his
    spleen.'

Well, I don't know, but I've been told
The streets in heaven are lined with gold
I ask you how things could get much worse
If the Russians happen to get up there first.
Wowee! pretty scary!

Now, I'm liberal, but to a degree
I want ev'rybody to be free
But if you think that I'll let Barry Goldwater
Move in next door and marry my daughter
You must think I'm crazy!
I wouldn't let him do it for all the farms in Cuba.

Well, I set my monkey on the log
And ordered him to do the Dog
He wagged his tail and shook his head
And he went and did the Cat instead
He's a weird monkey, very funky.

I sat with my high-heeled sneakers on
Waiting to play tennis in the noonday sun
I had my white shorts rolled up past my waist
And my wig-hat was falling in my face
But they wouldn't let me on the tennis court.

I gotta woman, she's so mean
She sticks my boots in the washing machine
Sticks me with buckshot when I'm nude
Puts bubblegum in my food
She's funny, wants my money, calls me 'honey.'

Now I gotta friend who spends his life
Stabbing my picture with a bowie-knife
Dreams of strangling me with a scarf
When my name comes up he pretends to barf.
I've got a million friends!

Now they asked me to read a poem
At the sorority sister's home
I got knocked down and my head was swimmin'
I wound up with the Dean of Women
Yippee! I'm a poet, and I know it.
Hope I don't blow it.

I'm gonna grow my hair down to my feet so strange
So I look like a walking mountain range
And I'm gonna ride into Omaha on a horse
Out to the country club and the golf course.
Carry the New York Times, shoot a few holes, blow their minds.

Now you're probably wondering by now
Just what this song is all about
What's probably got you baffled more

Is what this thing here is for.
It's nothing
It's something I learned over in England.

# To Ramona

Ramona, come closer,
Shut softly your watery eyes.
The pangs of your sadness
Shall pass as your senses will rise.
The flowers of the city
Though breathlike, get deathlike at times.
And there's no use in tryin'
T' deal with the dyin',
Though I cannot explain that in lines.

Your cracked country lips,
I still wish to kiss,
As to be under the strength of your skin.
Your magnetic movements
Still capture the minutes I'm in.
But it grieves my heart, love,
To see you tryin' to be a part of
A world that just don't exist.
It's all just a dream, babe,
A vacuum, a scheme, babe,
That sucks you into feelin' like this.

I can see that your head
Has been twisted and fed
By worthless foam from the mouth.
I can tell you are torn
Between stayin' and returnin'
On back to the South.
You've been fooled into thinking
That the finishin' end is at hand.
Yet there's no one to beat you,
No one t' defeat you,
'Cept the thoughts of yourself feeling bad.

I've heard you say many times
That you're better 'n no one
And no one is better 'n you.
If you really believe that,
You know you got
Nothing to win and nothing to lose.
From fixtures and forces and friends,
Your sorrow does stem,
That hype you and type you,
Making you feel
That you must be exactly like them.

I'd forever talk to you,
But soon my words,
They would turn into a meaningless ring.
For deep in my heart
I know there is no help I can bring.
Everything passes,
Everything changes,
Just do what you think you should do.
And someday maybe,
Who knows, baby,
I'll come and be cryin' to you.

# Motorpsycho Nightmare

I pounded on a farmhouse
Lookin' for a place to stay.
I was mighty, mighty tired,
I had gone a long, long way.
I said, 'Hey, hey, in there,
Is there anybody home?'
I was standin' on the steps
Feelin' most alone.
Well, out comes a farmer,
He must have thought that I was nuts.
He immediately looked at me
And stuck a gun into my guts.

I fell down
To my bended knees,
Saying, 'I dig farmers,
Don't shoot me, please!'
He cocked his rifle
And began to shout,
'You're that travelin' salesman
That I have heard about.'
I said, 'No! No! No!
I'm a doctor and it's true,
I'm a clean-cut kid
And I been to college, too.'

Then in comes his daughter
Whose name was Rita.
She looked like she stepped out of
La Dolce Vita.
I immediately tried to cool it
With her dad,
And told him what a
Nice, pretty farm he had.

He said, 'What do doctors
Know about farms, pray tell?'
I said, 'I was born
At the bottom of a wishing well.'

Well, by the dirt 'neath my nails
I guess he knew I wouldn't lie.
'I guess you're tired,'
He said, kinda sly.
I said, 'Yes, ten thousand miles
Today I drove.'
He said, 'I got a bed for you
Underneath the stove.
Just one condition
And you go to sleep right now,
That you don't touch my daughter
And in the morning, milk the cow.'

I was sleepin' like a rat
When I heard something jerkin'.
There stood Rita
Lookin' just like Tony Perkins.
She said, 'Would you like to take a shower?
I'll show you up to the door.'
I said, 'Oh, no! no!
I've been through this before.'
I knew I had to split
But I didn't know how,
When she said,
'Would you like to take that shower, now?'

Well, I couldn't leave
Unless the old man chased me out,
'Cause I'd already promised

That I'd milk his cows.
I had to say something
To strike him very weird,
So I yelled out,
'I like Fidel Castro and his beard.'
Rita looked offended
But she got out of the way,
As he came charging down the stairs
Sayin', 'What's that I heard you say?'

I said, 'I like Fidel Castro,
I think you heard me right,'
And ducked as he swung
At me with all his might.
Rita mumbled something
'Bout her mother on the hill,
As his fist hit the icebox,
He said he's going to kill me
If I don't get out the door
In two seconds flat,
'You unpatriotic,
Rotten doctor Commie rat.'

Well, he threw a Reader's Digest
At my head and I did run,
I did a somersault
As I seen him get his gun
And crashed through the window
At a hundred miles an hour,
And landed fully blast
In his garden flowers.
Rita said, 'Come back!'
As he started to load

The sun was comin' up
And I was runnin' down the road.

Well, I don't figure I'll be back
There for a spell,
Even though Rita moved away
And got a job in a motel.
He still waits for me,
Constant, on the sly.
He wants to turn me in
To the FBI.
Me, I romp and stomp,
Thankful as a romp,
Without freedom of speech,
I might be in the swamp.

# My Back Pages

Crimson flames tied through my ears
Rollin' high and mighty traps
Pounced with fire on flaming roads
Using ideas as my maps
'We'll meet on edges, soon,' said I
Proud 'neath heated brow.
Ah, but I was so much older then,
I'm younger than that now.

Half-racked prejudice leaped forth
'Rip down all hate,' I screamed
Lies that life is black and white
Spoke from my skull. I dreamed
Romantic facts of musketeers
Foundationed deep, somehow.
Ah, but I was so much older then,
I'm younger than that now.

Girls' faces formed the forward path
From phony jealousy
To memorizing politics
Of ancient history
Flung down by corpse evangelists
Unthought of, though, somehow.
Ah, but I was so much older then,
I'm younger than that now.

A self-ordained professor's tongue
Too serious to fool
Spouted out that liberty
Is just equality in school
'Equality,' I spoke the word
As if a wedding vow.

Ah, but I was so much older then,
I'm younger than that now.

In a soldier's stance, I aimed my hand
At the mongrel dogs who teach
Fearing not that I'd become my enemy
In the instant that I preach
My pathway led by confusion boats
Mutiny from stern to bow.
Ah, but I was so much older then,
I'm younger than that now.

Yes, my guard stood hard when abstract threats
Too noble to neglect
Deceived me into thinking
I had something to protect
Good and bad, I define these terms
Quite clear, no doubt, somehow.
Ah, but I was so much older then,
I'm younger than that now.

# I Don't Believe You
# (She Acts Like We Never Have Met)


I can't understand,
She let go of my hand
An' left me here facing the wall.
I'd sure like t' know
Why she did go,
But I can't get close t' her at all.
Though we kissed through the wild blazing nighttime,
She said she would never forget.
But now mornin's clear,
It's like I ain't here,
She just acts like we never have met.

It's all new t' me,
Like some mystery,
It could even be like a myth.
Yet it's hard t' think on,
That she's the same one
That last night I was with.
From darkness, dreams're deserted,
Am I still dreamin' yet?
I wish she'd unlock
Her voice once an' talk,
'Stead of acting like we never have met.

If she ain't feelin' well,
Then why don't she tell
'Stead of turnin' her back t' my face?
Without any doubt,
She seems too far out
For me t' return t' her chase.
Though the night ran swirling an' whirling,
I remember her whispering yet.
But evidently she don't

An' evidently she won't,
She just acts like we never have met.

If I didn't have t' guess,
I'd gladly confess
T' anything I might've tried.
If I was with 'er too long
Or have done something wrong,
I wish she'd tell me what it is, I'll run an' hide.
Though her skirt it swayed as a guitar played,
Her mouth was watery and wet.
But now something has changed
For she ain't the same,
She just acts like we never have met.

I'm leavin' today,
I'll be on my way
Of this I can't say very much.
But if you want me to,
I can be just like you
An' pretend that we never have touched.
An' if anybody asks me, 'Is it easy to forget?'
I'll say, 'It's easily done,
You just pick anyone,
An' pretend that you never have met!'

# Ballad in Plain D

I once loved a girl, her skin it was bronze.
With the innocence of a lamb, she was gentle like a fawn.
I courted her proudly but now she is gone,
Gone as the season she's taken.

Through young summer's breeze, I stole her away
From her mother and sister, though close did they stay.
Each one of them suffering from the failures of their day,
With strings of guilt they tried hard to guide us.

Of the two sisters, I loved the young.
With sensitive instincts, she was the creative one.
The constant scapegoat, she was easily undone
By the jealousy of others around her.

For her parasite sister, I had no respect,
Bound by her boredom, her pride to protect.
Countless visions of the other she'd reflect
As a crutch for her scenes and her society.

Myself, for what I did, I cannot be excused,
The changes I was going through can't even be used,
For the lies that I told her in hopes not to lose
The could-be dream-lover of my lifetime.

With unknown consciousness, I possessed in my grip
A magnificent mantelpiece, though its heart being chipped,
Noticing not that I'd already slipped
To a sin of love's false security.

From silhouetted anger to manufactured peace,
Answers of emptiness, voice vacancies,

Till the tombstones of damage read me no questions but,
 'Please,
What's wrong and what's exactly the matter?'

And so it did happen like it could have been foreseen,
The timeless explosion of fantasy's dream.
At the peak of the night, the king and the queen
Tumbled all down into pieces.

'The tragic figure!' her sister did shout,
'Leave her alone, God damn you, get out!'
And I in my armor, turning about
And nailing her to the ruins of her pettiness.

Beneath a bare light bulb the plaster did pound
Her sister and I in a screaming battleground.
And she in between, the victim of sound,
Soon shattered as a child 'neath her shadows.

All is gone, all is gone, admit it, take flight.
I gagged twice, doubled, tears blinding my sight.
My mind it was mangled, I ran into the night
Leaving all of love's ashes behind me.

The wind knocks my window, the room it is wet.
The words to say I'm sorry, I haven't found yet.
I think of her often and hope whoever she's met
Will be fully aware of how precious she is.

Ah, my friends from the prison, they ask unto me,
'How good, how good does it feel to be free?'
And I answer them most mysteriously,
'Are birds free from the chains of the skyway?'

# It Ain't Me, Babe

Go 'way from my window,
Leave at your own chosen speed.
I'm not the one you want, babe,
I'm not the one you need.
You say you're lookin' for someone
Never weak but always strong,
To protect you an' defend you
Whether you are right or wrong,
Someone to open each and every door,
But it ain't me, babe,
No, no, no, it ain't me, babe,
It ain't me you're lookin' for, babe.

Go lightly from the ledge, babe,
Go lightly on the ground.
I'm not the one you want, babe,
I will only let you down.
You say you're lookin' for someone
Who will promise never to part,
Someone to close his eyes for you,
Someone to close his heart,
Someone who will die for you an' more,
But it ain't me, babe,
No, no, no, it ain't me, babe,
It ain't me you're lookin' for, babe.

Go melt back into the night, babe,
Everything inside is made of stone.
There's nothing in here moving
An' anyway I'm not alone.
You say you're looking for someone
Who'll pick you up each time you fall,
To gather flowers constantly
An' to come each time you call,

A lover for your life an' nothing more,
But it ain't me, babe,
No, no, no, it ain't me, babe,
It ain't me you're lookin' for, babe.

# Some Other Kinds of Songs . . . (jacket notes)

baby black's
been had
ain't bad
smokestacked
chicken shacked
dressed in black
silver monkey
on her back
mammy ma
juiced pa
janitored
between the law
brothers ten
rat-faced
gravestoned
ditch dug
firescaped an' substroked
choked
baby black
hits back
robs, pawns
lives by trade
sits an' waits on fire plug
digs the heat
eyes meet
picket line
across the street
head rings
of bed springs
freedom's holler
you ask of order
she'd hock
the world
for a dollar an' a quarter

baby black
dressed in black
gunny sack
about t' crack
been gone
carry on
i'm givin' you
myself t' pawn

———————

for françoise hardy
at the seine's edge
a giant shadow
of notre dame
seeks t' grab my foot
sorbonne students
whirl by on thin bicycles
swirlin' lifelike colors of leather spin
the breeze yawns food
far from the bellies
of erhard meetin' johnson
piles of lovers
fishing
kissing
lay themselves on their books. boats.
old men
clothed in curly mustaches
float on the benches
blankets of tourists
in bright red nylon shirts
with straw hats of ambassadors
(cannot hear nixon's
dawg bark now)

218

will sail away
as the sun goes down
the doors of the river are open
i must remember that
i too play the guitar
it's easy t' stand here
more lovers pass
on motorcycles
roped together
from the walls of the water then
i look across t' what they call
the right bank
an' envy
your
trumpet
player

———————

'i could make you crawl
if i was payin' attention'
he said munchin' a sandwich
in between chess moves
'what d' you wanna make
me crawl for?'
'i mean i just could'
'could make me crawl'
'yeah, make you crawl!'
'humm, funny guy you are'
'no, i just play t' win,
that's all'
'well if you can't win me,
then you're the worst player
i ever played'

'what d' you mean?'
'i mean i lose all the time'
his jaw tightened an' he took
a deep breath
'hummm, now i gotta beat you'

straight away an' into the ring
juno takes twenty pills an'
paints all day. life he says
is a head kinda thing. outside
of chicago, private come down
junkie nurse home heals countless
common housewives strung out
fully on drugstore dope, legally
sold t' help clean the kitchen.
lenny bruce shows his seventh
avenue hand-made movies, while a
bunch of women sneak little white
tablets into shoes, stockings, hats
an' other hidin' places. newspapers
tell neither. irma goes t' israel
an' writes me that there, they
hate nazis much more 'n we over here
do. eichmann dies yes, an' west
germany sends eighty-year-old
pruned-out gestapo hermit off t'
the penitentiary. in east berlin
renata tells me that i must wear
tie t' get in t' this certain place
i wanna go. back here, literate
old man with rebel flag above
home sweet home sign says he won't
vote for goldwater. 'talks too
much. should keep his mouth shut'

i walk between backyards an' see
little boy with feather in his hair
lyin' dead on the grass. he gets
up an' hands feather t' another
little boy who immediately falls
down. 'it's my turn t' be the good
guy . . . take that, redskin' bang bang.
henry miller stands on other side
of ping pong table an' keeps
talkin' about me. 'did you ask
the poet fellow if he wants
something t' drink' he says t'
someone gettin' all the drinks.
i drop my ping pong paddle
an' look at the pool. my worst
enemies don't even put me down
in such a mysterious way.
college student trails me with
microphone an' tape machine.
what d' you think a the communist
party? what communist party?
he rattles off names an' numbers.
he can't answer my question. he
tries harder. i say 'you don't
have t' answer my question' he
gets all squishy. i say
there's no answer t' my question
any more 'n there's an answer t'
your question. ferris wheel runs
in california park an' the sky trembles.
turns red. above hiccups an' pointed
fingers. i tell reporter lady that yes
i'm monstrously against the house
unamerican activities committee

an' also the cia an' i beg her please
not t' ask me why for it would take
too long t' tell she asks me about
humanity an' i say i'm not sure
what that word means. she wants me
t' say what she wants me t' say. she
wants me t' say what she
can understand. a loose-tempered fat
man in borrowed stomach slams wife
in the face an' rushes off t' civil
rights meeting. while some strange
girl chases me up smoky mountain
tryin' t' find out what sign i am.
i take allen ginsberg t' meet fantastic
great beautiful artist an' no trespassin'

boards block up all there is t' see.
eviction. infection gangrene an'
atom bombs. both ends exist only
because there is someone who wants
profit. boy loses eyesight. becomes
airplane pilot. people pound their
chests an' other people's chests an'
interpret bibles t' suit their own
means. respect is just a misinterpreted word
an' if Jesus Christ himself came
down through these streets, Christianity
would start all over again. standin'
on the stage of all ground. insects
play in their own world. snakes
slide through the weeds. ants come an'
go through the grass. turtles an' lizards
make their way through the sand. everything

crawls. everything . . .
    an' everything still crawls

———————

jack o' diamonds
jack o' diamonds
one-eyed knave
on the move
hits the street
sneaks. leaps
between pillars of chips
springs on them like samson
thumps thumps
strikes
is on the prowl
you'll only lose
shouldn't stay
jack o' diamonds
is a hard t' play

jack o' diamonds
wrecked my hand
left me here t' stand
little tin men play
their drums now
upside my head
in the midst of cheers
flowers
four queens
with pawed out hearts
make believe
they're still good
but i should drop

223

fold
an' dean martin should apologize
t' the rolling stones
ho hum
weird tablestakes
young babies horseback ride
their fathers' necks
two dudes in hopped-up ford
for the tenth time
have rolled through town
it's your turn baby t'
cut the deck
on you're goin' under
stayed too long
chinese gong
down the way
says jack o' diamonds
(a high card)
jack o' diamonds
(but ain't high enough)

jack o' diamonds
is a hard card t' play

jack o' diamonds used t' laugh at me
now wants t' collect from me
used t' be ashamed of me
now wants t' walk 'long side of me
jack o' diamonds
one armed prince
wears but a single glove
as he shoves
never loves
the moon's too bright

as he's fixed mirrors
'round the room at night
it's hard t' think
there's probably somethin'
in my drink
should pour it out
inside the sink
would throw it in his face
but it'd do no good
give no gain
just leave a stain
jack o' diamonds
an' all his crap
needs some acid
in his lap
what hour now
it feels late somehow
my hounddog bays
need more ashtrays
i can't even remember
the early days
please don't stay
gather your bells an' go
jack o' diamonds
(can open for riches)
jack o' diamonds
(but then it switches)
a colorful picture but
beats only the ten
jack o' diamonds
is a hard card t' play

jack o' diamonds stays indoors
wants me t' fight his wars

jack o' diamonds is a hard card t' play
never certain. in the middle
commentin' on the songs of birds
chucklin' at screamin' mothers
jack o' diamonds drains
fish brains
raffles what's left over
across the table
t' little boy card sharks
who just sat down
t' get off their feet
bad luck run's all in fun
it's your choice. your voice
you choose
you lose
run for cover
hallaluyah
you choose t' lose
take yourself
disappear
jack o' diamonds
(a king's death)
jack o' diamonds
(at the ace's breath)
jack o' diamonds
is a hard card t' play

———

run go get out of here
quick
leave joshua
split
go fit your battle

do your thing
i lost my glasses
can't see jericho
the wind is tyin' knots
in my hair
nothin' seems
t' be straight
out there
no i shan't go with you
i can't go with you

on the brooklyn bridge
he was cockeyed
an' stood on the edge
there was a priest talkin' to him
i was shiftin' myself around
so i could see from all sides
in an' out of stretched necks
an' things
cops held people back
the lady in back of me
burst into my groin
'sick sick some are so sick'
like a circus trapeze act
'oh i hope he don't do it'
he was on the other side of the railin'
both eyes fiery wide
wet with sweat
the mouth of a shark
rolled up soiled sleeves
his arms were thick an' tattooed
an' he wore a silver watch
i could tell at a glance
he was uselessly lonely

227

i couldn't stay an' look at him
i couldn't stay an' look at him
because i suddenly realized that
deep in my heart
i really wanted
t' see him jump

(a mob. each member knowin'
that they all know an' see the same thing
they have the same thing in common.
can stare at each other in total blankness
they do not have t' speak an' not feel guilty
about havin' nothin' t' say. everyday boredom
soaked by the temporary happiness
of that their search is finally over
for findin' a way t' communicate a leech cookout
giant cop out. all mobs i would think.
an' i was in it an' caught by the excitement of it)

an' i walked away
i wanted t' see him jump so bad
that i had t' walk away an' hide
uptown uptown
orchard street
through all those people on
orchard street
pants legs in my face
'comere! comere!'
i don't need no clothes
an' cross the street
skull caps climb
by themselves out of manholes
an' shoeboxes ride
the cracks of the sidewalk
fishermen —

i've suddenly been turned into
a fish
but does anybody
wanna be a fisherman
any more 'n i
don't wanna be a fish

(swingin' wanda's
down in new orleans
rumbles across
brick written
swear word
vulgar wall
in new york city)

no they can't make it
off the banks of their river
i am in their river
(i wonder if he jumped
i really wonder if he jumped)
i turn corner
t' get off river
an' get off river
still goin' up
i about face
an' discover
that i'm on another river

(this time. king rex
blesses me with plastic beads
an' toot toot whistles
paper rings an' things.
royal street.
bourbon street

st claude an' esplanade
pass an' pull
everything out of shape
joe b. stuart
white southern poet
holds me up
we charge through casa
blazin' jukebox
gumbo overflowin'
get kicked out of colored bar
streets jammed
hypnotic stars explode
in louisiana murder night
everything's wedged
arm in arm
stoned galore
must see you in mobile then
down governor nichel
an' gone)

ok i can get off this river too
on bleeker street
i meet many friends
who look at me
as if they know something
i dont know
rocco an' his brothers
say that some people
are worse hung up than me
i don't wanna hear it
a basketball drops through
the hoop
an' i recall that the
living theater's been busted

(has the guy jumped yet?)
intellectual spiders
weave down sixth avenue
with colt forty-fives
stickin' out of their
belly buttons
an' for the first time
in my life
i'm proud that
i haven't read into
any masterpiece books
(an' why did i wanna see that
poor soul so dead?)

first of all two people get
together an' they want their doors
enlarged. second of all, more
people see what's happenin an'
come t' help with the door
enlargement. the ones that arrive
however have nothin' more than
'let's get these doors enlarged'
t' say t' the ones who were
there in the first place. it follows then that
the whole thing revolves around
nothing but this door enlargement idea.
third of all, there's a group now existin'
an' the only thing that keeps them friends
is that they all want the doors enlarged.
obviously, the doors're then enlarged
fourth of all,
after this enlargement
the group has t' find
something else t' keep

them together or
else the door enlargement
will prove t' be
embarrassing

on fourteenth street
i meet someone
who i know in front
wants t' put me
uptight
wants me t' be on
his level
in all honesty
he wants t' drag
me down there
i realize gravity
is my only enemy
loneliness has clutched
hands an' squeezes you
into wrongin' others
everybody has t' do things
keep themselves occupied
the workin' ones
have their minds on
the weekends
victims of the system
pack movie theaters
an' who an' of what
sadistic company is he
from that has the right
t' condemn others as trivial
whose fault
an' who really is t' blame
for one man carryin' a gun

it is impossible that
it's him
slaves are of no special color
an' the links of chains
fall into no special order
how good an actor do you have to be
and play God

(in greece, a little old lady
a worker lady
looks at me
rubs her chin
an' by sign language asks
how come i'm so unshaven
'the sea is very beautiful here'

i reply
pointin' t' my chin.
an' she believes me
needs no other answer
i strum the guitar
she dances
laughs
her bandana flies
i too realize that
she will die here
on the side of this sea
her death is certain here
my death is unknown
an' i come t' think that
i love her)

i talk t' people every day
involved in some scene

233

good an' evil are but words
invented by those
that are trapped in scenes

on what grounds are the
grounds for judgment
an' i think also
that there is not
one thing anyplace
anywhere that makes any
sense. there are only tears
an' there is only sorrow
there are no problems

i have seen what i've loved
slip away an' vanish. i still
love what i've lost but t' run
an' try t' catch it'd
be very greedy
for the rest of my life
i will never chase a livin' soul
into the prison grasp
of my own self-love

i can't believe that i have
t' hate anybody
an' when i do
it will only be out of fear
an' i'll know it

i know no answers an' no truth
for absolutely no soul alive
i will listen t' no one
who tells me morals

there are no morals
an' i dream a lot

so go joshua
go fit your battle
i have t' go t' the woods
for a while
i hope you understand
but if you don't
it doesn't matter
i will be with you
nex' time around
don't think about me
i'll be ok
just go ahead out there
right out there
do what you say
you're gonna do
an' who knows
someday
someone might even
write
    a song
       about you

————

i used t' hate enzo
i used t' hate him
so much that i could've killed him
he was rotten an' ruthless
an' after what he could get
i was sure of that
my beloved one met him

235

in a far-off land
an' she stayed longer there
because of him
i croaked with exhaustion
that he was actually makin' her happy
i never knew him
sometimes i would see him
on my ceilin'
i could've shot him
the rovin' phony
the romantic idiot
i know about guys for
i myself am a guy
poison swings its pendulums
with a seasick sensation
an' i used t' want t' trample on him
i used t' want t' massacre him
i used t' want t' murder him
i wanted t' be like him so much
that i ached
i used t' hate enzo

———

michelangelo would've wept
if he saw but once where charlie slept
(whoa, charlie, i'm afraid you've stepped
beyond the borders of being kept)
what price what price what price disgrace
for sleepin' on a cherub's face?

———

an amazon chick
with an amazin' pancho villa face

thumb out on highway
stands in the boilin' sun
countin' cars go by
zoom
catch that
u-turn
watch truck
yes i knew zapata well
some of my friends
my very best
have even looked
like the japanese
at certain times
i myself think they're
grand . . . make great radios
do you ever see liz taylor
down there
pack is heavy
there is ink
runnin' down its dusty straps
amarillo
ain't far
am going there too
won't need floor scrubbed
voice dubbed
or anything
won't need anything
a plane fumbles in the sky
must make it t' trinidad
tonight
a flyin' saucer texan
covered in cuff links
ate his steak for breakfast
an' now his car radiator

has blown up down the road
back here, a sixty-three
mercury convertible
crashes into girl
an' ten birds
just crossed
the colorado border

———————

johnny (little johnny)
with his father's hammer
nailed five flies
t' the kitchen window
trapped baby bumblebees
in orange juice bottles
rib whipped his
younger brother
an' stuck his sister's hand
in the garbage disposal
pleasin' johnny
dad's football star
named all the girls
that did it
he did
an' never knew a
one that didn't
bruiser johnny
sore loser johnny
bad in math
but his parents fixed it
got too drunk in bars
an' his parents fixed
that too

lovin' johnny
crew-cut johnny
well molded
clean lived in
something his parents
could be proud of
no matter what the
cost to him
a structure of a manly duckling
but his parents
couldn't buy him
into the college
where he wanted t' go
genius johnny
poutin' johnny
punchin' johnny
crashed his
here son have a car good boy
cadillac into
a couldn't care less
railroad bridge
his parents supported him still
they bought new hankies
an' johnny got lots of flowers

an' so as spoked prongs
pierce from perilous heights
plungin'
through soft pillows,
there IS a sound
that rings
no praise
no praise
but you must be

239

aware of poor johnny
t' hear it

———————

you tell me about politics
this that
you speak of rats.
geese. a world of peace
you stumble stammer
pound your fist
an' i tell you there are no politics
you swear
tell me how much you care
you cheat the lunch counter man
out of a pack of cigarettes
an' i tell you there are no politics
you tell me of goons'
graves. ginks an' finks
an' of what you've read
an' how things should be
an' what you'd do if . . .
an' i say someone's been
tamperin' with your head
you jump
raise your voice
an' gyrate yourself
t' the tone of principles
your arm is raised
an' i tell you there are no politics
in the afternoon you run
t' keep appointments
with false lovers
an' this leaves you

drained by nightfall
you ask me questions
an' i say that every question
if it's a truthful question
can be answered by askin' it
you stomp
get mad
i say it's got nothin' t' do with
gertrude stein
you turn your eyes
t' the radio
an' tell me what a
wasteland exists in television
you rant an' rave
of poverty
your fingers crawl the walls
the screen door leaves black marks
across your nose
your breath remains on
window glass
bullfight posters hang crooked above your head
an' the phone rings constantly
you tell me how much i've changed
as if that is all there is t' say
out of the side of your mouth
while talkin' on the wires
in a completely different
tone of voice
than you had a minute ago
when speakin' t' me about something else
i say what's this about changes?
you say 'let's go get drunk'
light a cigarette

'an' throw up on the world'
you go t' your closet
mumblin' about the phoniness of churches
an' spastic national leaders
i say groovy but
also holy hollowness too
yes hollow holiness
an' that some of my best friends
know people that go t' church
you blow up
slam doors
say 'can't no one say nothin' t' you'
i say 'what do You think?'
your face laughs
you say 'oh yeeeeeaah?'
i'm gonna break up i say
an' reach for your coat
'neath piles of paper slogans
i say your house is dirty
you say you should talk
your hallway stinks as
we walk through it
your stairs tilt drastically
your railing's rotted
an' there's blood at the
bottom of your steps
you say t' meet bricks with bricks
i say t' meet bricks with chalk
you tell me monster floor plans
an' i tell you about a bookie shop
in boston givin' odds on the presidential
race
i'm not gonna bet for a while i say
little children
shoot craps

242

in the alley garbage pot
you say 'nothin's perfect'
an' i tell you again
there are no
politics

———————

high treachery sails
unveils
its last wedding song
bang sing the bells
the low pauper's prayer
rice rags in blossom
blow in a fleet
ribbons in the street
white as a sheet
(a Mexican cigarette)
the people've been set
t' try t' forget
that their
whole life's a honeymoon
over soon
i'm not gettin' caught
by all this rot
as i vanish down the road
with a starving actress
on each arm
(for better or best
in sickness an' madness)
i do take thee
i'm already married
so i'll continue as one
faithful done

243

ah fair blondy
ye lead me blindly
I am in the gravel
an' down on the gamut
for our anniversary
you can make me nervous
clink sings the tower
clang sang the preacher
inside of the altar
outside of the theater
mystery fails
when treachery prevails
the forgotten rosary
nails
itself t' a cross
of sand
an' rich men
stare t' their
private own-ed murals
all is lost Cinderella
all is lost

# Denise

Denise, Denise,
Gal, what's on your mind?
Denise, Denise,
Gal, what's on your mind?
You got your eyes closed,
Heaven knows that you ain't blind.

Well, I can see you smiling,
But oh your mouth is inside out.
I can see you smiling,
But you're smiling inside out.
Well, I know you're laughin'
But what are you laughin' about.

Well, if you're tryin' to throw me,
Babe, I've already been tossed.
If you're tryin' to throw me,
Babe, I've already been tossed.
Babe, you're tryin' to lose me.
Babe, I'm already lost.

Well, what are you doing,
Are you flying or have you flipped?
Oh, what are you doing,
Are you flying or have you flipped?
Well, you call my name
And then say your tongue just slipped.

Denise, Denise,
You're concealed here on the shelf.
Denise, Denise,
You're concealed here on the shelf.
I'm looking deep in your eyes, babe,
And all I can see is myself.

# If You Gotta Go, Go Now

Listen to me, baby,
There's something you must see.
I want to be with you, gal,
If you want to be with me.

But if you got to go,
It's all right.
But if you got to go, go now,
Or else you gotta stay all night.

It ain't that I'm questionin' you.
To take part in any quiz.
It's just that I ain't got no watch
An' you keep askin' me what time it is.

But if you got to go,
It's all right.
But if you got to go, go now,
Or else you gotta stay all night.

I am just a poor boy, baby,
Lookin' to connect.
But I certainly don't want you thinkin'
That I ain't got any respect.

But if you got to go,
It's all right.
But if you got to go, go now,
Or else you gotta stay all night.

You know I'd have nightmares
And a guilty conscience, too,
If I kept you from anything
That you really wanted to do.

But if you got to go,
It's all right.
But if you got to go, go now,
Or else you gotta stay all night.

It ain't that I'm wantin'
Anything you never gave before.
It's just that I'll be sleepin' soon,
It'll be too dark for you to find the door.

But if you got to go,
It's all right.
But if you got to go, go now,
Or else you gotta stay all night.

# Mama, You Been on My Mind

Perhaps it's the color of the sun cut flat
An' cov'rin' the crossroads I'm standing at,
Or maybe it's the weather or something like that,
But mama, you been on my mind.

I don't mean trouble, please don't put me down or get upset,
I am not pleadin' or sayin', 'I can't forget.'
I do not walk the floor bowed down an' bent, but yet,
Mama, you been on my mind.

Even though my mind is hazy an' my thoughts they might be
    narrow,
Where you been don't bother me nor bring me down in
    sorrow.
It don't even matter to me where you're wakin' up tomorrow,
But mama, you're just on my mind.

I am not askin' you to say words like 'yes' or 'no,'
Please understand me, I got no place for you t' go.
I'm just breathin' to myself, pretendin' not that I don't know,
Mama, you been on my mind.

When you wake up in the mornin', baby, look inside your
    mirror.
You know I won't be next to you, you know I won't be near.
I'd just be curious to know if you can see yourself as clear
As someone who has had you on his mind.

# Playboys and Playgirls

Oh, ye playboys and playgirls
Ain't a-gonna run my world,
Ain't a-gonna run my world,
Ain't a-gonna run my world.
Ye playboys and playgirls
Ain't a-gonna run my world,
Not now or no other time.

You fallout shelter sellers
Can't get in my door,
Can't get in my door,
Can't get in my door.
You fallout shelter sellers
Can't get in my door,
Not now or no other time.

Your Jim Crow ground
Can't turn me around,
Can't turn me around,
Can't turn me around.
Your Jim Crow ground
Can't turn me around,
Not now or no other time.

The laughter in the lynch mob
Ain't a-gonna do no more,
Ain't a-gonna do no more,
Ain't a-gonna do no more.
The laughter in the lynch mob
Ain't a-gonna do no more,
Not now or no other time.

You insane tongues of war talk
Ain't a-gonna guide my road,

Ain't a-gonna guide my road,
Ain't a-gonna guide my road.
You insane tongues of war talk
Ain't a-gonna guide my road,
Not now or no other time.

You red baiters and race haters
Ain't a-gonna hang around here,
Ain't a-gonna hang around here,
Ain't a-gonna hang around here.
You red baiters and race haters,
Ain't a-gonna hang around here,
Not now or no other time.

Ye playboys and playgirls
Ain't a-gonna own my world,
Ain't a-gonna own my world,
Ain't a-gonna own my world.
Ye playboys and playgirls,
Ain't a-gonna own my world,
Not now or no other time.

# Bringing It All Back Home

**She Belongs to Me**
**Subterranean Homesick Blues**
**Maggie's Farm**
**Love Minus Zero/No Limit**
**Outlaw Blues**
**On the Road Again**
**Bob Dylan's 115th Dream**
**Mr Tambourine Man**
**Gates of Eden**
**It's Alright, Ma (I'm Only Bleeding)**
**It's All Over Now, Baby Blue**
**Bringing It All Back Home** *(jacket notes)*

California *(early version of 'Outlaw Blues')*
Farewell Angelina
Love Is Just a Four-Letter Word
Off the Top of My Head

# She Belongs to Me

She's got everything she needs,
She's an artist, she don't look back.
She's got everything she needs,
She's an artist, she don't look back.
She can take the dark out of nighttime
And paint the daytime black.

You will start out standing
Proud to steal her anything she sees.
You will start out standing
Proud to steal her anything she sees.
But you will wind up peeking through her keyhole
Down upon your knees.

She never stumbles,
She's got no place to fall.
She never stumbles,
She's got no place to fall.
She's nobody's child,
The Law can't touch her at all.

She wears an Egyptian ring
That sparkles before she speaks.
She wears an Egyptian ring
That sparkles before she speaks.
She's a hypnotist collector,
You are a walking antique.

Bow down to her on Sunday,
Salute her when her birthday comes.
Bow down to her on Sunday,
Salute her when her birthday comes.
For Halloween give her a trumpet
And for Christmas, buy her a drum.

# Subterranean Homesick Blues

Johnny's in the basement
Mixing up the medicine
I'm on the pavement
Thinking about the government
The man in the trench coat
Badge out, laid off
Says he's got a bad cough
Wants to get it paid off
Look out kid
It's somethin' you did
God knows when
But you're doin' it again
You better duck down the alley way
Lookin' for a new friend
The man in the coon-skin cap
In the big pen
Wants eleven dollar bills
You only got ten

Maggie comes fleet foot
Face full of black soot
Talkin' that the heat put
Plants in the bed but
The phone's tapped anyway
Maggie says that many say
They must bust in early May
Orders from the DA
Look out kid
Don't matter what you did
Walk on your tip toes
Don't try 'No Doz'
Better stay away from those
That carry around a fire hose
Keep a clean nose

Watch the plain clothes
You don't need a weather man
To know which way the wind blows

Get sick, get well
Hang around a ink well
Ring bell, hard to tell
If anything is goin' to sell
Try hard, get barred
Get back, write braille
Get jailed, jump bail
Join the army, if you fail
Look out kid
You're gonna get hit
But users, cheaters
Six-time losers
Hang around the theaters
Girl by the whirlpool
Lookin' for a new fool
Don't follow leaders
Watch the parkin' meters

Ah get born, keep warm
Short pants, romance, learn to dance
Get dressed, get blessed
Try to be a success
Please her, please him, buy gifts
Don't steal, don't lift
Twenty years of schoolin'
And they put you on the day shift
Look out kid
They keep it all hid
Better jump down a manhole
Light yourself a candle

Don't wear sandals
Try to avoid the scandals
Don't wanna be a bum
You better chew gum
The pump don't work
'Cause the vandals took the handles

man in a coonskin cap in the pigpen wants lldollars bills an i only got
i stumble downtown                                                    ten

                        man wants a pay off

a voice com  sounding like a passenger train
look out kid, it's something you did
go  nows when but you're doing it again
better duck down the doorway/ looking for a new friend
man in a coonskin cap ~~does~~ a back bend/
here comes maggie/ strutting donw the ~~xxinxx~~ fifth street
~~maggie~~ comes fleetfoot/ face full of black soot
talking that the heat cut/plants in the bed/ but
the phone's tapped anyway/maggie says that many say
they mu t bust  n early May/ orders from the da
look out  id/ it dont matter what you did
~~mabe~~ careful that they sell yuh/ or else try t sell yuh
they only try t tail you if they wanna nail yo
~~xxxxxxxxxxxxxxxxxxxxxxxx~~    dont be bashful but please be careful
mailman coming down the chimney like sata claus

dont be bashful if you see they wanna try you            keep a clean nose
                                                        an eyes upon the
                                                             plain clothes


careful if they tail ou/they only  wanna nail you


            ~~xxxxxx~~
walking  own ~~xxixxxxkxx/~~ thinking bout the govt/
daddy's in the dimestore/ ~~fxxx~~ ~~txxinxxxk~~getting 10 cent medicine
man  n the trench coat/ b dge out/laid off
wants t  ee paid off/ ~~xxkxinxxxxsxmxxkxbxxxuff~~
says he's  ot a bad c ugh, wants t get paid off



get sic./ get well/ hang around the ink well
r'n  ball/ hard t tell if anything is gonna sell
try hard/ get barred/ get back/ get stale
~~jxxx~~ get nailed/ his  bail
join the  rmy if you fail
look out  id you  anna get hit
by teachers, preacher, (timelowers hanging round threatres

get born/ keep warm/~~xaxixxxkm~~ short pants, romance
learn t dance/ ~~ixxxxxxxdk~~/ get blessed/ try t be a success
please her  ple se him/ buy gifts/ dont steal/ dont lift
2- years of school an        put you on the day shift
   look out kid/ ~~txxk~~ they got it all hid
~~xxxxxxxxxxxxxxxxxxxxxxxxxxxxxxxxxxxxxxxxxxxxx~~
  it's nowhere, all bare/ they just pay you f re there
~~in~~ t the smog/thick fog/they tell you hthat it's fresh air
  (sic)
  get down/ drop down/ make it out the back door
  or else quit laying on the floor before you get your back sore
                        (closet)



dont be bashful/ check where the ~~ind~~ wind blows/rain flows
keep a clean nose an be careful of the plain clothes


257

# Maggie's Farm

I ain't gonna work on Maggie's farm no more.
No, I ain't gonna work on Maggie's farm no more.
Well, I wake in the morning,
Fold my hands and pray for rain.
I got a head full of ideas
That are drivin' me insane.
It's a shame the way she makes me scrub the floor.
I ain't gonna work on Maggie's farm no more.

I ain't gonna work for Maggie's brother no more.
No, I ain't gonna work for Maggie's brother no more.
Well, he hands you a nickel,
He hands you a dime,
He asks you with a grin
If you're havin' a good time,
Then he fines you every time you slam the door.
I ain't gonna work for Maggie's brother no more.

I ain't gonna work for Maggie's pa no more.
No, I ain't gonna work for Maggie's pa no more.
Well, he puts his cigar
Out in your face just for kicks.
His bedroom window
It is made out of bricks.
The National Guard stands around his door.
Ah, I ain't gonna work for Maggie's pa no more.

I ain't gonna work for Maggie's ma no more.
No, I ain't gonna work for Maggie's ma no more.
Well, she talks to all the servants
About man and God and law.
Everybody says
She's the brains behind pa.

She's sixty-eight, but she says she's twenty-four.
I ain't gonna work for Maggie's ma no more.

I ain't gonna work on Maggie's farm no more.
No, I ain't gonna work on Maggie's farm no more.
Well, I try my best
To be just like I am,
But everybody wants you
To be just like them.
They sing while you slave and I just get bored.
I ain't gonna work on Maggie's farm no more.

# Love Minus Zero/No Limit

My love she speaks like silence,
Without ideals or violence,
She doesn't have to say she's faithful,
Yet she's true, like ice, like fire.
People carry roses,
Make promises by the hours,
My love she laughs like the flowers,
Valentines can't buy her.

In the dime stores and bus stations,
People talk of situations,
Read books, repeat quotations,
Draw conclusions on the wall.
Some speak of the future,
My love she speaks softly,
She knows there's no success like failure
And that failure's no success at all.

The cloak and dagger dangles,
Madams light the candles.
In ceremonies of the horsemen,
Even the pawn must hold a grudge.
Statues made of match sticks,
Crumble into one another,
My love winks, she does not bother,
She knows too much to argue or to judge.

The bridge at midnight trembles,
The country doctor rambles,
Bankers' nieces seek perfection,
Expecting all the gifts that wise men bring.

The wind howls like a hammer,
The night blows cold and rainy,
My love she's like some raven
At my window with a broken wing.

# Outlaw Blues

Ain't it hard to stumble
And land in some funny lagoon?
Ain't it hard to stumble
And land in some muddy lagoon?
Especially when it's nine below zero
And three o'clock in the afternoon.

Ain't gonna hang no picture,
Ain't gonna hang no picture frame.
Ain't gonna hang no picture,
Ain't gonna hang no picture frame.
Well, I might look like Robert Ford
But I feel just like a Jesse James.

Well, I wish I was on some
Australian mountain range.
Oh, I wish I was on some
Australian mountain range.
I got no reason to be there, but I
Imagine it would be some kind of change.

I got my dark sunglasses,
I got for good luck my black tooth.
I got my dark sunglasses,
I'm carryin' for good luck my black tooth.
Don't ask me nothin' about nothin',
I just might tell you the truth.

I got a woman in Jackson,
I ain't gonna say her name.
I got a woman in Jackson,
I ain't gonna say her name.
She's a brown-skin woman, but I
Love her just the same.

# On the Road Again

Well, I woke up in the morning
There's frogs inside my socks
Your mama, she's a-hidin'
Inside the icebox
Your daddy walks in wearin'
A Napoleon Bonaparte mask
Then you ask why I don't live here
Honey, do you have to ask?

Well, I go to pet your monkey
I get a face full of claws
I ask who's in the fireplace
And you tell me Santa Claus
The milkman comes in
He's wearing a derby hat
Then you ask why I don't live here
Honey, how come you have to ask me that?

Well, I asked for something to eat
I'm hungry as a hog
So I get brown rice, seaweed
And a dirty hot dog
I've got a hole
Where my stomach disappeared
Then you ask why I don't live here
Honey, I gotta think you're really weird.

Your grandpa's cane
It turns into a sword
Your grandma prays to pictures
That are pasted on a board
Everything inside my pockets
Your uncle steals

Then you ask why I don't live here
Honey, I can't believe that you're for real.

Well, there's fist fights in the kitchen
They're enough to make me cry
The mailman comes in
Even he's gotta take a side
Even the butler
He's got something to prove
Then you ask why I don't live here
Honey, how come you don't move?

# Bob Dylan's 115th Dream

I was riding on the Mayflower
When I thought I spied some land
I yelled for Captain Arab
I have yuh understand
Who came running to the deck
Said, 'Boys, forget the whale
Look on over yonder
Cut the engines
Change the sail
Haul on the bowline'
We sang that melody
Like all tough sailors do
When they are far away at sea

'I think I'll call it America'
I said as we hit land
I took a deep breath
I fell down, I could not stand
Captain Arab he started
Writing up some deeds
He said, 'Let's set up a fort
And start buying the place with beads'
Just then this cop comes down the street
Crazy as a loon
He throw us all in jail
For carryin' harpoons

Ah me I busted out
Don't even ask me how
I went to get some help
I walked by a Guernsey cow
Who directed me down
To the Bowery slums
Where people carried signs around

Saying, 'Ban the bums'
I jumped right into line
Sayin', 'I hope that I'm not late'
When I realized I hadn't eaten
For five days straight

I went into a restaurant
Lookin' for the cook
I told them I was the editor
Of a famous etiquette book
The waitress he was handsome
He wore a powder blue cape
I ordered some suzette, I said
'Could you please make that crepe'
Just then the whole kitchen exploded
From boilin' fat
Food was flying everywhere
And I left without my hat

Now, I didn't mean to be nosy
But I went into a bank
To get some bail for Arab
And all the boys back in the tank
They asked me for some collateral
And I pulled down my pants
They threw me in the alley
When up comes this girl from France
Who invited me to her house
I went, but she had a friend
Who knocked me out
And robbed my boots
And I was on the street again

Well, I rapped upon a house
With the US flag upon display

266

I said, 'Could you help me out
I got some friends down the way'
The man says, 'Get out of here
I'll tear you limb from limb'
I said, 'You know they refused Jesus, too'
He said, 'You're not Him
Get out of here before I break your bones
I ain't your pop'
I decided to have him arrested
And I went looking for a cop

I ran right outside
And I hopped inside a cab
I went out the other door
This Englishman said, 'Fab'
As he saw me leap a hot dog stand
And a chariot that stood
Parked across from a building
Advertising brotherhood
I ran right through the front door
Like a hobo sailor does
But it was just a funeral parlor
And the man asked me who I was

I repeated that my friends
Were all in jail, with a sigh
He gave me his card
He said, 'Call me if they die'
I shook his hand and said goodbye
Ran out to the street
When a bowling ball came down the road
And knocked me off my feet
A pay phone was ringing
It just about blew my mind

When I picked it up and said hello
This foot came through the line

Well, by this time I was fed up
At tryin' to make a stab
At bringin' back any help
For my friends and Captain Arab
I decided to flip a coin
Like either heads or tails
Would let me know if I should go
Back to ship or back to jail
So I hocked my sailor suit
And I got a coin to flip
It came up tails
It rhymed with sails
So I made it back to the ship

Well, I got back and took
The parkin' ticket off the mast
I was ripping it to shreds
When this coastguard boat went past
They asked me my name
And I said, 'Captain Kidd'
They believed me but
They wanted to know
What exactly that I did
I said for the Pope of Eruke
I was employed
They let me go right away
They were very paranoid

Well, the last I heard of Arab
He was stuck on a whale
That was married to the deputy

Sheriff of the jail
But the funniest thing was
When I was leavin' the bay
I saw three ships a-sailin'
They were all heading my way
I aked the captain what his name was
And how come he didn't drive a truck
He said his name was Columbus
I just said, 'Good luck.'

# Mr Tambourine Man

Hey! Mr Tambourine Man, play a song for me,
I'm not sleepy and there is no place I'm going to.
Hey! Mr Tambourine Man, play a song for me,
In the jingle jangle morning I'll come followin' you.

Though I know that evenin's empire has returned into sand,
Vanished from my hand,
Left me blindly here to stand but still not sleeping.
My weariness amazes me, I'm branded on my feet,
I have no one to meet
And the ancient empty street's too dead for dreaming.

Hey! Mr Tambourine Man, play a song for me,
I'm not sleepy and there is no place I'm going to.
Hey! Mr Tambourine Man, play a song for me,
In the jingle jangle morning I'll come followin' you.

Take me on a trip upon your magic swirlin' ship,
My senses have been stripped, my hands can't feel to grip,
My toes too numb to step, wait only for my boot heels
To be wanderin'.
I'm ready to go anywhere, I'm ready for to fade
Into my own parade, cast your dancing spell my way,
I promise to go under it.

Hey! Mr Tambourine Man, play a song for me,
I'm not sleepy and there is no place I'm going to.
Hey! Mr Tambourine Man, play a song for me,
In the jingle jangle morning I'll come followin' you.

Though you might hear laughin', spinnin', swingin' madly
     across the sun,
It's not aimed at anyone, it's just escapin' on the run
And but for the sky there are no fences facin'.

And if you hear vague traces of skippin' reels of rhyme
To your tambourine in time, it's just a ragged clown behind,
I wouldn't pay it any mind, it's just a shadow you're
Seein' that he's chasing.

Hey! Mr Tambourine Man, play a song for me,
I'm not sleepy and there is no place I'm going to.
Hey! Mr Tambourine Man, play a song for me,
In the jingle jangle morning I'll come followin' you.

Then take me disappearin' through the smoke rings of my mind,
Down the foggy ruins of time, far past the frozen leaves,
The haunted, frightened trees, out to the windy beach,
Far from the twisted reach of crazy sorrow.
Yes, to dance beneath the diamond sky with one hand waving
    free,
Silhouetted by the sea, circled by the circus sands,
With all memory and fate driven deep beneath the waves,
Let me forget about today until tomorrow.

Hey! Mr Tambourine Man, play a song for me,
I'm not sleepy and there is no place I'm going to.
Hey! Mr Tambourine Man, play a song for me,
In the jingle jangle morning I'll come followin' you.

# Gates of Eden

Of war and peace the truth just twists
Its curfew gull just glides
Upon four-legged forest clouds
The cowboy angel rides
With his candle lit into the sun
Though its glow is waxed in black
All except when 'neath the trees of Eden

The lamppost stands with folded arms
Its iron claws attached
To curbs 'neath holes where babies wail
Though it shadows metal badge
All and all can only fall
With a crashing but meaningless blow
No sound ever comes from the Gates of Eden

The savage soldier sticks his head in sand
And then complains
Unto the shoeless hunter who's gone deaf
But still remains
Upon the beach where hound dogs bay
At ships with tattooed sails
Heading for the Gates of Eden

With a time-rusted compass blade
Aladdin and his lamp
Sits with Utopian hermit monks
Side saddle on the Golden Calf
And on their promises of paradise
You will not hear a laugh
All except inside the Gates of Eden

Relationships of ownership
They whisper in the wings

To those condemned to act accordingly
And wait for succeeding kings
And I will try to harmonize with songs
The lonesome sparrow sings
There are no kings inside the Gates of Eden

The motorcycle black madonna
Two-wheeled gypsy queen
And her silver-studded phantom cause
The gray flannel dwarf to scream
As he weeps to wicked birds of prey
Who pick up on his bread crumb sins
And there are no sins inside the Gates of Eden

The kingdoms of Experience
In the precious wind they rot
While paupers change possessions
Each one wishing for what the other has got
And the princess and the prince
Discuss what's real and what is not
It doesn't matter inside the Gates of Eden

The foreign sun, it squints upon
A bed that is never mine
As friends and other strangers
From their fates try to resign
Leaving men wholly, totally free
To do anything they wish to do but die
And there are no trials inside the Gates of Eden

At dawn my lover comes to me
And tells me of her dreams
With no attempts to shovel the glimpse
Into the ditch of what each one means

At times I think there are no words
But these to tell what's true
And there are no truths outside the Gates of Eden

# It's Alright, Ma
# (I'm Only Bleeding)

Darkness at the break of noon
Shadows even the silver spoon
The handmade blade, the child's balloon
Eclipses both the sun and moon
To understand you know too soon
There is no sense in trying.

Pointed threats, they bluff with scorn
Suicide remarks are torn
From the fools gold mouthpiece
The hollow horn plays wasted words
Proves to warn
That he not busy being born
Is busy dying.

Temptation's page flies out the door
You follow, find yourself at war
Watch waterfalls of pity roar
You feel to moan but unlike before
You discover
That you'd just be
One more person crying.

So don't fear if you hear
A foreign sound to your ear
It's alright, Ma, I'm only sighing.

As some warn victory, some downfall
Private reasons great or small
Can be seen in the eyes of those that call
To make all that should be killed to crawl
While others say don't hate nothing at all
Except hatred.

Disillusioned words like bullets bark
As human gods aim for their mark
Made everything from toy guns that spark
To flesh-colored Christs that glow in the dark
It's easy to see without looking too far
That not much
Is really sacred.

While preachers preach of evil fates
Teachers teach that knowledge waits
Can lead to hundred-dollar plates
Goodness hides behind its gates
But even the president of the United States
Sometimes must have
To stand naked.

An' though the rules of the road have been lodged
It's only people's games that you got to dodge
And it's alright, Ma, I can make it.

Advertising signs that con you
Into thinking you're the one
That can do what's never been done
That can win what's never been won
Meantime life outside goes on
All around you.

You lose yourself, you reappear
You suddenly find you got nothing to fear
Alone you stand with nobody near
When a trembling distant voice, unclear
Startles your sleeping ears to hear
That somebody thinks
They really found you.

A question in your nerves is lit
Yet you know there is no answer fit to satisfy
Insure you not to quit
To keep it in your mind and not fergit
That it is not he or she or them or it
That you belong to.

Although the masters make the rules
For the wise men and the fools
I got nothing, Ma, to live up to.

For them that must obey authority
That they do not respect in any degree
Who despise their jobs, their destinies
Speak jealously of them that are free
Cultivate their flowers to be
Nothing more than something
They invest in.

While some on principles baptized
To strict party platform ties
Social clubs in drag disguise
Outsiders they can freely criticize
Tell nothing except who to idolize
And then say God bless him.

While one who sings with his tongue on fire
Gargles in the rat race choir
Bent out of shape from society's pliers
Cares not to come up any higher
But rather get you down in the hole
That he's in.

277

But I mean no harm nor put fault
On anyone that lives in a vault
But it's alright, Ma, if I can't please him.

Old lady judges watch people in pairs
Limited in sex, they dare
To push fake morals, insult and stare
While money doesn't talk, it swears
Obscenity, who really cares
Propaganda, all is phony.

While them that defend what they cannot see
With a killer's pride, security
It blows the minds most bitterly
For them that think death's honesty
Won't fall upon them naturally
Life sometimes
Must get lonely.

My eyes collide head-on with stuffed graveyards
False gods, I scuff
At pettiness which plays so rough
Walk upside-down inside handcuffs
Kick my legs to crash it off
Say okay, I have had enough
What else can you show me?

And if my thought-dreams could be seen
They'd probably put my head in a guillotine
But it's alright, Ma, it's life, and life only.

# It's All Over Now, Baby Blue

You must leave now, take what you need, you think will last.
But whatever you wish to keep, you better grab it fast.
Yonder stands your orphan with his gun,
Crying like a fire in the sun.
Look out the saints are comin' through
And it's all over now, Baby Blue.

The highway is for gamblers, better use your sense.
Take what you have gathered from coincidence.
The empty-handed painter from your streets
Is drawing crazy patterns on your sheets.
This sky, too, is folding under you
And it's all over now, Baby Blue.

All your seasick sailors, they are rowing home.
All your reindeer armies, are all going home.
The lover who just walked out your door
Has taken all his blankets from the floor.
The carpet, too, is moving under you
And it's all over now, Baby Blue.

Leave your stepping stones behind, something calls for you.
Forget the dead you've left, they will not follow you.
The vagabond who's rapping at your door
Is standing in the clothes that you once wore.
Strike another match, go start anew
And it's all over now, Baby Blue.

# Bringing It All Back Home (jacket notes)

i'm standing there watching the parade/
feeling combination of sleepy john estes.
jayne mansfield. humphrey bogart/morti-
mer snerd. murph the surf and so forth/
erotic hitchhiker wearing japanese
blanket. gets my attention by asking didn't
he see me at this hootenanny down in
puerto vallarta, mexico/i say no you must
be mistaken. i happen to be one of the
Supremes/then he rips off his blanket
an' suddenly becomes a middle-aged druggist.
up for district attorney. he starts scream-
ing at me you're the one. you're the one
that's been causing all them riots over in
vietnam. immediately turns t' a bunch of
people an' says if elected, he'll have me
electrocuted publicly on the next fourth
of july. i look around an' all these people
he's talking to are carrying blowtorches/
needless t' say, i split fast go back t' the
nice quiet country. am standing there writing
WHAAAT? on my favorite wall when who should
pass by in a jet plane but my recording
engineer 'i'm here t' pick up you and your
latest works of art. do you need any help
with anything?'
                  (pause)
my songs're written with the kettledrum
in mind/a touch of any anxious color. un-
mentionable. obvious. an' people perhaps
like a soft brazilian singer . . . i have
given up at making any attempt at perfection/
the fact that the white house is filled with
leaders that've never been t' the apollo

theater amazes me. why allen ginsberg was
not chosen t' read poetry at the inauguration
boggles my mind/if someone thinks norman
mailer is more important than hank williams,
that's fine. i have no arguments an' i
never drink milk. i would rather model har-
monica holders than discuss aztec anthropology/
english literature. or history of the united
nations. i accept chaos. i am not sure whether
it accepts me. i know there're some people terrified
of the bomb. but there are other people terrified
t' be seen carrying a modern screen magazine.
experience teaches that silence terrifies people
the most . . . i am convinced that all souls have
some superior t' deal with/like the school
system, an invisible circle of which no one
can think without consulting someone/ in the
face of this, responsibility/security. success
mean absolutely nothing . . . i would not want
t' be bach. mozart. tolstoy. joe hill. gertrude
stein or james dean/they are all dead. the
Great books've been written. the Great sayings
have all been said/I am about t' sketch You
a picture of what goes on around here some-
times. though I don't understand too well
myself what's really happening. i do know
that we're all gonna die someday an' that no
death has ever stopped the world. my poems
are written in a rhythm of unpoetic distortion/
divided by pierced ears. false eyelashes/sub-
tracted by people constantly torturing each
other. with a melodic purring line of descriptive
hollowness — seen at times through dark sunglasses
an' other forms of psychic explosion. a song is

anything that can walk by itself/i am called
a songwriter. a poem is a naked person . . . some
people say that i am a poet
                    (end of pause)
an' so i answer my recording engineer
'yes. well i could use some help in getting
this wall in the plane'

# California <small>(early version of 'Outlaw Blues')</small>

I'm goin' down south,
'Neath the borderline.
I'm goin' down south,
'Neath the borderline.
Some fat momma
Kissed my mouth one time.

Well, I needed it this morning
Without a shadow of doubt.
My suitcase is packed,
My clothes are hangin' out.

San Francisco's fine,
You sure get lots of sun.
San Francisco is fine.
You sure get lots of sun.
But I'm used to four seasons,
California's got but one.

Well, I got my dark sunglasses,
I got for good luck my black tooth.
I got my dark sunglasses,
And for good luck I got my black tooth.
Don't ask me nothin' about nothin',
I just might tell you the truth.

# Farewell Angelina

Farewell Angelina
The bells of the crown
Are being stolen by bandits
I must follow the sound
The triangle tingles
And the trumpets play slow
Farewell Angelina
The sky is on fire
And I must go.

There's no need for anger
There's no need for blame
There's nothing to prove
Ev'rything's still the same
Just a table standing empty
By the edge of the sea
Farewell Angelina
The sky is trembling
And I must leave.

The jacks and the queens
Have forsaken the courtyard
Fifty-two gypsies
Now file past the guards
In the space where the deuce
And the ace once ran wild
Farewell Angelina
The sky is folding
I'll see you in a while.

See the cross-eyed pirates sitting
Perched in the sun
Shooting tin cans
With a sawed-off shotgun

And the neighbors they clap
And they cheer with each blast
Farewell Angelina
The sky's changing color
And I must leave fast.

King Kong, little elves
On the rooftops they dance
Valentino-type tangos
While the make-up man's hands
Shut the eyes of the dead
Not to embarrass anyone
Farewell Angelina
The sky is embarrassed
And I must be gone.

The machine guns are roaring
The puppets heave rocks
The fiends nail time bombs
To the hands of the clocks
Call me any name you like
I will never deny it
Farewell Angelina
The sky is erupting
I must go where it's quiet.

# Love Is Just a Four-Letter Word

Seems like only yesterday
I left my mind behind
Down in the Gypsy Café
With a friend of a friend of mine
She sat with a baby heavy on her knee
Yet spoke of life most free from slavery
With eyes that showed no trace of misery
A phrase in connection first with she I heard
That love is just a four-letter word

Outside a rambling store-front window
Cats meowed to the break of day
Me, I kept my mouth shut, too
To you I had no words to say
My experience was limited and underfed
You were talking while I hid
To the one who was the father of your kid
You probably didn't think I did, but I heard
You say that love is just a four-letter word

I said goodbye unnoticed
Pushed towards things in my own games
Drifting in and out of lifetimes
Unmentionable by name
Searching for my double, looking for
Complete evaporation to the core
Though I tried and failed at finding any door
I must have thought that there was nothing more
Absurd than that love is just a four-letter word

Though I never knew just what you meant
When you were speaking to your man
I can only think in terms of me
And now I understand

After waking enough times to think I see
The Holy Kiss that's supposed to last eternity
Blow up in smoke, its destiny
Falls on strangers, travels free
Yes, I know now, traps are only set by me
And I do not really need to be
Assured that love is just a four-letter word

# Off the Top of My Head

All right, then — next on the pole was Horseman and his friend
Photochick. Photochick is wearing a Hoover button in her
mouth and this keeps her lips together.

Horseman was first up the pole and he's shouting back,
'Hurry up, Photochick. Get up here.' But then his pants fall
down. Photochick, blinded, reaches for her banjo and
Horseman screams, 'What you doing? Get rid of that thing.
Hurry. God, the cops are coming!'

Photochick snarls, 'Don't call me no God,' and she starts in a'
singing, 'Coming through the rye, coming through the rye, oh
yeah, baby-o, we-all just coming through the rye.' Horseman
gives her a kick in the mouth and her lips pry open and she
stops her singing. 'Now get the hell up this pole' Horseman
sighs, vomits and looks out toward the slums . . . 'Good God,
there's a thousand angry plumbers all in chrome suits. They've
smashed the gates.' Photochick, she squints. Horseman looks
down. His face is dirty. 'Didja hear me? Stop squinting! Didja
hear me?'

'The sun's hot. I'm getting down off this pole' says
Photochick. Meanwhile, back at the kazoo factory, Prez is
walking back and forth dictating a letter. 'Yes, I want the holes
much bigger in these kazoos. I also want them cut sharper and
to kind of pinch the tongue a little. I want a higher pitch,
perhaps like a girl screaming. Also in the ads, I want to see a
young hunchback. Perhaps with his nose broken. I want to see
him sitting. Oh, I'd say, in front of a swamp with lots of
mosquitoes. I want to see more of a poverty-type mood in the
displays, also.'

SCREAM from the closet. 'Who's in there?' says the Prez.
'Could you check on that, please, Miss Flunk.' Miss Flunk opens
the closet. Tattler, the errand boy, falls out. His arm tied behind
his back. His shoes gone. 'What's the matter there boy! Speak
up! I'll have you demolished!' says Prez. 'Sorry sir. The dykes

have broken down. They're beating everybody up and putting them in the closets.' 'Oh my Gawaud' says the Prez. 'When? When has all this happened? Where are they finding all the closets? There aren't enough closets! Oh my Gawaud! What'll my wife say? Miss Flunk! Miss Flunk! Cancel my appointments for today. Order me my lunch?'

Miss Flunk slowly puts down her pen. Shuffles up to the Prez. Punches him in the gut and heaves him into the encyclopedias. 'What! What's happening here! What, dear Gawaud, is happening here?' Prez, in a gust of anguish. 'Get your hands behind your back, you fat fiend' says Miss Flunk. 'You're going into the closet.'

BAP and the Prez lands in the closet. Tattler escapes out an air-vent. Miss Flunk takes a bottle of ink and starts to polish her muscles. It begins to rain . . .

Meanwhile, back at the pole, Horseman is shouting, 'Don't get down Photochick! I want you! I need you! I love you!' Photochick shouting back, 'The sun's in my eyes! I can't do a thing with it! I fear my banjo is missing.' The plumbers arrive. They take off their chrome suits. 'What you guys want?' says Horseman. 'We want you to ask each one of us for our autographs' says the chief plumber, who used to be one helluva banjo player himself and now spends most of his free time propositioning old ladies down on Highway 90. 'That's what we want you to do.'

'Nonsense!' says Horseman. 'Just a minute' says Photochick. 'Hold it just a minute. I'm game. I'll do it. Who do I ask first?' 'What do you mean YOU will!' growls Horseman. 'I'll do it. I'll ask 'm. I wanna do it. I'll do it.'

'Good' says the chief plumber. 'Now that we got that straightened out, we can chop down this pole without feeling too guilty and we won't have to join any lumberjack's union besides.' Good. Everything's looking good today and WHAM down comes the pole and they all walk back through the gates and go to the movies. Horseman and Photochick. They all sprawled out on the ground clutching the grass. A giant billboard sign faces them. It, being a musical instrument advertisement. Showing a picture of two women racing car drivers. Holding hands and each smoking a kazoo.

The sign smiles handsomely and just squats there like the moon. 'Notice anything strange?' says Horseman to Photochick. 'About what?' says Photochick. 'About the pole being chopped down' says Horseman. 'No. Nothing strange about that. Just that the sun's still in my eyes and that sign over there looks like it wasn't here before.' 'You mean that racing-car advertisement?' 'I thought it was a government report warning against cigars.' 'Oh, yeah' says Horseman. 'Yeah, it is.' 'Yeah, it is. I know it is' says Photochick, who begins now to look for her Hoover button . . . Meanwhile, back at the Newport Folk Festival . . .

# Highway 61 Revisited

**Like a Rolling Stone**
**Tombstone Blues**
**It Takes a Lot to Laugh,**
   **It Takes a Train to Cry**
**From a Buick 6**
**Ballad of a Thin Man**
**Queen Jane Approximately**
**Highway 61 Revisited**
**Desolation Row**
**Just Like Tom Thumb's Blues**

Highway 61 Revisited (liner notes)
Positively 4th Street
Can You Please Crawl Out Your Window?
Sitting on a Barbed-Wire Fence
Alternatives to College

# Like a Rolling Stone

Once upon a time you dressed so fine
You threw the bums a dime in your prime, didn't you?
People'd call, say, 'Beware doll, you're bound to fall'
You thought they were all kiddin' you
You used to laugh about
Everybody that was hangin' out
Now you don't talk so loud
Now you don't seem so proud
About having to be scrounging for your next meal.

How does it feel
How does it feel
To be without a home
Like a complete unknown
Like a rolling stone?

You've gone to the finest school all right, Miss Lonely
But you know you only used to get juiced in it
And nobody has ever taught you how to live on the street
And now you find out you're gonna have to get used to it
You said you'd never compromise
With the mystery tramp, but now you realize
He's not selling any alibis
As you stare into the vacuum of his eyes
And ask him do you want to make a deal?

How does it feel
How does it feel
To be on your own
With no direction home
Like a complete unknown
Like a rolling stone?

You never turned around to see the frowns on the jugglers and
    the clowns
When they all come down and did tricks for you
You never understood that it ain't no good
You shouldn't let other people get your kicks for you
You used to ride on the chrome horse with your diplomat
Who carried on his shoulder a Siamese cat
Ain't it hard when you discover that
He really wasn't where it's at
After he took from you everything he could steal.

How does it feel
How does it feel
To be on your own
With no direction home
Like a complete unknown
Like a rolling stone?

Princess on the steeple and all the pretty people
They're drinkin', thinkin' that they got it made
Exchanging all kinds of precious gifts and things
But you'd better lift your diamond ring, you'd better pawn it
    babe
You used to be so amused
At Napoleon in rags and the language that he used
Go to him now, he calls you, you can't refuse
When you got nothing, you got nothing to lose
You're invisible now, you got no secrets to conceal.

How does it feel
How does it feel
To be on your own
With no direction home
Like a complete unknown

# Like a rolling stone?

# Tombstone Blues

The sweet pretty things are in bed now of course
The city fathers they're trying to endorse
The reincarnation of Paul Revere's horse
But the town has no need to be nervous

The ghost of Belle Starr she hands down her wits
To Jezebel the nun she violently knits
A bald wig for Jack the Ripper who sits
At the head of the chamber of commerce

Mama's in the fact'ry
She ain't got no shoes
Daddy's in the alley
He's lookin' for the fuse
I'm in the streets
With the tombstone blues

The hysterical bride in the penny arcade
Screaming she moans, 'I've just been made'
Then sends out for the doctor who pulls down the shade
Says, 'My advice is to not let the boys in'

Now the medicine man comes and he shuffles inside
He walks with a swagger and he says to the bride
'Stop all this weeping, swallow your pride
You will not die, it's not poison'

Mama's in the fact'ry
She ain't got no shoes
Daddy's in the alley
He's lookin' for the fuse
I'm in the streets
With the tombstone blues

Well, John the Baptist after torturing a thief
Looks up at his hero the Commander-in-Chief
Saying, 'Tell me great hero, but please make it brief
Is there a hole for me to get sick in?'

The Commander-in-Chief answers him while chasing a fly
Saying, 'Death to all those who would whimper and cry'
And dropping a bar bell he points to the sky
Saying, 'The sun's not yellow it's chicken'

Mama's in the fact'ry
She ain't got no shoes
Daddy's in the alley
He's lookin' for the fuse
I'm in the streets
With the tombstone blues

The king of the Philistines his soldiers to save
Put jawbones on their tombstones and flatters their graves
Puts the pied pipers in prison and fattens the slaves
Then sends them out to the jungle

Gypsy Davey with a blowtorch he burns out their camps
With his faithful slave Pedro behind him he tramps
With a fantastic collection of stamps
To win friends and influence his uncle

Mama's in the fact'ry
She ain't got no shoes
Daddy's in the alley
He's lookin' for the fuse
I'm in the streets
With the tombstone blues

The geometry of innocence flesh on the bone
Causes Galileo's math book to get thrown
At Delilah who sits worthlessly alone
But the tears on her cheeks are from laughter

Now I wish I could give Brother Bill his great thrill
I would set him in chains at the top of the hill
Then send out for some pillars and Cecil B. DeMille
He could die happily ever after

Mama's in the fact'ry
She ain't got no shoes
Daddy's in the alley
He's lookin' for the fuse
I'm in the streets
With the tombstone blues

Where Ma Raney and Beethoven once unwrapped their bed
    roll
Tuba players now rehearse around the flagpole
And the National Bank at a profit sells road maps for the soul
To the old folks home and the college

Now I wish I could write you a melody so plain
That could hold you dear lady from going insane
That could ease you and cool you and cease the pain
Of your useless and pointless knowledge

Mama's in the fact'ry
She ain't got no shoes
Daddy's in the alley
He's lookin' for the fuse
I'm in the streets
With the tombstone blues

# It Takes a Lot to Laugh,
# It Takes a Train to Cry

Well, I ride on a mailtrain, baby,
Can't buy a thrill.
Well, I've been up all night, baby,
Leanin' on the window sill.
Well, if I die
On top of the hill
And if I don't make it,
You know my baby will.

Don't the moon look good, mama,
Shinin' through the trees?
Don't the brakeman look good, mama,
Flagging down the 'Double E'?
Don't the sun look good
Goin' down over the sea?
Don't my gal look fine
When she's comin' after me?

Now the wintertime is coming,
The windows are filled with frost.
I went to tell everybody,
But I could not get across.
Well, I wanna be your lover, baby,
I don't wanna be your boss.
Don't say I never warned you
When your train gets lost.

# From a Buick 6

I got this graveyard woman, you know she keeps my kid
But my soulful mama, you know she keeps me hid
She's a junkyard angel and she always gives me bread
Well, if I go down dyin', you know she bound to put a blanket
   on my bed.

Well, when the pipeline gets broken and I'm lost on the river
   bridge
I'm cracked up on the highway and on the water's edge
She comes down the thruway ready to sew me up with thread
Well, if I go down dyin', you know she bound to put a blanket
   on my bed.

Well, she don't make me nervous, she don't talk too much
She walks like Bo Diddley and she don't need no crutch
She keeps this four-ten all loaded with lead
Well, if I go down dyin', you know she bound to put a blanket
   on my bed.

Well, you know I need a steam shovel mama to keep away the
   dead
I need a dump truck mama to unload my head
She brings me everything and more, and just like I said
Well, if I go down dyin', you know she bound to put a blanket
   on my bed.

# Ballad of a Thin Man

You walk into the room
With your pencil in your hand
You see somebody naked
And you say, 'Who is that man?'
You try so hard
But you don't understand
Just what you'll say
When you get home

Because something is happening here
But you don't know what it is
Do you, Mister Jones?

You raise up your hand
And you ask, 'Is this where it is?'
And somebody points to you and says
'It's his'
And you say, 'What's mine?'
And somebody else says, 'Where what is?'
And you say, 'Oh my God
Am I here all alone?'

Because something is happening here
But you don't know what it is
Do you, Mister Jones?

You hand in your ticket
And you go watch the geek
Who immediately walks up to you
When he hears you speak
And says, 'How does it feel
To be such a freak?'
And you say, 'Impossible'
As he hands you a bone

Because something is happening here
But you don't know what it is
Do you, Mister Jones?

You have many contacts
Among the lumberjacks
To get you facts
When someone attacks your imagination
But nobody has any respect
Anyway they already expect you
To just give a check
To tax-deductible charity organizations

You've been with the professors
And they've all liked your looks
With great lawyers you have
Discussed lepers and crooks
You've been through all of
F. Scott Fitzgerald's books
You're very well read
It's well known

Because something is happening here
But you don't know what it is
Do you, Mister Jones?

Well, the sword swallower, he comes up to you
And then he kneels
He crosses himself
And then he clicks his high heels
And without further notice
He asks you how it feels

And he says, 'Here is your throat back
Thanks for the loan'

Because something is happening here
But you don't know what it is
Do you, Mister Jones?

Now you see this one-eyed midget
Shouting the word 'NOW'
And you say, 'For what reason?'
And he says, 'How?'
And you say, 'What does this mean?'
And he screams back, 'You're a cow
Give me some milk
or else go home'

Because something is happening here
But you don't know what it is
Do you, Mister Jones?

Well, you walk into the room
Like a camel and then you frown
You put your eyes in your pocket
And your nose on the ground
There ought to be a law
Against you comin' around
You should be made
To wear earphones

Because something is happening here
But you don't know what it is
Do you, Mister Jones?

# Queen Jane Approximately

When your mother sends back all your invitations
And your father to your sister he explains
That you're tired of yourself and all of your creations
Won't you come see me, Queen Jane?
Won't you come see me, Queen Jane?

Now when all of the flower ladies want back what they have
    lent you
And the smell of their roses does not remain
And all of your children start to resent you
Won't you come see me, Queen Jane?
Won't you come see me, Queen Jane?

Now when all the clowns that you have commissioned
Have died in battle or in vain
And you're sick of all this repetition
Won't you come see me, Queen Jane?
Won't you come see me, Queen Jane?

When all of your advisers heave their plastic
At your feet to convince you of your pain
Trying to prove that your conclusions should be more drastic
Won't you come see me, Queen Jane?
Won't you come see me, Queen Jane?

Now when all the bandits that you turned your other cheek to
All lay down their bandanas and complain
And you want somebody you don't have to speak to
Won't you come see me, Queen Jane?
Won't you come see me, Queen Jane?

# Highway 61 Revisited

Oh God said to Abraham, 'Kill me a son'
Abe says, 'Man, you must be puttin' me on'
God say, 'No.' Abe say, 'What?'
God say, 'You can do what you want Abe, but
The next time you see me comin' you better run'
Well Abe says, 'Where do you want this killin' done?'
God says, 'Out on Highway 61.'

Well Georgia Sam he had a bloody nose
Welfare Department they wouldn't give him no clothes
He asked poor Howard where can I go
Howard said there's only one place I know
Sam said tell me quick man I got to run
Ol' Howard just pointed with his gun
And said that way down on Highway 61.

Well Mack the Finger said to Louie the King
I got forty red white and blue shoe strings
And a thousand telephones that don't ring
Do you know where I can get rid of these things
And Louie the King said let me think for a minute son
And he said yes I think it can be easily done
Just take everything down to Highway 61.

Now the fifth daughter on the twelfth night
Told the first father that things weren't right
My complexion she said is much too white
He said come here and step into the light he says hmm you're
    right
Let me tell the second mother this has been done
But the second mother was with the seventh son
And they were both out on Highway 61.

Now the rovin' gambler he was very bored
He was tryin' to create a next world war
He found a promoter who nearly fell off the floor
He said I never engaged in this kind of thing before
But yes I think it can be very easily done
We'll just put some bleachers out in the sun
And have it on Highway 61.

The image shows a gasoline tanker truck with "GASOLINE" written on the tank.

# Desolation Row

They're selling postcards of the hanging
They're painting the passports brown
The beauty parlor is filled with sailors
The circus is in town
Here comes the blind commissioner
They've got him in a trance
One hand is tied to the tight-rope walker
The other is in his pants
And the riot squad they're restless
They need somewhere to go
As Lady and I look out tonight
From Desolation Row

Cinderella, she seems so easy
'It takes one to know one,' she smiles
And puts her hands in her back pockets
Bette Davis style
And in comes Romeo, he's moaning
'You Belong to Me I Believe'
And someone says, 'You're in the wrong place, my friend
You better leave'
And the only sound that's left
After the ambulances go
Is Cinderella sweeping up
On Desolation Row

Now the moon is almost hidden
The stars are beginning to hide
The fortunetelling lady
Has even taken all her things inside
All except for Cain and Abel
And the hunchback of Notre Dame
Everybody is making love
Or else expecting rain

And the Good Samaritan, he's dressing
He's getting ready for the show
He's going to the carnival tonight
On Desolation Row

Now Ophelia, she's 'neath the window
For her I feel so afraid
On her twenty-second birthday
She already is an old maid
To her, death is quite romantic
She wears an iron vest
Her profession's her religion
Her sin is her lifelessness
And though her eyes are fixed upon
Noah's great rainbow
She spends her time peeking
Into Desolation Row

Einstein, disguised as Robin Hood
With his memories in a trunk
Passed this way an hour ago
With his friend, a jealous monk
He looked so immaculately frightful
As he bummed a cigarette
Then he went off sniffing drainpipes
And reciting the alphabet
Now you would not think to look at him
But he was famous long ago
For playing the electric violin
On Desolation Row

Dr Filth, he keeps his world
Inside of a leather cup
But all his sexless patients

They're trying to blow it up
Now his nurse, some local loser
She's in charge of the cyanide hole
And she also keeps the cards that read
'Have Mercy on His Soul'
They all play on penny whistles
You can hear them blow
If you lean your head out far enough
From Desolation Row

Across the street they've nailed the curtains
They're getting ready for the feast
The Phantom of the Opera
A perfect image of a priest
They're spoonfeeding Casanova
To get him to feel more assured
Then they'll kill him with self-confidence
After poisoning him with words
And the Phantom's shouting to skinny girls
'Get Outa Here If You Don't Know
Casanova is just being punished for going
To Desolation Row'

Now at midnight all the agents
And the superhuman crew
Come out and round up everyone
That knows more than they do
Then they bring them to the factory
Where the heart-attack machine
Is strapped across their shoulders
And then the kerosene
Is brought down from the castles
By insurance men who go

Check to see that nobody is escaping
To Desolation Row

Praise be to Nero's Neptune
The Titanic sails at dawn
And everybody's shouting
'Which Side Are You On?'
And Ezra Pound and T. S. Eliot
Fighting in the captain's tower
While calypso singers laugh at them
And fishermen hold flowers
Between the windows of the sea
Where lovely mermaids flow
And nobody has to think too much
About Desolation Row

Yes, I received your letter yesterday
(About the time the door knob broke)
When you asked how I was doing
Was that some kind of joke?
All these people that you mention
Yes, I know them, they're quite lame
I had to rearrange their faces
And give them all another name
Right now I can't read too good
Don't send me no more letters no
Not unless you mail them
From Desolation Row

# Just Like Tom Thumb's Blues

When you're lost in the rain in Juarez
And it's Eastertime too
And your gravity fails
And negativity don't pull you through
Don't put on any airs
When you're down on Rue Morgue Avenue
They got some hungry women there
And they really make a mess outa you

Now if you see Saint Annie
Please tell her thanks a lot
I cannot move
My fingers are all in a knot
I don't have the strength
To get up and take another shot
And my best friend, my doctor
Won't even say what it is I've got

Sweet Melinda
The peasants call her the goddess of gloom
She speaks good English
And she invites you up into her room
And you're so kind
And careful not to go to her too soon
And she takes your voice
And leaves you howling at the moon

Up on Housing Project Hill
It's either fortune or fame
You must pick up one or the other
Though neither of them are to be what they claim
If you're lookin' to get silly
You better go back to from where you came

Because the cops don't need you
And man they expect the same

Now all the authorities
They just stand around and boast
How they blackmailed the sergeant-at-arms
Into leaving his post
And picking up Angel who
Just arrived here from the coast
Who looked so fine at first
But left looking just like a ghost

I started out on burgundy
But soon hit the harder stuff
Everybody said they'd stand behind me
When the game got rough
But the joke was on me
There was nobody even there to call my bluff
I'm going back to New York City
I do believe I've had enough

# Highway 61 Revisited (liner notes)

On the slow train time does not interfere & at the Arabian
crossing waits White Heap, the man from the newspaper &
behind him the hundred Inevitables made of solid rock & stone –
the Cream Judge & the Clown – the doll house where Savage
Rose & Fixable live simply in their wild animal luxury . . .
Autumn, with two zeros above her nose arguing over the sun
being dark or Bach is as famous as its commotion & that she
herself – not Orpheus – is the logical poet 'I am the logical
poet!' she screams 'Spring? Spring is only the beginning!' she
attempts to make Cream Judge jealous by telling him of down-
to-earth people & while the universe is erupting, she points to
the slow train & prays for rain and for time to interfere – she is
not extremely fat but rather progressively unhappy . . . the
hundred Inevitables hide their predictions & go to bars & drink
& get drunk in their very special conscious way & when tom
dooley, the kind of person you think you've seen before,
comes strolling in with White Heap, the hundred Inevitables all
say 'who's that man who looks so white?' & the bartender, a
good boy & one who keeps a buffalo in his mind, says 'I don't
know, but I'm sure I've seen the other fellow someplace' &
when Paul Sargent, a plainclothes man from 4th street, comes
in at three in the morning & busts everybody for being
incredible, nobody really gets angry – just a little illiterate most
people get & Rome, one of the hundred Inevitables whispers 'I
told you so' to Madam John . . . Savage Rose & Fixable are
bravely blowing kisses to the Jade Hexagram-Carnaby Street &
to all the mysterious juveniles & the Cream Judge is writing a
book on the true meaning of a pear – last year, he wrote one
on famous dogs of the civil war & now he has false teeth & no
children . . . when the Cream met Savage Rose & Fixable, he
was introduced to them by none other than Lifelessness –
Lifelessness is the Great Enemy & always wears a hip guard –
he is very hipguard . . . Lifelessness said when introducing
everybody 'go save the world' & 'involvement! that's the issue'
& things like that & Savage Rose winked at Fixable & the Cream

went off with his arm in a sling singing 'summertime & the livin is easy' . . . the Clown appears – puts a gag over Autumn's mouth & says 'there are two kinds of people – simple people & normal people' this usually gets a big laugh from the sandpit & White Heap sneezes – passes out & rips open Autumn's gag & says 'What do you mean you're Autumn and without you there'd be no spring! you fool! without spring, there'd be no you! what do you think of that???.' then Savage Rose & Fixable come by & kick him in the brains & color him pink for being a phony philosopher – then the Clown comes by and screams 'You phony philosopher!' & jumps on his head – Paul Sargent comes by again in an umpire's suit & some college kid who's read all about Nietzsche comes by & says 'Nietzsche never wore an umpire's suit' & Paul says 'You wanna buy some clothes, kid?' & then Rome & John come out of the bar & they're going up to Harlem . . . we are singing today of the WIPE-OUT GANG – the WIPE-OUT GANG buys, owns & operates the Insanity Factory – if you do not know where the Insanity Factory is located, you should hereby take two steps to the right, paint your teeth & go to sleep . . . the songs on this specific record are not so much songs but rather exercises in tonal breath control . . . the subject matter – though meaningless as it is – has something to do with the beautiful strangers . . . the beautiful strangers, Vivaldi's green jacket & the holy slow train

you are right john cohen – quasimodo was right – mozart was right . . . I cannot say the word eye any more . . . when I speak this word eye, it is as if I am speaking of somebody's eye that I faintly remember . . . there is no eye – there is only a series of mouths – long live the mouths – your rooftop – if you don't already know – has been demolished . . . eye is plasma & you are right about that too – you are lucky – you don't have to think about such things as eyes & rooftops & quasimodo.

# Positively 4th Street

You got a lotta nerve
To say you are my friend
When I was down
You just stood there grinning

You got a lotta nerve
To say you gota helping hand to lend
You just want to be on
The side that's winning

You say I let you down
You know it's not like that
If you're so hurt
Why then don't you show it

You say you lost your faith
But that's not where it's at
You had no faith to lose
And you know it

I know the reason
That you talk behind my back
I used to be among the crowd
You're in with

Do you take me for such a fool
To think I'd make contact
With the one who tries to hide
What he don't know to begin with

You see me on the street
You always act surprised
You say, 'How are you?' 'Good luck'
But you don't mean it

When you know as well as me
You'd rather see me paralyzed
Why don't you just come out once
And scream it

No, I do not feel that good
When I see the heartbreaks you embrace
If I was a master thief
Perhaps I'd rob them

And now I know you're dissatisfied
With you position and your place
Don't you understand
It's not my problem

I wish that for just one time
You could stand inside my shoes
And just for that one moment
I could be you

Yes, I wish that for just one time
You could stand inside my shoes
You'd know what a drag it is
To see you

# Can You Please
# Crawl Out Your Window?

He sits in your room, his tomb, with a fist full of tacks
Preoccupied with his vengeance
Cursing the dead that can't answer him back
I'm sure that he has no intentions
Of looking your way, unless it's to say
That he needs you to test his inventions.

Can you please crawl out your window?
Use your arms and legs it won't ruin you
How can you say he will haunt you?
You can go back to him any time you want to.

He looks so truthful, is this how he feels
Trying to peel the moon and expose it
With his businesslike anger and his bloodhounds that kneel
If he needs a third eye he just grows it
He just needs you to talk or to hand him his chalk
Or pick it up after he throws it.

Can you please crawl out your window?
Use your arms and legs it won't ruin you
How can you say he will haunt you?
You can go back to him any time you want to.

Why does he look so righteous while your face is so changed
Are you frightened of the box you keep him in
While his genocide fools and his friends rearrange
Their religion of the little ten women
That backs up their views but your face is so bruised
Come on out the dark is beginning

Can you please crawl out your window?
Use your arms and legs it won't ruin you

How can you say he will haunt you?
You can go back to him any time you want to.

# Sitting on a Barbed-Wire Fence

I paid fifteen million dollars, twelve hundred and seventy-two
   cents
I paid one thousand two hundred twenty-seven dollars and
   fifty-five cents
See my hound dog bite a rabbit
And my football's sittin' on a barbed-wire fence

Well, my temperature rises and my feet don't walk so fast
Yes, my temperature rises and my feet don't walk so fast
Well, this Arabian doctor came in, gave me a shot
But wouldn't tell me if what I had would last

Well, this woman I've got, she's filling me with her drive
Yes, this woman I've got, she's thrillin' me with her hive
She's calling me Stan
Or else she calls me Mister Clive

Of course, you're gonna think this song is a riff
I know you're gonna think this song is a cliff
Unless you've been inside a tunnel
And fell down 69, 70 feet over a barbed-wire fence

All night!

# Alternatives to College

retreat by dawn but love this bed – this cult – this wolf & cell of
smelling mouth – tongue in hand & faint little lord, the bounty
hunter playing flute & you, the younger, playing the tramp . . .
one pale virgin with a plastic hammer FLASH & the cardboard
birds & thousand teachers looking for Tibet & mathematics –
they, constipated, moving slowly, bulky across the constipation
. . . this virgin eats her hammer & holy mackerel she's a college
girl – the porkypine attacking Down with Breath & she's killed
by a flying tooth – bounty hunter now reincarnated into a fire
hydrant – he sleeps on your dog – neath your window –
Phoenix rising – he say 'God'll save the moon' & using this
dawn for a blanket you part with sleep & accept this tomb –
this want of Recollection & reward & the star gazer making
petty fun of the farmer, the angel, the generous cowboy & your
father who is just another person . . . welcome this notorious
moment wearing the robe & blindfold – smile & let mad doctor
sell his technicolor wigs to Maid Marian & you passing to dream
with voices down the window but say farewell to health, fake
laws, maturity & the visible imbecile becoming randolph . . .
enter with your sponge & friends & wave good-bye to gramma
   Lover, she moves like the seasons – she doesnt fight the
clock – her strength is in her weakness & that is why she is my
lover . . . Penrod, Cain – they offend themselves & take
responsibility they have no right to take & leading others' lives,
they lose their own & break their thumbs & dwell in madness &
define this madness as success & they follow BLASPHEMY &
touch of goodness exit – cutting out the eyes of lambs &
hanging in the evil hallway – the dead shepherd in the closet
. . . the only floor, a floor of sound BLASPHEMY it leads them
. . . Lover, she knows better & doesnt fall for MATRON GIFTS
disguised as book & proper
   hitchhiking with the gas mask on & thumbing the queens, the
paul reveres & meet Nick the Nail for he exists & he's real like
Sing Sing & snowplows in the sewer . . . Sunday comes & the

old maid – but are you joking – she's just twenty-two & her
name is Nancy or Peggy or Brunella & she squats in a cornfield
& weaving brooms from roses, she reeks of heroes & paints her
face the color of Custer's last massacre – she peeks from tanks
& repeats herself – she stays away from the merry-go-round &
you must love her too/ she lives in armor & prejudice . . . she is
frightened of the clowns & may God have mercy on her soul –
may her pupils grow trees from their ears & shout about the
eclipse, whimpers from the farm girls & the counter
revolutionary crucifixion & damn the saints & make a profit the
vandal from his gamut & baby cupid, the roustabout forcing
you to store away velvet bonnet of barbarian funnel & drinking
& drinking until pay day & graduation & Sunday coming &
going just like Monday & some other people . . . throbbing & to
the pendulum strapped 'til Christmas may these teachers of the
shade be rot for committing the problems of past & future &
omitting the weather, the drunken eagle & the holy present . . .
Sunday being prisoner of the castle sleeping on & Nancy or
Peggy or Brunella – she turning into twenty-three & you
concluding that even gas masks can be worn in freedom, but
who are you really talking & thinking about when you discuss
your destiny? your problem? your freedom? . . . Sphinx & the
tango partner, her professor busy writing a book about the
bums, sit like wallflowers & you being taught by Felix the Cat &
how dare you have the nerve to pass! how dare you search for
pain! for self pity! for decisions!

Aunt Fang from the witch-hunt, her left jab weakened – the
flame in her arm & poor potbrain Shakespeare, a wire for his
halo . . . hand in hand, they whisper of cannibals & the poet & I
WISH I WAS JAYNE MANSFIELD/ STANDING ON THE
MOON/ I'D ORDER ME A LEPRECHAUN/ & SHOOT YOU
WITH MY SPOON/ while White Stoveman with earrings that
jingle from his toes & who sings of Hiroshima & Tokyo &
Hollywood happenings pulls out his leaflets, his plum & I WISH

325

I WAS A DIPLOMAT/ NOT A DOORMAT OR A MOVIE/ I'D
BURN MY OFFICE OFF THE EARTH/ & MAKE THE WORLD
MORE GROOVY/ & ho ho ho amazing & get two corsets free
with each butter sandwich & Plato with his flask of verbs
building his buildings on ground where there is no ground at all
& his mother in the tower wringing her head & moaning & oh
great screech of help! & crippled mermaid singing & listen
that's her singing now & she meows too . . . (1) get yourself a
harness. be avant garde. eat lots of mushrooms & end up as a
country music expert (2) get yourself a torn calendar, some
leftover birthday cake. buy a flagpole & you will indeed wind
up as a good librarian (3) steal a pink rake. carry a burnt
balloon. wash your neck with egg yolk & if you dont find
yourself a successful plantation owner within a matter of time,
then something is wrong . . . on & on & on sweet mermaid she
sings of ideals, different formulas & wild cookbooks/ dark
Scary, the weeper at the drop of anybody's hat but his,
sentimental – sentimental like the shock patient who recalls his
refrigerator with a slight tear & Right Lie, himself being whipped
to death by a pigtail – both of them right now being pasteurized
in a quart of milk & Gimmick hailing the armies of intelligence,
Jerry Lewis & used french fries . . . all right then, if you must go,
go with the jack of spades, the honky tonk lady & take care the
woman at the well – for kicks, see with your third eye & dream
of being mr deserted fox but dont depend on him. dont use
him. dont count on him

yonder at your funeral, you will see this pauper – dressed like
your face, he will have a wedding present for you – it will be a
mirror & in it, you will see the world as it sees you . . . behind
this mirror there will be a common worker looking like Little
Lulu. he'll be teaching a boy scout the Ten Commandments & if
you run from the mirror, they will both seize you & take you
with them to the desert. they will stick a fishing pole in your
hand & immediately tell you of backaches, Buicks, senate seats

& ant poison – forks & knives – Stork, the magic gladiator will appear from a trunk locker & say he brought you here & now he wants to collect & you saying 'no no i'm a student! i'm a student of life!' & him saying 'i'll give you a student of life! yuh just better pay up yuh dig, i'm the stork, yuh dig?' SHAZAAAAM & the mighty mirror cracking & you seeing yourself oh you cant believe it & youre vanishing – the boy scout saying 'fish! fish!' & you saying 'help me, common worker!' & the common worker saying 'call me C.W. yuh dig?' & you saying 'oweee strange & tell me what's happening!' – Bull Flipt, the way out method actor who sleeps in peanuts to get the feel of being a hog & Sabu Jones coming out of the subway & he say 'now what's so important about being a hog & gimme some of those peanuts – i gotta go hunt me some tiger today Baby!' & the geese charging – thinking theyre scarecrows & you seeking goats in the midst of novelists who eat shot glasses – write books about other people's masters – each one in a mustache & wishing he was Frank Buck & you getting rather salty & everything begins & is forming into one Great big strangle-shape & the corpse, the voice – the struggle & you saying 'is it true that children who die at birth really have committed suicide?' but there's nobody to ask . . . forget these delusions find your opposite – be like Jonah – go deep & there will be no pauper at your ceremony . . . be him civilian – disciple or bellydancer . . . long live catastrophe

Josie & the hermit, King of the Blues – ragged at the motel – a wheel being invented in the barn & here come the innkeeper with bars from the window . . . Lady Chance & Superstition, the cleaning woman – she holler fresh quarters f' sale & Ritz Deaf paying all he has to get into this dungeon & he cant even hear . . . blank stares, caves & the in-crowd grinning & banners with little bo peep – simple simon & here come Standing Room Only . . . he's wearing a sucker & conning for better or worse – he's blowing the toot toot – Gigantic Push & the gingerbread sergeant growls & dies & the low rank gobble up the pieces & then they die from poison groin – malnutrition & thinking theyre too smart & you with the dice & forever uniform . . . receiving some degree & while giving it to your wall, somebody steals your enemy – your pride – your existence – your chum, Slop, leaving you to the dogs & defenders of mankind – ghost of Einstein like the raven & Miss Prune the Terror, trying to convince you that there was no edgar allan poe & then you straightening the tie that either Eileen or Punk Roger gave you for pennies on the brain & saying 'take me to your leader for change! i'm sick of these vincent price people!' . . . Homer on the gallows – his feet swollen & you wondering why there is no eternity & that you make your own eternity & why there is no music & that you make your own music & why there are no alternatives & that you make your own alternatives

# Blonde on Blonde

Rainy Day Women # 12 & 35
Pledging My Time
Visions of Johanna
One of Us Must Know
    (Sooner or Later)
I Want You
Stuck Inside of Mobile
    with the Memphis Blues Again
Leopard-Skin Pill-Box Hat
Just Like a Woman
Most Likely You Go Your Way
    (and I'll Go Mine)
Absolutely Sweet Marie
Temporary Like Achilles
Obviously Five Believers
Fourth Time Around
Sad-Eyed Lady of the Lowlands

I'll Keep It with Mine
I Wanna Be Your Lover
Tell Me, Momma
She's Your Lover Now

# Rainy Day Women #12 & 35

Well, they'll stone ya when you're trying to be so good,
They'll stone ya just a-like they said they would.
They'll stone ya when you're tryin' to go home.
Then they'll stone ya when you're there all alone.
But I would not feel so all alone,
Everybody must get stoned.

Well, they'll stone ya when you're walkin' 'long the street.
They'll stone ya when you're tryin' to keep your seat.
They'll stone ya when you're walkin' on the floor.
They'll stone ya when you're walkin' to the door.
But I would not feel so all alone,
Everybody must get stoned.

They'll stone ya when you're at the breakfast table.
They'll stone ya when you are young and able.
They'll stone ya when you're tryin' to make a buck.
They'll stone ya and then they'll say, 'good luck.'
Tell ya what, I would not feel so all alone,
Everybody must get stoned.

Well, they'll stone you and say that it's the end.
Then they'll stone you and then they'll come back again.
They'll stone you when you're riding in your car.
They'll stone you when you're playing your guitar.
Yes, but I would not feel so all alone,
Everybody must get stoned.

Well, they'll stone you when you walk all alone.
They'll stone you when you are walking home.
They'll stone you and then say you are brave.
They'll stone you when you are set down in your grave.
But I would not feel so all alone,
Everybody must get stoned.

# Pledging My Time

Well, early in the mornin'
'Til late at night,
I got a poison headache,
But I feel all right.
I'm pledging my time to you,
Hopin' you'll come through, too.

Well, the hobo jumped up,
He came down natur'lly.
After he stole my baby,
Then he wanted to steal me.
But I'm pledging my time to you,
Hopin' you'll come through, too.

Won't you come with me, baby?
I'll take you where you wanna go.
And if it don't work out,
You'll be the first to know.
I'm pledging my time to you,
Hopin' you'll come through, too.

Well, the room is so stuffy,
I can hardly breathe.
Ev'rybody's gone but me and you
And I can't be the last to leave.
I'm pledging my time to you,
Hopin' you'll come through, too.

Well, they sent for the ambulance
And one was sent.
Somebody got lucky
But it was an accident.
Now I'm pledging my time to you,
Hopin' you'll come through, too.

# Visions of Johanna

Ain't it just like the night to play tricks when you're tryin' to be
   so quiet?
We sit here stranded, though we're all doin' our best to deny it
And Louise holds a handful of rain, temptin' you to defy it
Lights flicker from the opposite loft
In this room the heat pipes just cough
The country music station plays soft
But there's nothing, really nothing to turn off
Just Louise and her lover so entwined
And these visions of Johanna that conquer my mind

In the empty lot where the ladies play blindman's bluff with the
   key chain
And the all-night girls they whisper of escapades out on the 'D'
   train
We can hear the night watchman click his flashlight
Ask himself if it's him or them that's really insane
Louise, she's all right, she's just near
She's delicate and seems like the mirror
But she just makes it all too concise and too clear
That Johanna's not here
The ghost of 'lectricity howls in the bones of her face
Where these visions of Johanna have now taken my place

Now, little boy lost, he takes himself so seriously
He brags of his misery, he likes to live dangerously
And when bringing her name up
He speaks of a farewell kiss to me
He's sure got a lotta gall to be so useless and all
Muttering small talk at the wall while I'm in the hall
How can I explain?
Oh, it's so hard to get on
And these visions of Johanna, they kept me up past the dawn

Inside the museums, Infinity goes up on trial
Voices echo this is what salvation must be like after a while
But Mona Lisa musta had the highway blues
You can tell by the way she smiles
See the primitive wallflower freeze
When the jelly-faced women all sneeze
Hear the one with the mustache say, 'Jeeze
I can't find my knees'
Oh, jewels and binoculars hang from the head of the mule
But these visions of Johanna, they make it all seem so cruel

The peddler now speaks to the countess who's pretending to
    care for him
Sayin', 'Name me someone that's not a parasite and I'll go out
    and say a prayer for him'
But like Louise always says
'Ya can't look at much, can ya man?'
As she, herself, prepares for him
And Madonna, she still has not showed
We see this empty cage now corrode
Where her cape of the stage once had flowed
The fiddler, he now steps to the road
He writes ev'rything's been returned which was owed
On the back of the fish truck that loads
While my conscience explodes
The harmonicas play the skeleton keys and the rain
And these visions of Johanna are now all that remain

# One of Us Must Know
# (Sooner or Later)

I didn't mean to treat you so bad
You shouldn't take it so personal
I didn't mean to make you so sad
You just happened to be there, that's all
When I saw you say 'goodbye' to your friends and smile
I thought that it was well understood
That you'd be comin' back in a little while
I didn't know that you were sayin' 'goodbye' for good

But, sooner or later, one of us must know
You just did what you're supposed to do
Sooner or later, one of us must know
That I really did try to get close to you

I couldn't see what you could show me
Your scarf had kept your mouth well hid
I couldn't see how you could know me
But you said you knew me and I believed you did
When you whispered in my ear
And asked me if I was leavin' with you or her
I didn't realize just what I did hear
I didn't realize how young you were

But, sooner or later, one of us must know
You just did what you're supposed to do
Sooner or later, one of us must know
That I really did try to get close to you

I couldn't see when it started snowin'
Your voice was all that I heard
I couldn't see where we were goin'
But you said you knew an' I took your word
And then you told me later, as I apologized

That you were just kiddin' me, you weren't really from the farm
An' I told you, as you clawed out my eyes
That I never really meant to do you any harm

But, sooner or later, one of us must know
You just did what you're supposed to do
Sooner or later, one of us must know
That I really did try to get close to you

# I Want You

The guilty undertaker sighs,
The lonely organ grinder cries,
The silver saxophones say I should refuse you.
The cracked bells and washed-out horns
Blow into my face with scorn,
But it's not that way,
I wasn't born to lose you.
I want you, I want you,
I want you so bad,
Honey, I want you.

The drunken politician leaps
Upon the street where mothers weep
And the saviors who are fast asleep,
They wait for you.
And I wait for them to interrupt
Me drinkin' from my broken cup
And ask me to
Open up the gate for you.
I want you, I want you,
I want you so bad,
Honey, I want you.

Now all my fathers, they've gone down,
True love they've been without it.
But all their daughters put me down
'Cause I don't think about it.

Well, I return to the Queen of Spades
And talk with my chambermaid.
She knows that I'm not afraid
To look at her.
She is good to me
And there's nothing she doesn't see.

She knows where I'd like to be
But it doesn't matter.
I want you, I want you,
I want you so bad,
Honey, I want you.

Now your dancing child with his Chinese suit,
He spoke to me, I took his flute.
No, I wasn't very cute to him,
Was I?
But I did it, though, because he lied
Because he took you for a ride
And because time was on his side
And because I . . .
I want you, I want you,
I want you so bad,
Honey, I want you.

# Stuck Inside of Mobile
# with the Memphis Blues Again

Oh, the ragman draws circles
Up and down the block.
I'd ask him what the matter was
But I know that he don't talk.
And the ladies treat me kindly
And furnish me with tape,
But deep inside my heart
I know I can't escape.
Oh, Mama, can this really be the end,
To be stuck inside of Mobile
With the Memphis blues again.

Well, Shakespeare, he's in the alley
With his pointed shoes and his bells,
Speaking to some French girl,
Who says she knows me well.
And I would send a message
To find out if she's talked,
But the post office has been stolen
And the mailbox is locked.
Oh, Mama, can this really be the end,
To be stuck inside of Mobile
With the Memphis blues again.

Mona tried to tell me
To stay away from the train line.
She said that all the railroad men
Just drink up your blood like wine.
An' I said, 'Oh, I didn't know that,
But then again, there's only one I've met
An' he just smoked my eyelids
An' punched my cigarette.'
Oh, Mama, can this really be the end,

To be stuck inside of Mobile
With the Memphis blues again.

Grandpa died last week
And now he's buried in the rocks,
But everybody still talks about
How badly they were shocked.
But me, I expected it to happen,
I knew he'd lost control
When he built a fire on Main Street
And shot it full of holes.
Oh, Mama, can this really be the end,
To be stuck inside of Mobile
With the Memphis blues again.

Now the senator came down here
Showing ev'ryone his gun,
Handing out free tickets
To the wedding of his son.
An' me, I nearly got busted
An' wouldn't it be my luck
To get caught without a ticket
And be discovered beneath a truck.
Oh, Mama, can this really be the end,
To be stuck inside of Mobile
With the Memphis blues again.

Now the preacher looked so baffled
When I asked him why he dressed
With twenty pounds of headlines
Stapled to his chest.
But he cursed me when I proved it to him,
Then I whispered, 'Not even you can hide.
You see, you're just like me,

I hope you're satisfied.'
Oh, Mama, can this really be the end,
To be stuck inside of Mobile
With the Memphis blues again.

Now the rainman gave me two cures,
Then he said, 'Jump right in.'
The one was Texas medicine,
The other was just railroad gin.
An' like a fool I mixed them
An' it strangled up my mind,
An' now people just get uglier
An' I have no sense of time.
Oh, Mama, can this really be the end,
To be stuck inside of Mobile
With the Memphis blues again.

When Ruthie says come see her
In her honky-tonk lagoon,
Where I can watch her waltz for free
'Neath her Panamanian moon.
An' I say, 'Aw come on now,
You must know about my debutante.'
An' she says, 'Your debutante just knows what you need
But I know what you want.'
Oh, Mama, can this really be the end,
To be stuck inside of Mobile
With the Memphis blues again.

Now the bricks lay on Grand Street
Where the neon madmen climb.
They all fall there so perfectly,
It all seems so well timed.
An' here I sit so patiently

Waiting to find out what price
You have to pay to get out of
Going through all these things twice.
Oh, Mama, can this really be the end,
To be stuck inside of Mobile
With the Memphis blues again.

# Leopard-Skin Pill-Box Hat

Well, I see you got your brand new leopard-skin pill-box hat
Yes, I see you got your brand new leopard-skin pill-box hat
Well, you must tell me, baby
How your head feels under somethin' like that
Under your brand new leopard-skin pill-box hat

Well, you look so pretty in it
Honey, can I jump on it sometime?
Yes, I just wanna see
If it's really that expensive kind
You know it balances on your head
Just like a mattress balances
On a bottle of wine
Your brand new leopard-skin pill-box hat

Well, if you wanna see the sun rise
Honey, I know where
We'll go out and see it sometime
We'll both just sit there and stare
Me with my belt
Wrapped around my head
And you just sittin' there
In your brand new leopard-skin pill-box hat

Well, I asked the doctor if I could see you
It's bad for your health, he said
Yes, I disobeyed his orders
I came to see you
But I found him there instead
You know, I don't mind him cheatin' on me
But I sure wish he'd take that off his head
Your brand new leopard-skin pill-box hat

Well, I see you got a new boyfriend
You know, I never seen him before
Well, I saw him
Makin' love to you
You forgot to close the garage door
You might think he loves you for your money
But I know what he really loves you for
It's your brand new leopard-skin pill-box hat

# Just Like a Woman

Nobody feels any pain
Tonight as I stand inside the rain
Ev'rybody knows
That Baby's got new clothes
But lately I see her ribbons and her bows
Have fallen from her curls.
She takes just like a woman, yes, she does
She makes love just like a woman, yes, she does
And she aches just like a woman
But she breaks just like a little girl.

Queen Mary, she's my friend
Yes, I believe I'll go see her again
Nobody has to guess
That Baby can't be blessed
Till she sees finally that she's like all the rest
With her fog, her amphetamine and her pearls.
She takes just like a woman, yes, she does
She makes love just like a woman, yes, she does
And she aches just like a woman
But she breaks just like a little girl.

It was raining from the first
And I was dying there of thirst
So I came in here
And your long-time curse hurts
But what's worse
Is this pain in here
I can't stay in here
Ain't it clear that —

I just can't fit
Yes, I believe it's time for us to quit
When we meet again

Introduced as friends
Please don't let on that you knew me when
I was hungry and it was your world.
Ah, you fake just like a woman, yes, you do
You make love just like a woman, yes, you do
Then you ache just like a woman
But you break just like a little girl.

# Most Likely You Go Your Way
# (and I'll Go Mine)

You say you love me
And you're thinkin' of me,
But you know you could be wrong.
You say you told me
That you wanna hold me,
But you know you're not that strong.
I just can't do what I done before,
I just can't beg you any more.
I'm gonna let you pass
And I'll go last.
Then time will tell just who fell
And who's been left behind,
When you go your way and I go mine.

You say you disturb me
And you don't deserve me,
But you know sometimes you lie.
You say you're shakin'
And you're always achin',
But you know how hard you try.
Sometimes it gets so hard to care,
It can't be this way ev'rywhere.
And I'm gonna let you pass,
Yes, and I'll go last.
Then time will tell just who fell
And who's been left behind,
When you go your way and I go mine.

The judge, he holds a grudge,
He's gonna call on you.
But he's badly built
And he walks on stilts,
Watch out he don't fall on you.

You say you're sorry
For tellin' stories
That you know I believe are true.
You say ya got some
Other kinda lover
And yes, I believe you do.
You say my kisses are not like his,
But this time I'm not gonna tell you why that is.
I'm just gonna let you pass,
Yes, and I'll go last.
Then time will tell who fell
And who's been left behind,
When you go your way and I go mine.

# Absolutely Sweet Marie

Well, your railroad gate, you know I just can't jump it
Sometimes it gets so hard, you see
I'm just sitting here beating on my trumpet
With all these promises you left for me
But where are you tonight, sweet Marie?

Well, I waited for you when I was half sick
Yes, I waited for you when you hated me
Well, I waited for you inside of the frozen traffic
When you knew I had some other place to be
Now, where are you tonight, sweet Marie?

Well, anybody can be just like me, obviously
But then, now again, not too many can be like you, fortunately.

Well, six white horses that you did promise
Were fin'lly delivered down to the penitentiary
But to live outside the law, you must be honest
I know you always say that you agree
But where are you tonight, sweet Marie?

Well, I don't know how it happened
But the river-boat captain, he knows my fate
But ev'rybody else, even yourself
They're just gonna have to wait.

Well, I got the fever down in my pockets
The Persian drunkard, he follows me
Yes, I can take him to your house but I can't unlock it
You see, you forgot to leave me with the key
Oh, where are you tonight, sweet Marie?

Now, I been in jail when all my mail showed
That a man can't give his address out to bad company

And now I stand here lookin' at your yellow railroad
In the ruins of your balcony
Wond'ring where you are tonight, sweet Marie.

# Temporary Like Achilles

Standing on your window, honey,
Yes, I've been here before.
Feeling so harmless,
I'm looking at your second door.
How come you don't send me no regards?
You know I want your lovin',
Honey, why are you so hard?

Kneeling 'neath your ceiling,
Yes, I guess I'll be here for a while.
I'm tryin' to read your portrait, but,
I'm helpless, like a rich man's child.
How come you send someone out to have me barred?
You know I want your lovin',
Honey, why are you so hard?

Like a poor fool in his prime,
Yes, I know you can hear me walk,
But is your heart made out of stone, or is it lime,
Or is it just solid rock?

Well, I rush into your hallway,
Lean against your velvet door.
I watch upon your scorpion
Who crawls across your circus floor.
Just what do you think you have to guard?
You know I want your lovin',
Honey, but you're so hard.

Achilles is in your alleyway,
He don't want me here,
He does brag,
He's pointing to the sky
And he's hungry, like a man in drag.
How come you get someone like him to be your guard?

351

You know I want your lovin',
Honey, but you're so hard.

# Obviously Five Believers

Early in the mornin'
Early in the mornin'
I'm callin' you to
I'm callin' you to
Please come home
Yes, I guess I could make it without you
If I just didn't feel so all alone

Don't let me down
Don't let me down
I won't let you down
I won't let you down
No I won't
You know I can if you can, honey
But, honey, please don't

I got my black dog barkin'
Black dog barkin'
Yes it is now
Yes it is now
Outside my yard
Yes, I could tell you what he means
If I just didn't have to try so hard

Your mama's workin'
Your mama's moanin'
She's cryin' you know
She's tryin' you know
You better go now
Well, I'd tell you what she wants
But I just don't know how

Fifteen jugglers
Fifteen jugglers

Five believers
Five believers
All dressed like men
Tell yo' mama not to worry because
They're just my friends

Early in the mornin'
Early in the mornin'
I'm callin' you to
I'm callin' you to
Please come home
Yes, I could make it without you
If I just didn't feel so all alone

# Fourth Time Around

When she said,
'Don't waste your words, they're just lies,'
I cried she was deaf.
And she worked on my face until breaking my eyes,
Then said, 'What else you got left?'
It was then that I got up to leave
But she said, 'Don't forget,
Everybody must give something back
For something they get.'

I stood there and hummed,
I tapped on her drum and asked her how come.
And she buttoned her boot,
And straightened her suit,
Then she said, 'Don't get cute.'
So I forced my hands in my pockets
And felt with my thumbs,
And gallantly handed her
My very last piece of gum.

She threw me outside,
I stood in the dirt where ev'ryone walked.
And after finding I'd
Forgotten my shirt,
I went back and knocked.
I waited in the hallway, she went to get it,
And I tried to make sense
Out of that picture of you in your wheelchair
That leaned up against . . .

Her Jamaican rum
And when she did come, I asked her for some.
She said, 'No, dear.'
I said, 'Your words aren't clear,

You'd better spit out your gum.'
She screamed till her face got so red,
Then she fell on the floor,
And I covered her up and then
Thought I'd go look through her drawer.

And when I was through,
I filled up my shoe
And brought it to you.
And you, you took me in,
You loved me then,
You didn't waste time.
And I, I never took much,
I never asked for your crutch,
Now don't ask for mine.

# Sad-Eyed Lady of the Lowlands

With your mercury mouth in the missionary times,
And your eyes like smoke and your prayers like rhymes,
And your silver cross, and your voice like chimes,
Oh, who among them do they think could bury you?
With your pockets well protected at last,
And your streetcar visions which you place on the grass,
And your flesh like silk, and your face like glass,
Who among them do they think could carry you?
Sad-eyed lady of the lowlands,
Where the sad-eyed prophet says that no man comes,
My warehouse eyes, my Arabian drums,
Should I leave them by your gate,
Or, sad-eyed lady, should I wait?

With your sheets like metal and your belt like lace,
And your deck of cards missing the jack and the ace,
And your basement clothes and your hollow face,
Who among them can think he could outguess you?
With your silhouette when the sunlight dims
Into your eyes where the moonlight swims,
And your match-book songs and your gypsy hymns,
Who among them would try to impress you?
Sad-eyed lady of the lowlands,
Where the sad-eyed prophet says that no man comes,
My warehouse eyes, my Arabian drums,
Should I leave them by your gate,
Or, sad-eyed lady, should I wait?

The kings of Tyrus with their convict list
Are waiting in line for their geranium kiss,
And you wouldn't know it would happen like this,
But who among them really wants just to kiss you?
With your childhood flames on your midnight rug,

And your Spanish manners and your mother's drugs,
And your cowboy mouth and your curfew plugs,
Who among them do you think could resist you?
Sad-eyed lady of the lowlands,
Where the sad-eyed prophet says that no man comes,
My warehouse eyes, my Arabian drums,
Should I leave them by your gate,
Or, sad-eyed lady, should I wait?


Oh, the farmers and the businessmen, they all did decide
To show you the dead angels that they used to hide.
But why did they pick you to sympathize with their side?
Oh, how could they ever mistake you?
They wished you'd accepted the blame for the farm,
But with the sea at your feet and the phony false alarm,
And with the child of a hoodlum wrapped up in your arms,
How could they ever, ever persuade you?
Sad-eyed lady of the lowlands,
Where the sad-eyed prophet says that no man comes,
My warehouse eyes, my Arabian drums,
Should I leave them by your gate,
Or, sad-eyed lady, should I wait?


With your sheet-metal memory of Cannery Row,
And your magazine-husband who one day just had to go,
And your gentleness now, which you just can't help but show,
Who among them do you think would employ you?
Now you stand with your thief, you're on his parole
With your holy medallion which your fingertips fold,
And your saintlike face and your ghostlike soul,
Oh, who among them do you think could destroy you?
Sad-eyed lady of the lowlands,

Where the sad-eyed prophet says that no man comes,
My warehouse eyes, my Arabian drums,
Should I leave them by your gate,
Or, sad-eyed lady, should I wait?

# I'll Keep It with Mine

You will search, babe,
At any cost.
But how long, babe,
Can you search for what's not lost?
Ev'rybody will help you,
Some people are very kind.
But if I can save you any time,
Come on, give it to me,
I'll keep it with mine.

I can't help it
If you might think I'm odd,
If I say I'm not loving you for what you are
But for what you're not.
Everybody will help you
Discover what you set out to find.
But if I can save you any time,
Come on, give it to me,
I'll keep it with mine.

The train leaves
At half past ten,
But it'll be back tomorrow,
Same time again.
The conductor he's weary,
He's still stuck on the line.
But if I can save you any time,
Come on, give it to me,
I'll keep it with mine.

# I Wanna Be Your Lover

Well, the rainman comes with his magic wand
And the judge says, 'Mona can't have no bond.'
And the walls collide, Mona cries,
And the rainman leaves in the wolfman's disguise.

I wanna be your lover, baby, I wanna be your man.
I wanna be your lover, baby,
I don't wanna be hers, I wanna be yours.

Well, the undertaker in his midnight suit
Says to the masked man, 'Ain't you cute!'
Well, the mask man he gets up on the shelf
And he says, 'You ain't so bad, yourself.'

I wanna be your lover, baby, I wanna be your man.
I wanna be your lover, baby,
I don't wanna be hers, I wanna be yours.

Well, jumpin' Judy can't go no higher.
She had bullets in her eyes, and they fire.
Rasputin he's so dignified,
He touched the back of her head an' he died.

I wanna be your lover, baby, I wanna be your man.
I wanna be your lover, baby,
I don't wanna be hers, I wanna be yours.

Well, Phaedra with her looking glass,
Stretchin' out upon the grass.
She gets all messed up and she faints –
That's 'cause she's so obvious and you ain't.

I wanna be your lover, baby, I wanna be your man.
I wanna be your lover, baby,
I don't wanna be hers, I wanna be yours.

# Tell Me, Momma

Ol' black Bascom, don't break no mirrors
Cold black water dog, make no tears
You say you love me with what may be love
Don't you remember makin' baby love?
Got your steam drill built and you're lookin' for some kid
To get it to work for you like your nine-pound hammer did
But I know that you know that I know what you show
Something is tearing up your mind.

Tell me, momma,
Tell me, momma,
Tell me, momma, what is it?
What's wrong with you this time?

Hey, John, come and get me some candy goods
Shucks, it sure feels like it's in the woods
Spend some time on your January trips
You got tombstone moose up and your brave-yard whips
If you're anxious to find out when your friendship's gonna end
Come on, baby, I'm your friend!
And I know that you know that I know that you show
Something is tearing up your mind.

Tell me, momma,
Tell me, momma,
Tell me, momma, what is it?
What's wrong with you this time?

Ohh, we bone the editor, can't get read
But his painted sled, instead it's a bed
Yes, I see you on your window ledge
But I can't tell just how far away you are from the edge
And, anyway, you're just gonna make people jump and roar
Whatcha wanna go and do that for?

For I know that you know that I know that you know
Something is tearing up your mind.

Ah, tell me, momma,
Tell me, momma,
Tell me, momma, what is it?
What's wrong with you this time?

# She's Your Lover Now

The pawnbroker roared
Also, so, so did the landlord
The scene was so crazy, wasn't it?
Both were so glad
To watch me destroy what I had
Pain sure brings out the best in people, doesn't it?
Why didn't you just leave me if you didn't want to stay?
Why'd you have to treat me so bad?
Did it have to be that way?
Now you stand here expectin' me to remember somethin' you
　　forgot to say
Yes, and you, I see you're still with her, well
That's fine 'cause she's comin' on so strange, can't you tell?
Somebody had better explain
She's got her iron chain
I'd do it, but I, I just can't remember how
You talk to her
She's your lover now.

I already assumed
That we're in the felony room
But I ain't a judge, you don't have to be nice to me
But please tell that
To your friend in the cowboy hat
You know he keeps on sayin' ev'rythin' twice to me
You know I was straight with you
You know I've never tried to change you in any way
You know if you didn't want to be with me
That you could . . . didn't have to stay.
Now you stand here sayin' you forgive and forget. Honey, what
　　can I say?
Yes, you, you just sit around and ask for ashtrays, can't you
　　reach?
I see you kiss her on the cheek ev'rytime she gives a speech

With her picture books of the pyramid
And her postcards of Billy the Kid
(Why must everybody bow?)
You better talk to her 'bout it
You're her lover now.

Oh, ev'rybody that cares
Is goin' up the castle stairs
But I'm not up in your castle, honey
It's true, I just can't recall
San Francisco at all
I can't even remember El Paso, uh, honey
You never had to be faithful
I didn't want you to grieve
Oh, why was it so hard for you
If you didn't want to be with me, just to leave?
Now you stand here while your finger's goin' up my sleeve
An' you, just what do you do anyway? Ain't there nothin' you
    can say?
She'll be standin' on the bar soon
With a fish head an' a harpoon
An' a fake beard plastered on her brow
You'd better do somethin' quick
She's your lover now.

# John Wesley Harding

John Wesley Harding
As I Went Out One Morning
All Along the Watchtower
The Ballad of Frankie Lee
    and Judas Priest
I Dreamed I Saw St Augustine
Drifter's Escape
Dear Landlord
I Am a Lonesome Hobo
I Pity the Poor Immigrant
The Wicked Messenger
Down Along the Cove
I'll Be Your Baby Tonight

John Wesley Harding (liner notes)

# John Wesley Harding

John Wesley Harding
Was a friend to the poor,
He trav'led with a gun in ev'ry hand.
All along this countryside,
He opened a many a door,
But he was never known
To hurt a honest man.

'Twas down in Chaynee County,
A time they talk about,
With his lady by his side
He took a stand.
And soon the situation there
Was all but straightened out,
For he was always known
To lend a helping hand.

All across the telegraph
His name it did resound,
But no charge held against him
Could they prove.
And there was no man around
Who could track or chain him down,
He was never known
To make a foolish move.

# As I Went Out One Morning

As I went out one morning
To breathe the air around Tom Paine's,
I spied the fairest damsel
That ever did walk in chains.
I offer'd her my hand,
She took me by the arm.
I knew that very instant,
She meant to do me harm.

'Depart from me this moment,'
I told her with my voice.
Said she, 'But I don't wish to,'
Said I, 'But you have no choice.'
'I beg you, sir,' she pleaded
From the corners of her mouth,
'I will secretly accept you
And together we'll fly south.'

Just then Tom Paine, himself,
Came running from across the field,
Shouting at this lovely girl
And commanding her to yield.
And as she was letting go her grip,
Up Tom Paine did run,
'I'm sorry, sir,' he said to me,
'I'm sorry for what she's done.'

# All Along the Watchtower

'There must be some way out of here,' said the joker to the
    thief,
'There's too much confusion, I can't get no relief.
Businessmen, they drink my wine, plowmen dig my earth,
None of them along the line know what any of it is worth.'

'No reason to get excited,' the thief, he kindly spoke,
'There are many here among us who feel that life is but a joke.
But you and I, we've been through that, and this is not our fate,
So let us not talk falsely now, the hour is getting late.'

All along the watchtower, princes kept the view
While all the women came and went, barefoot servants, too.

Outside in the distance a wildcat did growl,
Two riders were approaching, the wind began to howl.

# The Ballad of Frankie Lee
# and Judas Priest

Well, Frankie Lee and Judas Priest,
They were the best of friends.
So when Frankie Lee needed money one day,
Judas quickly pulled out a roll of tens
And placed them on a footstool
Just above the plotted plain,
Sayin', 'Take your pick, Frankie Boy,
My loss will be your gain.'

Well, Frankie Lee, he sat right down
And put his fingers to his chin,
But with the cold eyes of Judas on him,
His head began to spin.
'Would ya please not stare at me like that,' he said,
'It's just my foolish pride,
But sometimes a man must be alone
And this is no place to hide.'

Well, Judas, he just winked and said,
'All right, I'll leave you here,
But you'd better hurry up and choose
Which of those bills you want,
Before they all disappear.'
'I'm gonna start my pickin' right now,
Just tell me where you'll be.'

Judas pointed down the road
And said, 'Eternity!'
'Eternity?' said Frankie Lee,
With a voice as cold as ice.
'That's right,' said Judas Priest, 'Eternity,
Though you might call it "Paradise."'

'I don't call it anything,'
Said Frankie Lee with a smile.
'All right,' said Judas Priest,
'I'll see you after a while.'

Well, Frankie Lee, he sat back down,
Feelin' low and mean,
When just then a passing stranger
Burst upon the scene,
Saying, 'Are you Frankie Lee, the gambler,
Whose father is deceased?
Well, if you are,
There's a fellow callin' you down the road
And they say his name is Priest.'

'Oh, yes, he is my friend,'
Said Frankie Lee in fright,
'I do recall him very well,
In fact, he just left my sight.'
'Yes, that's the one,' said the stranger,
As quiet as a mouse,
'Well, my message is, he's down the road,
Stranded in a house.'

Well, Frankie Lee, he panicked,
He dropped ev'rything and ran
Until he came up to the spot
Where Judas Priest did stand.
'What kind of house is this,' he said,
'Where I have come to roam?'
'It's not a house,' said Judas Priest,
'It's not a house . . . it's a home.'

Well, Frankie Lee, he trembled,
He soon lost all control
Over ev'rything which he had made
While the mission bells did toll.
He just stood there staring
At that big house as bright as any sun,
With four and twenty windows
And a woman's face in ev'ry one.


Well, up the stairs ran Frankie Lee
With a soulful, bounding leap,
And, foaming at the mouth,
He began to make his midnight creep.
For sixteen nights and days he raved,
But on the seventeenth he burst
Into the arms of Judas Priest,
Which is where he died of thirst.


No one tried to say a thing
When they took him out in jest,
Except, of course, the little neighbor boy
Who carried him to rest.
And he just walked along, alone,
With his guilt so well concealed,
And muttered underneath his breath,
'Nothing is revealed.'


Well, the moral of the story,
The moral of this song,
Is simply that one should never be
Where one does not belong.

So when you see your neighbor carryin' somethin',
Help him with his load,
And don't go mistaking Paradise
For that home across the road.

# I Dreamed
# I Saw St Augustine

I dreamed I saw St Augustine,
Alive as you or me,
Tearing through these quarters
In the utmost misery,
With a blanket underneath his arm
And a coat of solid gold,
Searching for the very souls
Whom already have been sold.

'Arise, arise,' he cried so loud,
In a voice without restraint,
'Come out, ye gifted kings and queens
And hear my sad complaint.
No martyr is among ye now
Whom you can call your own,
So go on your way accordingly
But know you're not alone.'

I dreamed I saw St Augustine,
Alive with fiery breath,
And I dreamed I was amongst the ones
That put him out to death.
Oh, I awoke in anger,
So alone and terrified,
I put my fingers against the glass
And bowed my head and cried.

# Drifter's Escape

'Oh, help me in my weakness,'
I heard the drifter say,
As they carried him from the courtroom
And were taking him away.
'My trip hasn't been a pleasant one
And my time it isn't long,
And I still do not know
What it was that I've done wrong.'

Well, the judge, he cast his robe aside,
A tear came to his eye,
'You fail to understand,' he said,
'Why must you even try?'
Outside, the crowd was stirring,
You could hear it from the door.
Inside, the judge was stepping down,
While the jury cried for more.

'Oh, stop that cursed jury,'
Cried the attendant and the nurse,
'The trial was bad enough,
But this is ten times worse.'
Just then a bolt of lightning
Struck the courthouse out of shape,
And while ev'rybody knelt to pray
The drifter did escape.

# Dear Landlord

Dear landlord,
Please don't put a price on my soul.
My burden is heavy,
My dreams are beyond control.
When that steamboat whistle blows,
I'm gonna give you all I got to give,
And I do hope you receive it well,
Dependin' on the way you feel that you live.

Dear landlord,
Please heed these words that I speak.
I know you've suffered much,
But in this you are not unique.
All of us, at times, we might work too hard
To have it too fast and too much,
And anyone can fill his life up
With things he can see but he just cannot touch.

Dear landlord,
Please don't dismiss my case.
I'm not about to argue,
I'm not about to move to no other place.
Now, each of us has his own special gift
And you know this was meant to be true,
And if you don't underestimate me,
I won't underestimate you.

# I Am a Lonesome Hobo

I am a lonesome hobo
Without family or friends,
Where another man's life might begin,
That's exactly where mine ends.
I have tried my hand at bribery,
Blackmail and deceit,
And I've served time for ev'rything
'Cept beggin' on the street.

Well, once I was rather prosperous,
There was nothing I did lack.
I had fourteen-karat gold in my mouth
And silk upon my back.
But I did not trust my brother,
I carried him to blame,
Which led me to my fatal doom,
To wander off in shame.

Kind ladies and kind gentlemen,
Soon I will be gone,
But let me just warn you all,
Before I do pass on;
Stay free from petty jealousies,
Live by no man's code,
And hold your judgment for yourself
Lest you wind up on this road.

# I Pity the Poor Immigrant

I pity the poor immigrant
Who wishes he would've stayed home,
Who uses all his power to do evil
But in the end is always left so alone.
That man whom with his fingers cheats
And who lies with ev'ry breath,
Who passionately hates his life
And likewise, fears his death.

I pity the poor immigrant
Whose strength is spent in vain,
Whose heaven is like Ironsides,
Whose tears are like rain,
Who eats but is not satisfied,
Who hears but does not see,
Who falls in love with wealth itself
And turns his back on me.

I pity the poor immigrant
Who tramples through the mud,
Who fills his mouth with laughing
And who builds his town with blood,
Whose visions in the final end
Must shatter like the glass.
I pity the poor immigrant
When his gladness comes to pass.

# The Wicked Messenger

There was a wicked messenger
From Eli he did come,
With a mind that multiplied
The smallest matter.
When questioned who had sent for him,
He answered with his thumb,
For his tongue it could not speak, but only flatter.

He stayed behind the assembly hall,
It was there he made his bed,
Oftentimes he could be seen returning.
Until one day he just appeared
With a note in his hand which read,
'The soles of my feet, I swear they're burning.'

Oh, the leaves began to fallin'
And the seas began to part,
And the people that confronted him were many.
And he was told but these few words,
Which opened up his heart,
'If ye cannot bring good news, then don't bring any.'

# Down Along the Cove

Down along the cove,
I spied my true love comin' my way.
Down along the cove,
I spied my true love comin' my way.
I say, 'Lord, have mercy, mama,
It sure is good to see you comin' today.'

Down along the cove,
I spied my little bundle of joy.
Down along the cove,
I spied my little bundle of joy.
She said, 'Lord, have mercy, honey,
I'm so glad you're my boy!'

Down along the cove,
We walked together hand in hand.
Down along the cove,
We walked together hand in hand.
Ev'rybody watchin' us go by
Knows we're in love, yes, and they understand.

# I'll Be Your Baby Tonight

Close your eyes, close the door,
You don't have to worry any more.
I'll be your baby tonight.

Shut the light, shut the shade,
You don't have to be afraid.
I'll be your baby tonight.

Well, that mockingbird's gonna sail away,
We're gonna forget it.
That big, fat moon is gonna shine like a spoon,
But we're gonna let it,
You won't regret it.

Kick your shoes off, do not fear,
Bring that bottle over here.
I'll be your baby tonight.

# John Wesley Harding (liner notes)

There were three kings and a jolly three too. The first one had a broken nose, the second, a broken arm and the third was broke. 'Faith is the key!' said the first king. 'No, froth is the key!' said the second. 'You're both wrong,' said the third, 'the key is Frank!'

It was late in the evening and Frank was sweeping up, preparing the meat and dishing himself out when there came a knock upon the door. 'Who is it?' he mused. 'It's us, Frank,' said the three kings in unison, 'and we'd like to have a word with you!' Frank opened the door and the three kings crawled in.

Terry Shute was in the midst of prying open a hairdresser when Frank's wife came in and caught him. 'They're here!' she gasped. Terry dropped his drawer and rubbed the eye. 'What do they appear to be like?' 'One's got a broken vessel and that's the truth, the other two I'm not so sure about.' 'Fine, thank you, that'll be all.' 'Good' she turned and puffed. Terry tightened his belt and in an afterthought, stated: 'Wait!' 'Yes?' 'How many of them would you say there were?' Vera smiled, she tapped her toe three times. Terry watched her foot closely. 'Three?' he asked, hesitating. Vera nodded.

'Get up off my floor!' shouted Frank. The second king, who was first to rise, mumbled, 'Where's the better half, Frank?' Frank, who was in no mood for jokes, took it lightly, replied, 'She's in the back of the house, flaming it up with an arrogant man, now come on, out with it, what's on our minds today?' Nobody answered.

Terry Shute then entered the room with a bang, looking the three kings over and fondling his mop. Getting down to the source of things, he proudly boasted: 'There is a creeping consumption in the land. It begins with these three fellas and it travels outward. Never in my life have I seen such a motley crew. They ask nothing and they receive nothing. Forgiveness is not in them. The wilderness is rotten all over their foreheads. They scorn the widow and abuse the child but I am afraid that they shall not prevail over the young man's destiny, not even them!' Frank turned with a blast, 'Get out of here, you ragged man! Come ye no more!' Terry left the room willingly.

'What seems to be the problem?' Frank turned back to the three kings who were astonished. The first king cleared his throat. His shoes were too big and his crown was wet and lopsided but nevertheless, he began to speak in the most meaningful way, 'Frank,' he began, 'Mr Dylan has come out with a new record. This record of course features none but his own songs and we understand that you're the key.' 'That's right,' said Frank, 'I am.' 'Well then,' said the king in a bit of excitement, 'could you please open it up for us?' Frank, who all this time had been reclining with his eyes closed, suddenly opened them both up as wide as a tiger. 'And just how far would you like to go in?' he asked and the three kings all looked at each other. 'Not too far but just far enough so's we can say that we've been there,' said the first chief. 'All right,' said Frank, 'I'll see what I can do,' and he commenced to doing it. First of all, he sat down and crossed his legs, then he sprung up, ripped off his shirt and began waving it in the air.
A lightbulb fell from one of his pockets and he stamped it out with his foot. Then he took a deep breath, moaned and punched his fist through the plate-glass window.
Settling back in his chair, he pulled out a knife, 'Far enough?' he asked. 'Yeah, sure, Frank,' said the second king. The third king just shook his head and said he didn't know. The first king remained silent. The door opened and Vera stepped in. 'Terry Shute will be leaving us soon and he desires to know if you kings got any gifts you wanna lay on him.' Nobody answered.

It was just before the break of day and the three kings were tumbling along the road. The first one's nose had been mysteriously fixed, the second one's arm had healed and the third one was rich. All three of them were blowing horns. 'I've never been so happy in all my life!' sang the one with all the money.

'Oh mighty thing!' said Vera to Frank, 'Why didn't you just tell them you were a moderate man and leave it at that instead of goosing yourself all over the room?' 'Patience, Vera,' said Frank. Terry Shute, who was sitting over by the curtain cleaning an ax, climbed to his feet, walked over to Vera's husband and placed his hand on his shoulder. 'Yuh didn't hurt yer hand, didja Frank?' Frank just sat there watching the workmen replace the window. 'I don't believe so,' he said.

# Nashville Skyline

**To Be Alone with You**
**I Threw It All Away**
**Peggy Day**
**Lay, Lady, Lay**
**One More Night**
**Tell Me That It Isn't True**
**Country Pie**
**Tonight I'll Be Staying Here with You**

Living the Blues
Wanted Man
Mistrel Boy

# To Be Alone with You

To be alone with you
Just you and me
Now won't you tell me true
Ain't that the way it oughta be?
To hold each other tight
The whole night through
Ev'rything is always right
When I'm alone with you.

To be alone with you
At the close of the day
With only you in view
While evening slips away
It only goes to show
That while life's pleasures be few
The only one I know
Is when I'm alone with you.

They say that nighttime is the right time
To be with the one you love
Too many thoughts get in the way in the day
But you're always what I'm thinkin' of
I wish the night were here
Bringin' me all of your charms
When only you are near
To hold me in your arms.

I'll always thank the Lord
When my working day's through
I get my sweet reward
To be alone with you.

# I Threw It All Away

I once held her in my arms,
She said she would always stay.
But I was cruel,
I treated her like a fool,
I threw it all away.

Once I had mountains in the palm of my hand,
And rivers that ran through ev'ry day.
I must have been mad,
I never knew what I had,
Until I threw it all away.

Love is all there is, it makes the world go 'round,
Love and only love, it can't be denied.
No matter what you think about it
You just won't be able to do without it.
Take a tip from one who's tried.

So if you find someone that gives you all of her love,
Take it to your heart, don't let it stray,
For one thing that's certain,
You will surely be a-hurtin',
If you throw it all away.

# Peggy Day

Peggy Day stole my poor heart away,
By golly, what more can I say,
Love to spend the night with Peggy Day.

Peggy night makes my future look so bright,
Man, that girl is out of sight,
Love to spend the day with Peggy night.

Well, you know that even before I learned her name,
You know I loved her just the same.
An' I tell 'em all, wherever I may go,
Just so they'll know, that she's my little lady
And I love her so.

Peggy Day stole my poor heart away,
Turned my skies to blue from gray,
Love to spend the night with Peggy Day.

Peggy Day stole my poor heart away,
By golly, what more can I say,
Love to spend the night with Peggy Day.
Love to spend the night with Peggy Day.

# Lay, Lady, Lay

Lay, lady, lay, lay across my big brass bed
Lay, lady, lay, lay across my big brass bed
Whatever colors you have in your mind
I'll show them to you and you'll see them shine

Lay, lady, lay, lay across my big brass bed
Stay, lady, stay, stay with your man awhile
Until the break of day, let me see you make him smile
His clothes are dirty but his hands are clean
And you're the best thing that he's ever seen

Stay, lady, stay, stay with your man awhile
Why wait any longer for the world to begin
You can have your cake and eat it too
Why wait any longer for the one you love
When he's standing in front of you

Lay, lady, lay, lay across my big brass bed
Stay, lady, stay, stay while the night is still ahead
I long to see you in the morning light
I long to reach for you in the night
Stay, lady, stay, stay while the night is still ahead

# One More Night

One more night, the stars are in sight
But tonight I'm as lonesome as can be.
Oh, the moon is shinin' bright,
Lighting ev'rything in sight,
But tonight no light will shine on me.

Oh, it's shameful and it's sad,
I lost the only pal I had,
I just could not be what she wanted me to be.
I will turn my head up high
To that dark and rolling sky,
For tonight no light will shine on me.

I was so mistaken when I thought that she'd be true,
I had no idea what a woman in love would do!

One more night, I will wait for the light
While the wind blows high above the tree.
Oh, I miss my darling so,
I didn't mean to see her go,
But tonight no light will shine on me.

One more night, the moon is shinin' bright
And the wind blows high above the tree.
Oh, I miss that woman so,
I didn't mean to see her go,
But tonight no light will shine on me.

# Tell Me That It Isn't True

I have heard rumors all over town,
They say that you're planning to put me down.
All I would like you to do,
Is tell me that it isn't true.

They say that you've been seen with some other man,
That he's tall, dark, and handsome, and you're holding his
    hand.
Darlin', I'm a-countin' on you,
Tell me that it isn't true.

To know that some other man is holdin' you tight,
It hurts me all over, it doesn't seem right.

All of those awful things that I have heard,
I don't want to believe them, all I want is your word.
So darlin', you better come through,
Tell me that it isn't true.

All of those awful things that I have heard,
I don't want to believe them, all I want is your word.
So darlin', I'm countin' on you,
Tell me that it isn't true.

# Country Pie

Just like old Saxophone Joe
When he's got the hogshead up on his toe
Oh me, oh my
Love that country pie

Listen to the fiddler play
When he's playin' 'til the break of day
Oh me, oh my
Love that country pie

Raspberry, strawberry, lemon and lime
What do I care?
Blueberry, apple, cherry, pumpkin and plum
Call me for dinner, honey, I'll be there

Saddle me up my big white goose
Tie me on 'er and turn her loose
Oh me, oh my
Love that country pie

I don't need much and that ain't no lie
Ain't runnin' any race
Give to me my country pie
I won't throw it up in anybody's face

Shake me up that old peach tree
Little Jack Horner's got nothin' on me
Oh me, oh my
Love that country pie

# Tonight I'll Be Staying Here with You

Throw my ticket out the window,
Throw my suitcase out there, too,
Throw my troubles out the door,
I don't need them any more
'Cause tonight I'll be staying here with you.

I should have left this town this morning
But it was more than I could do.
Oh, your love comes on so strong
And I've waited all day long
For tonight when I'll be staying here with you.

Is it really any wonder
The love that a stranger might receive.
You cast your spell and I went under,
I find it so difficult to leave.

I can hear that whistle blowin',
I see that stationmaster, too,
If there's a poor boy on the street,
Then let him have my seat
'Cause tonight I'll be staying here with you.

Throw my ticket out the window,
Throw my suitcase out there, too,
Throw my troubles out the door,
I don't need them any more
'Cause tonight I'll be staying here with you.

# Living the Blues

Since you've been gone,
I've been walking around
With my head bowed down to my shoes.
I've been living the blues
Ev'ry night without you.

I don't have to go far
To know where you are,
Strangers all give me the news.
I've been living the blues
Ev'ry night without you.

I think that it's best,
I soon get some rest
And forget my pride.
But I can't deny
This feeling that I
Carry for you deep down inside.

If you see me this way,
You'd come back and you'd stay,
Oh, how could you refuse.
I've been living the blues
Ev'ry night without you.

# Wanted Man

Wanted man in California, wanted man in Buffalo,
Wanted man in Kansas City, wanted man in Ohio,
Wanted man in Mississippi, wanted man in old Cheyenne,
Wherever you might look tonight, you might see this wanted
    man.

I might be in Colorado or Georgia by the sea,
Working for some man who may not know at all who I might
    be.
If you ever see me comin' and if you know who I am,
Don't you breathe it to nobody 'cause you know I'm on the
    lam.

Wanted man by Lucy Watson, wanted man by Jeannie Brown,
Wanted man by Nellie Johnson, wanted man in this next town.
But I've had all that I've wanted of a lot of things I had
And a lot more than I needed of some things that turned out
    bad.

I got sidetracked in El Paso, stopped to get myself a map,
Went the wrong way into Juarez with Juanita on my lap.
Then I went to sleep in Shreveport, woke up in Abilene
Wonderin' why the hell I'm wanted at some town halfway
    between.

Wanted man in Albuquerque, wanted man in Syracuse,
Wanted man in Tallahassee, wanted man in Baton Rouge,
There's somebody set to grab me anywhere that I might be
And wherever you might look tonight, you might get a glimpse
    of me.

Wanted man in California, wanted man in Buffalo,
Wanted man in Kansas City, wanted man in Ohio,
Wanted man in Mississippi, wanted man in old Cheyenne,

**Wherever you might look tonight, you might see this wanted man.**

# Minstrel Boy

Who's gonna throw that minstrel boy a coin?
Who's gonna let it roll?
Who's gonna throw that minstrel boy a coin?
Who's gonna let it down easy to save his soul?

Oh, Lucky's been drivin' a long, long time
And now he's stuck on top of the hill.
With twelve forward gears, it's been a long hard climb,
And with all of them ladies, though, he's lonely still.

Who's gonna throw that minstrel boy a coin?
Who's gonna let it roll?
Who's gonna throw that minstrel boy a coin?
Who's gonna let it down easy to save his soul?

Well, he deep in number and heavy in toil,
Mighty Mockingbird, he still has such a heavy load.
Beneath his bound'ries, what more can I tell,
With all of his trav'lin', but I'm still on that road.

Who's gonna throw that minstrel boy a coin?
Who's gonna let it roll?
Who's gonna throw that minstrel boy a coin?
Who's gonna let it down easy to save his soul?

# New Morning

**If Not for You**
**Day of the Locusts**
**Time Passes Slowly**
**Went to See the Gypsy**
**Winterlude**
**If Dogs Run Free**
**New Morning**
**Sign on the Window**
**One More Weekend**
**The Man in Me**
**Three Angels**
**Father of Night**

I'd Have You Any Time
Watching the River Flow
When I Paint My Masterpiece
Wallflower
George Jackson

# If Not for You

If not for you,
Babe, I couldn't find the door,
Couldn't even see the floor,
I'd be sad and blue,
If not for you.

If not for you,
Babe, I'd lay awake all night,
Wait for the mornin' light
To shine in through,
But it would not be new,
If not for you.

If not for you
My sky would fall,
Rain would gather too.
Without your love I'd be nowhere at all,
I'd be lost if not for you,
And you know it's true.

If not for you
My sky would fall,
Rain would gather too.
Without your love I'd be nowhere at all,
Oh! what would I do
If not for you.

If not for you,
Winter would have no spring,
Couldn't hear the robin sing,
I just wouldn't have a clue,
Anyway it wouldn't ring true,
If not for you.

# Day of the Locusts

Oh, the benches were stained with tears and perspiration,
The birdies were flying from tree to tree.
There was little to say, there was no conversation
As I stepped to the stage to pick up my degree.
And the locusts sang off in the distance,
Yeah, the locusts sang such a sweet melody.
Oh, the locusts sang off in the distance,
Yeah, the locusts sang and they were singing for me.

I glanced into the chamber where the judges were talking,
Darkness was everywhere, it smelled like a tomb.
I was ready to leave, I was already walkin',
But the next time I looked there was light in the room.
And the locusts sang, yeah, it give me a chill,
Oh, the locusts sang such a sweet melody.
Oh, the locusts sang their high whining trill,
Yeah, the locusts sang and they were singing for me.

Outside of the gates the trucks were unloadin',
The weather was hot, a-nearly 90 degrees.
The man standin' next to me, his head was exploding,
Well, I was prayin' the pieces wouldn't fall on me.
Yeah, the locusts sang off in the distance,
Yeah, the locusts sang such a sweet melody.
Oh, the locusts sang off in the distance,
And the locusts sang and they were singing for me.

I put down my robe, picked up my diploma,
Took hold of my sweetheart and away we did drive,
Straight for the hills, the black hills of Dakota,
Sure was glad to get out of there alive.
And the locusts sang, well, it give me a chill,
Yeah, the locusts sang such a sweet melody.
And the locusts sang with a high whinin' trill,

Yeah, the locusts sang and they was singing for me,
Singing for me, well, singing for me.

# Time Passes Slowly

Time passes slowly up here in the mountains,
We sit beside bridges and walk beside fountains,
Catch the wild fishes that float through the stream,
Time passes slowly when you're lost in a dream.

Once I had a sweetheart, she was fine and good-lookin',
We sat in her kitchen while her mama was cookin',
Stared out the window to the stars high above,
Time passes slowly when you're searchin' for love.

Ain't no reason to go in a wagon to town,
Ain't no reason to go to the fair.
Ain't no reason to go up, ain't no reason to go down,
Ain't no reason to go anywhere.

Time passes slowly up here in the daylight,
We stare straight ahead and try so hard to stay right,
Like the red rose of summer that blooms in the day,
Time passes slowly and fades away.

# Went to See the Gypsy

Went to see the gypsy,
Stayin' in a big hotel.
He smiled when he saw me coming,
and he said, 'Well, well, well.'
His room was dark and crowded,
Lights were low and dim.
'How are you?' he said to me,
I said it back to him.

I went down to the lobby
To make a small call out.
A pretty dancing girl was there,
And she began to shout,
'Go on back to see the gypsy.
He can move you from the rear,
Drive you from your fear,
Bring you through the mirror.
He did it in Las Vegas,
And he can do it here.'

Outside the lights were shining
On the river of tears,
I watched them from the distance
With music in my ears.

I went back to see the gypsy,
It was nearly early dawn.
The gypsy's door was open wide
But the gypsy was gone,
And that pretty dancing girl,
She could not be found.
So I watched that sun come rising
From that little Minnesota town.

# Winterlude

Winterlude, Winterlude, oh darlin',
Winterlude by the road tonight.
Tonight there will be no quarrelin',
Ev'rything is gonna be all right.
Oh, I see by the angel beside me
That love has a reason to shine.
You're the one I adore, come over here and give me more,
Then Winterlude, this dude thinks you're fine.

Winterlude, Winterlude, my little apple,
Winterlude by the corn in the field,
Winterlude, let's go down to the chapel,
Then come back and cook up a meal.
Well, come out when the skating rink glistens
By the sun, near the old crossroads sign.
The snow is so cold, but our love can be bold,
Winterlude, don't be rude, please be mine.

Winterlude, Winterlude, my little daisy,
Winterlude, by the telephone wire,
Winterlude, it's makin' me lazy,
Come on, sit by the logs in the fire.
The moonlight reflects from the window
Where the snowflakes, they cover the sand.
Come out tonight, ev'rything will be tight,
Winterlude, this dude thinks you're grand.

# If Dogs Run Free

If dogs run free, then why not we
Across the swooping plain?
My ears hear a symphony
Of two mules, trains and rain.
The best is always yet to come,
That's what they explain to me.
Just do your thing, you'll be king,
If dogs run free.

If dogs run free, why not me
Across the swamp of time?
My mind weaves a symphony
And tapestry of rhyme.
Oh, winds which rush my tale to thee
So it may flow and be,
To each his own, it's all unknown,
If dogs run free.

If dogs run free, then what must be,
Must be, and that is all.
True love can make a blade of grass
Stand up straight and tall.
In harmony with the cosmic sea,
True love needs no company,
It can cure the soul, it can make it whole,
If dogs run free.

# New Morning

Can't you hear that rooster crowin'?
Rabbit runnin' down across the road
Underneath the bridge where the water flowed through
So happy just to see you smile
Underneath the sky of blue
On this new morning, new morning
On this new morning with you.

Can't you hear that motor turnin'?
Automobile comin' into style
Comin' down the road for a country mile or two
So happy just to see you smile
Underneath the sky of blue
On this new morning, new morning
On this new morning with you.

The night passed away so quickly
It always does when you're with me.

Can't you feel that sun a-shinin'?
Ground hog runnin' by the country stream
This must be the day that all of my dreams come true
So happy just to be alive
Underneath the sky of blue
On this new morning, new morning
On this new morning with you.

So happy just to be alive
Underneath the sky of blue
On this new morning, new morning
On this new morning with you.
New morning . . .

# Sign on the Window

Sign on the window says 'Lonely,'
Sign on the door said 'No Company Allowed,'
Sign on the street says 'Y' Don't Own Me,'
Sign on the porch says 'Three's A Crowd,'
Sign on the porch says 'Three's A Crowd.'

Her and her boyfriend went to California,
Her and her boyfriend done changed their tune.
My best friend said, 'Now didn' I warn ya,
Brighton girls are like the moon,
Brighton girls are like the moon.'

Looks like a-nothing but rain . . .
Sure gonna be wet tonight on Main Street . . .
Hope that it don't sleet.

Build me a cabin in Utah,
Marry me a wife, catch rainbow trout,
Have a bunch of kids who call me 'Pa,'
That must be what it's all about,
That must be what it's all about.

# One More Weekend

Slippin' and slidin' like a weasel on the run,
I'm lookin' good to see you, yeah, and we can have some fun.
One more weekend, one more weekend with you,
One more weekend, one more weekend'll do.

Come on down to my ship, honey, ride on deck,
We'll fly over the ocean just like you suspect.
One more weekend, one more weekend with you,
One more weekend, one more weekend'll do.

We'll fly the night away,
Hang out the whole next day,
Things will be okay,
You wait and see.
We'll go someplace unknown,
Leave all the children home,
Honey, why not go alone
Just you and me.

Comin' and goin' like a rabbit in the wood,
I'm happy just to see you, yeah, lookin' so good.
One more weekend, one more weekend with you,
One more weekend, one more weekend'll do (yes, you will!).

Like a needle in a haystack, I'm gonna find you yet,
You're the sweetest gone mama that this boy's ever gonna get.
One more weekend, one more weekend with you,
One more weekend, one more weekend'll do.

# The Man in Me

The man in me will do nearly any task,
And as for compensation, there's little he would ask.
Take a woman like you
To get through to the man in me.

Storm clouds are raging all around my door,
I think to myself I might not take it any more.
Take a woman like your kind
To find the man in me.

But, oh, what a wonderful feeling
Just to know that you are near,
Sets my a heart a-reeling
From my toes up to my ears.

The man in me will hide sometimes to keep from bein' seen,
But that's just because he doesn't want to turn into some
    machine.
Took a woman like you
To get through to the man in me.

# Three Angels

Three angels up above the street,
Each one playing a horn,
Dressed in green robes with wings that stick out,
They've been there since Christmas morn.
The wildest cat from Montana passes by in a flash,
Then a lady in a bright orange dress,
One U-Haul trailer, a truck with no wheels,
The Tenth Avenue bus going west.
The dogs and pigeons fly up and they flutter around,
A man with a badge skips by,
Three fellas crawlin' on their way back to work,
Nobody stops to ask why.
The bakery truck stops outside of that fence
Where the angels stand high on their poles,
The driver peeks out, trying to find one face
In this concrete world full of souls.
The angels play on their horns all day,
The whole earth in progression seems to pass by.
But does anyone hear the music they play,
Does anyone even try?

# Father of Night

Father of night, Father of day,
Father, who taketh the darkness away,
Father, who teacheth the bird to fly,
Builder of rainbows up in the sky,
Father of loneliness and pain,
Father of love and Father of rain.

Father of day, Father of night,
Father of black, Father of white,
Father, who build the mountain so high,
Who shapeth the cloud up in the sky,
Father of time, Father of dreams,
Father, who turneth the rivers and streams.

Father of grain, Father of wheat,
Father of cold and Father of heat,
Father of air and Father of trees,
Who dwells in our hearts and our memories,
Father of minutes, Father of days,
Father of whom we most solemnly praise.

# I'd Have You Any Time (with George Harrison)

Let me in here, I know I've been here,
Let me into your heart.
Let me know you, let me show you,
Let me roll it to you.
All I have is yours,
All you see is mine
And I'm glad to have you in my arms,
I'd have you any time.

Let me say it, let me play it,
Let me lay it on you.
Let me know you, let me show you,
Let me grow it on you.
All I have is yours,
All you see is mine
And I'm glad to have you in my arms,
I'd have you any time.

Let me in here, I know I've been here,
Let me into your heart.
Let me know you, let me show you,
Let me roll it to you.
All I have is yours,
All you see is mine
And I'm glad to have you in my arms,
I'd have you any time.

# Watching the River Flow

What's the matter with me,
I don't have much to say,
Daylight sneakin' through the window
And I'm still in this all-night café.
Walkin' to and fro beneath the moon
Out to where the trucks are rollin' slow,
To sit down on this bank of sand
And watch the river flow.

Wish I was back in the city
Instead of this old bank of sand,
With the sun beating down over the chimney tops
And the one I love so close at hand.
If I had wings and I could fly,
I know where I would go.
But right now I'll just sit here so contentedly
And watch the river flow.

People disagreeing on all just about everything, yeah,
Makes you stop and all wonder why.
Why only yesterday I saw somebody on the street
Who just couldn't help but cry.
Oh, this ol' river keeps on rollin', though,
No matter what gets in the way and which way the wind does
    blow,
And as long as it does I'll just sit here
And watch the river flow.

People disagreeing everywhere you look,
Makes you wanna stop and read a book.
Why only yesterday I saw somebody on the street
That was really shook.
But this ol' river keeps on rollin', though,

No matter what gets in the way and which way the wind does
    blow,
And as long as it does I'll just sit here
And watch the river flow.

Watch the river flow,
Watchin' the river flow,
Watchin' the river flow,
But I'll sit down on this bank of sand
And watch the river flow.

# When I Paint My Masterpiece

Oh, the streets of Rome are filled with rubble,
Ancient footprints are everywhere.
You can almost think that you're seein' double
On a cold, dark night on the Spanish Stairs.
Got to hurry on back to my hotel room,
Where I've got me a date with Botticelli's niece.
She promised that she'd be right there with me
When I paint my masterpiece.

Oh, the hours I've spent inside the Coliseum,
Dodging lions and wastin' time.
Oh, those mighty kings of the jungle, I could hardly stand to see
   'em,
Yes, it sure has been a long, hard climb.
Train wheels runnin' through the back of my memory,
When I ran on the hilltop following a pack of wild geese.
Someday, everything is gonna be smooth like a rhapsody
When I paint my masterpiece.

Sailin' 'round the world in a dirty gondola.
Oh, to be back in the land of Coca-Cola!

I left Rome and landed in Brussels,
On a plane ride so bumpy that I almost cried.
Clergymen in uniform and young girls pullin' muscles,
Everyone was there to greet me when I stepped inside.
Newspapermen eating candy
Had to be held down by big police.
Someday, everything is gonna be diff'rent
When I paint my masterpiece.

# Wallflower

Wallflower, wallflower
Won't you dance with me?
I'm sad and lonely too.
Wallflower, wallflower
Won't you dance with me?
I'm fallin' in love with you.

Just like you I'm wondrin' what I'm doin' here.
Just like you I'm wondrin' what's goin' on.

Wallflower, wallflower
Won't you dance with me?
The night will soon be gone.

I have seen you standing in the smoky haze
And I know that you're gonna be mine one of these days,
Mine alone.

Wallflower, wallflower
Take a chance on me.
Please let me ride you home.

# George Jackson

I woke up this mornin',
There were tears in my bed.
They killed a man I really loved
Shot him through the head.
Lord, Lord,
They cut George Jackson down.
Lord, Lord,
They laid him in the ground.

Sent him off to prison
For a seventy-dollar robbery.
Closed the door behind him
And they threw away the key.
Lord, Lord,
They cut George Jackson down.
Lord, Lord,
They laid him in the ground.

He wouldn't take shit from no one
He wouldn't bow down or kneel.
Authorities, they hated him
Because he was just too real.
Lord, Lord,
They cut George Jackson down.
Lord, Lord,
They laid him in the ground.

Prison guards, they cursed him
As they watched him from above
But they were frightened of his power
They were scared of his love.
Lord, Lord,
They cut George Jackson down.

Lord, Lord,
They laid him in the ground.

Sometimes I think this whole world
Is one big prison yard.
Some of us are prisoners
The rest of us are guards.
Lord, Lord,
They cut George Jackson down.
Lord, Lord,
They laid him in the ground.

# Basement Tapes

**Odds and Ends**
**Million Dollar Bash**
**Goin' to Acapulco**
**Lo and Behold!**
**Clothes Line**
**Apple Suckling Tree**
**Please, Mrs Henry**
**Tears of Rage**
**Too Much of Nothing**
**Yea! Heavy and a Bottle of Bread**
**Down in the Flood**
**Tiny Montgomery**
**You Ain't Goin' Nowhere**
**Don't Ya Tell Henry**
**Nothing Was Delivered**
**Open the Door, Homer**
**Long-Distance Operator**
**This Wheel's on Fire**

Sign on the Cross
Quinn the Eskimo (The Mighty Quinn)
I Shall Be Released
Get Your Rocks Off!
Silent Weekend

# Odds and Ends

I plan it all and I take my place
You break your promise all over the place
You promised to love me, but what do I see
Just you comin' and spillin' juice over me
Odds and ends, odds and ends
Lost time is not found again

Now, you take your file and you bend my head
I never can remember anything that you said
You promised to love me, but what do I know
You're always spillin' juice on me like you got someplace to go
Odds and ends, odds and ends
Lost time is not found again

Now, I've had enough, my box is clean
You know what I'm sayin' and you know what I mean
From now on you'd best get on someone else
While you're doin' it, keep that juice to yourself
Odds and ends, odds and ends
Lost time is not found again

# Million Dollar Bash

Well, that big dumb blonde
With her wheel in the gorge
And Turtle, that friend of theirs
With his checks all forged
And his cheeks in a chunk
With his cheese in the cash
They're all gonna be there
At that million dollar bash
Ooh, baby, ooh-ee
Ooh, baby, ooh-ee
It's that million dollar bash

Ev'rybody from right now
To over there and back
The louder they come
The harder they crack
Come now, sweet cream
Don't forget to flash
We're all gonna meet
At that million dollar bash
Ooh, baby, ooh-ee
Ooh, baby, ooh-ee
It's that million dollar bash

Well, I took my counselor
Out to the barn
Silly Nelly was there
She told him a yarn
Then along came Jones
Emptied the trash
Ev'rybody went down
To that million dollar bash
Ooh, baby, ooh-ee

Ooh, baby, ooh-ee
It's that million dollar bash

Well, I'm hittin' it too hard
My stones won't take
I get up in the mornin'
But it's too early to wake
First it's hello, goodbye
Then push and then crash
But we're all gonna make it
At that million dollar bash
Ooh, baby, ooh-ee
Ooh, baby, ooh-ee
It's that million dollar bash

Well, I looked at my watch
I looked at my wrist
Punched myself in the face
With my fist
I took my potatoes
Down to be mashed
Then I made it over
To that million dollar bash
Ooh, baby, ooh-ee
Ooh, baby, ooh-ee
It's that million dollar bash

# Goin' to Acapulco

I'm going down to Rose Marie's
She never does me wrong.
She puts it to me plain as day
And gives it to me for a song.

It's a wicked life but what the hell
The stars ain't falling down.
I'm standing outside the Taj Mahal
I don't see no one around.

Goin' to Acapulco
Goin' on the run.
Goin' down to see fat gut
Goin' to have some fun.
Yeah
Goin' to have some fun.

Now, whenever I get up
And I ain't got what I see
I just make it down to Rose Marie's
'Bout a quarter after three.

There are worse ways of getting there
And I ain't complainin' none.
If the clouds don't drop and the train don't stop
I'm bound to meet the sun.

Goin' to Acapulco
Goin' on the run.
Goin' down to see some girl
Goin' to have some fun.
Yeah
Goin' to have some fun.

Now, if someone offers me a joke
I just say no thanks.
I try to tell it like it is
And keep away from pranks.

Well, sometime you know when the well breaks down
I just go pump on it some.
Rose Marie, she likes to go to big places
And just set there waitin' for me to come.

Goin' to Acapulco
Goin' on the run.
Goin' down to see some girl
Goin' to have some fun.
Yeah
Goin' to have some fun.

# Lo and Behold!

I pulled out for San Anton',
I never felt so good.
My woman said she'd meet me there
And of course, I knew she would.
The coachman, he hit me for my hook
And he asked me my name.
I give it to him right away,
Then I hung my head in shame.
Lo and behold! Lo and behold!
Lookin' for my lo and behold,
Get me outa here, my dear man!

I come into Pittsburgh
At six-thirty flat.
I found myself a vacant seat
An' I put down my hat.
'What's the matter, Molly, dear,
What's the matter with your mound?'
'What's it to ya, Moby Dick?
This is chicken town!'
Lo and behold! Lo and behold!
Lookin' for my lo and behold,
Get me outa here, my dear man!

I bought my girl
A herd of moose,
One she could call her own.
Well, she came out the very next day
To see where they had flown.
I'm goin' down to Tennessee,
Get me a truck 'r somethin'.
Gonna save my money and rip it up!
Lo and behold! Lo and behold!

Lookin' for my lo and behold,
Get me outa here, my dear man!

Now, I come in on a ferris wheel
An' boys, I sure was slick.
I come in like a ton of bricks,
Laid a few tricks on 'em.
Goin' back to Pittsburgh,
Count up to thirty,
Round that horn and ride that herd,
Gonna thread up!
Lo and behold! Lo and behold!
Lookin' for my lo and behold,
Get me outa here, my dear man!

# Clothes Line

After a while we took in the clothes,
Nobody said very much.
Just some old wild shirts and a couple pairs of pants
Which nobody really wanted to touch.
Mama come in and picked up a book
An' Papa asked her what it was.
Someone else asked, 'What do you care?'
Papa said, 'Well, just because.'
Then they started to take back their clothes,
Hang 'em on the line.
It was January the thirtieth
And everybody was feelin' fine.

The next day everybody got up
Seein' if the clothes were dry.
The dogs were barking, a neighbor passed,
Mama, of course, she said, 'Hi!'
'Have you heard the news?' he said, with a grin,
'The Vice-President's gone mad!'
'Where?' 'Downtown.' 'When?' 'Last night.'
'Hmm, say, that's too bad!'
'Well, there's nothin' we can do about it,' said the neighbor,
'It's just somethin' we're gonna have to forget.'
'Yes, I guess so,' said Ma,
Then she asked me if the clothes was still wet.

I reached up, touched my shirt,
And the neighbor said, 'Are those clothes yours?'
I said, 'Some of 'em, not all of 'em.'
He said, 'Ya always help out around here with the chores?'
I said, 'Sometime, not all the time.'
Then my neighbor, he blew his nose
Just as papa yelled outside,

'Mama wants you t' come back in the house and bring them
    clothes.'
Well, I just do what I'm told,
So, I did it, of course.
I went back in the house and Mama met me
And then I shut all the doors.

# Apple Suckling Tree

Old man sailin' in a dinghy boat
Down there
Old man down is baitin' a hook
On there
Gonna pull man down on a suckling hook
Gonna pull man into the suckling brook
Oh yeah!

Now, he's underneath that apple suckling tree
Oh yeah!
Under that apple suckling tree
Oh yeah!
That's underneath that tree
There's gonna be just you and me
Underneath that apple suckling tree
Oh yeah!

I push him back and I stand in line
Oh yeah!
Then I hush my Sadie and stand in line
Oh yeah!
Then I hush my Sadie and stand in line
I get on board in two-eyed time
Oh yeah!

Under that apple suckling tree
Oh yeah!
Under that apple suckling tree
Oh yeah!
Underneath that tree
There's just gonna be you and me
Underneath that apple suckling tree
Oh yeah!

Now, who's on the table, who's to tell me?
Oh yeah!
Who's on the table, who's to tell me?
Oh yeah!
Who should I tell, oh, who should I tell?
The forty-nine of you like bats out of hell
Oh underneath that old apple suckling tree

# Please, Mrs Henry

Well, I've already had two beers
I'm ready for the broom
Please, Missus Henry, won't you
Take me to my room?
I'm a good ol' boy
But I've been sniffin' too many eggs
Talkin' to too many people
Drinkin' too many kegs
Please, Missus Henry, Missus Henry, please!
Please, Missus Henry, Missus Henry, please!
I'm down on my knees
An' I ain't got a dime

Well, I'm groanin' in a hallway
Pretty soon I'll be mad
Please, Missus Henry, won't you
Take me to your dad?
I can drink like a fish
I can crawl like a snake
I can bite like a turkey
I can slam like a drake
Please, Missus Henry, Missus Henry, please!
Please, Missus Henry, Missus Henry, please!
I'm down on my knees
An' I ain't got a dime

Now, don't crowd me, lady
Or I'll fill up your shoe
I'm a sweet bourbon daddy
An' tonight I am blue
I'm a thousand years old
And I'm a generous bomb
I'm T-boned and punctured
But I'm known to be calm

Please, Missus Henry, Missus Henry, please!
Please, Missus Henry, Missus Henry, please!
I'm down on my knees
An' I ain't got a dime

Now, I'm startin' to drain
My stool's gonna squeak
If I walk too much farther
My crane's gonna leak
Look, Missus Henry
There's only so much I can do
Why don't you look my way
An' pump me a few?
Please, Missus Henry, Missus Henry, please!
Please, Missus Henry, Missus Henry, please!
I'm down on my knees
An' I ain't got a dime

# Tears of Rage

We carried you in our arms
On Independence Day,
And now you'd throw us all aside
And put us on our way.
Oh what dear daughter 'neath the sun
Would treat a father so,
To wait upon him hand and foot
And always tell him, 'No'?
Tears of rage, tears of grief,
Why must I always be the thief?
Come to me now, you know
We're so alone
And life is brief.

We pointed out the way to go
And scratched your name in sand,
Though you just thought it was nothing more
Than a place for you to stand.
Now, I want you to know that while we watched,
You discover there was no one true.
Most ev'rybody really thought
It was a childish thing to do.
Tears of rage, tears of grief,
Must I always be the thief?
Come to me now, you know
We're so low
And life is brief.

It was all very painless
When you went out to receive
All that false instruction
Which we never could believe.
And now the heart is filled with gold
As if it was a purse.

But, oh, what kind of love is this
Which goes from bad to worse?
Tears of rage, tears of grief,
Must I always be the thief?
Come to me now, you know
We're so low
And life is brief.

# Too Much of Nothing

Now, too much of nothing
Can make a man feel ill at ease.
One man's temper might rise
While another man's temper might freeze.
In the day of confession
We cannot mock a soul.
Oh, when there's too much of nothing,
No one has control.

Say hello to Valerie
Say hello to Vivian
Send them all my salary
On the waters of oblivion

Too much of nothing
Can make a man abuse a king.
He can walk the streets and boast like most
But he wouldn't know a thing.
Now, it's all been done before,
It's all been written in the book,
But when there's too much of nothing,
Nobody should look.

Say hello to Valerie
Say hello to Vivian
Send them all my salary
On the waters of oblivion

Too much of nothing
Can turn a man into a liar,
It can cause one man to sleep on nails
And another man to eat fire.
Ev'rybody's doin' somethin',
I heard it in a dream,

But when there's too much of nothing,
It just makes a fella mean.

Say hello to Valerie
Say hello to Vivian
Send them all my salary
On the waters of oblivion

# Yea! Heavy
# and a Bottle of Bread

Well, the comic book and me, just us, we caught the bus.
The poor little chauffeur, though, she was back in bed
On the very next day, with a nose full of pus.
Yea! Heavy and a bottle of bread
Yea! Heavy and a bottle of bread
Yea! Heavy and a bottle of bread


It's a one-track town, just brown, and a breeze, too,
Pack up the meat, sweet, we're headin' out
For Wichita in a pile of fruit.
Get the loot, don't be slow, we're gonna catch a trout
Get the loot, don't be slow, we're gonna catch a trout
Get the loot, don't be slow, we're gonna catch a trout


Now, pull that drummer out from behind that bottle.
Bring me my pipe, we're gonna shake it.
Slap that drummer with a pie that smells.
Take me down to California, baby
Take me down to California, baby
Take me down to California, baby


Well, the comic book and me, just us, we caught the bus.
The poor little chauffeur, though, she was back in bed
On the very next day, with a nose full of pus.
Yea! Heavy and a bottle of bread
Yea! Heavy and a bottle of bread
Yea! Heavy and a bottle of bread

# Down in the Flood

Crash on the levee, mama,
Water's gonna overflow,
Swamp's gonna rise,
No boat's gonna row.
Now, you can train on down
To Williams Point,
You can bust your feet,
You can rock this joint.
But oh mama, ain't you gonna miss your best friend now?
You're gonna have to find yourself
Another best friend, somehow.


Now, don't you try an' move me,
You're just gonna lose.
There's a crash on the levee
And, mama, you've been refused.
Well, it's sugar for sugar
And salt for salt,
If you go down in the flood,
It's gonna be your own fault.
Oh mama, ain't you gonna miss your best friend now?
You're gonna have to find yourself
Another best friend, somehow.


Well, that high tide's risin',
Mama, don't you let me down.
Pack up your suitcase,
Mama, don't you make a sound.
Now, it's king for king,
Queen for queen,
It's gonna be the meanest flood

That anybody's seen.
Oh mama, ain't you gonna miss your best friend now?
Yes, you're gonna have to find yourself
Another best friend, somehow.

# Tiny Montgomery

Well, you can tell ev'rybody
Down in ol' Frisco
Tell 'em
Tiny Montgomery says hello

Now ev'ry boy and girl's
Gonna get their bang
'Cause Tiny Montgomery's
Gonna shake that thing
Tell ev'rybody
Down in ol' Frisco
That Tiny Montgomery's comin'
Down to say hello

Skinny Moo and
Half-track Frank
They're gonna both be gettin'
Outa the tank
One bird book
And a buzzard and a crow
Tell 'em all
That Tiny's gonna say hello

Scratch your dad
Do that bird
Suck that pig
And bring it on home
Pick that drip
And bake that dough
Tell 'em all
That Tiny says hello

Now he's king of the drunks
An' he squeezes, too

Watch out, Lester
Take it, Lou
Join the monks
The CIO
Tell 'em all
That Tiny Montgomery says hello

Now grease that pig
And sing praise
Go on out
And gas that dog
Trick on in
Honk that stink
Take it on down
And watch it grow
Play it low
And pick it up
Take it on in
In a plucking cup
Three-legged man
And a hot-lipped hoe
Tell 'em all
Montgomery says hello

Well you can tell ev'rybody
Down in ol' Frisco
Tell 'em all
Montgomery says hello

# You Ain't Goin' Nowhere

Clouds so swift
Rain won't lift
Gate won't close
Railings froze
Get your mind off wintertime
You ain't goin' nowhere
Whoo-ee! Ride me high
Tomorrow's the day
My bride's gonna come
Oh, oh, are we gonna fly
Down in the easy chair!

I don't care
How many letters they sent
Morning came and morning went
Pick up your money
And pack up your tent
You ain't goin' nowhere
Whoo-ee! Ride me high
Tomorrow's the day
My bride's gonna come
Oh, oh, are we gonna fly
Down in the easy chair!

Buy me a flute
And a gun that shoots
Tailgates and substitutes
Strap yourself
To the tree with roots
You ain't goin' nowhere
Whoo-ee! Ride me high
Tomorrow's the day
My bride's gonna come

Oh, oh, are we gonna fly
Down in the easy chair!

Genghis Khan
He could not keep
All his kings
Supplied with sleep
We'll climb that hill no matter how steep
When we get up to it
Whoo-ee! Ride me high
Tomorrow's the day
My bride's gonna come
Oh, oh, are we gonna fly
Down in the easy chair!

# Don't Ya Tell Henry

Don't ya tell Henry,
Apple's got your fly.

I went down to the river on a Saturday morn,
A-lookin' around just to see who's born.
I found a little chicken down on his knees,
I went up and yelled to him,
'Please, please, please!'
He said, 'Don't ya tell Henry,
Don't ya tell Henry,
Don't ya tell Henry,
Apple's got your fly.'

I went down to the corner at a-half past ten,
I's lookin' around, I wouldn't say when.
I looked down low, I looked above,
And who did I see but the one I love.
She said, 'Don't ya tell Henry,
Don't ya tell Henry,
Don't ya tell Henry,
Apple's got your fly.'

Now, I went down to the beanery at half past twelve,
A-lookin' around just to see myself.
I spotted a horse and a donkey, too,
I looked for a cow and I saw me a few.
They said, 'Don't ya tell Henry,
Don't ya tell Henry,
Don't ya tell Henry,
Apple's got your fly.'

Now, I went down to the pumphouse the other night,
A-lookin' around, it was outa sight.
I looked high and low for that big ol' tree,

I did go upstairs but I didn't see nobody but me.
I said, 'Don't ya tell Henry,
Don'i ya tell Henry,
Don't ya tell Henry,
Apple's got your fly.'

# Nothing Was Delivered

Nothing was delivered
And I tell this truth to you,
Not out of spite or anger
But simply because it's true.
Now, I hope you won't object to this,
Giving back all of what you owe,
The fewer words you have to waste on this,
The sooner you can go.

Nothing is better, nothing is best,
Take heed of this and get plenty of rest.

Nothing was delivered
But I can't say I sympathize
With what your fate is going to be,
Yes, for telling all those lies.
Now you must provide some answers
For what you sell has not been received,
And the sooner you come up with them,
The sooner you can leave.

Nothing is better, nothing is best,
Take heed of this and get plenty of rest.

(Now you know)
Nothing was delivered
And it's up to you to say
Just what you had in mind
When you made ev'rybody pay.
No, nothing was delivered,
Yes, 'n' someone must explain
That as long as it takes to do this
Then that's how long that you'll remain.

Nothing is better, nothing is best,
Take heed of this and get plenty of rest.

# Open the Door, Homer

Now, there's a certain thing
That I learned from Jim
That he'd always make sure I'd understand
And that is that there's a certain way
That a man must swim
If he expects to live off
Of the fat of the land.
Open the door, Homer,
I've heard it said before.
Open the door, Homer,
I've heard it said before
But I ain't gonna hear it said no more.

Now, there's a certain thing
That I learned from my friend, Mouse
A fella who always blushes
And that is that ev'ryone
Must always flush out his house
If he don't expect to be
Goin' 'round housing flushes.
Open the door, Homer,
I've heard it said before.
Open the door, Homer,
I've heard it said before
But I ain't gonna hear it said no more.

'Take care of all your memories'
Said my friend, Mick
'For you cannot relive them
And remember when you're out there
Tryin' to heal the sick
That you must always
First forgive them.'
Open the door, Homer,

I've heard it said before.
Open the door, Homer,
I've heard it said before
But I ain't gonna hear it said no more.

# Long-Distance Operator

Long-distance operator,
Place this call, it's not for fun.
Long-distance operator,
Please, place this call, you know it's not for fun.
I gotta get a message to my baby,
You know, she's not just anyone.

There are thousands in the phone booth,
Thousands at the gate.
There are thousands in the phone booth,
Thousands at the gate.
Ev'rybody wants to make a long-distance call
But you know they're just gonna have to wait.

If a call comes from Louisiana,
Please, let it ride.
If a call comes from Louisiana,
Please, let it ride.
This phone booth's on fire,
It's getting hot inside.

Ev'rybody wants to be my friend,
But nobody wants to get higher.
Ev'rybody wants to be my friend,
But nobody wants to get higher.
Long-distance operator,
I believe I'm stranglin' on this telephone wire.

# This Wheel's on Fire

If your mem'ry serves you well,
We were goin' to meet again and wait,
So I'm goin' to unpack all my things
And sit before it gets too late.
No man alive will come to you
With another tale to tell,
But you know that we shall meet again
If your mem'ry serves you well.
This wheel's on fire,
Rolling down the road,
Best notify my next of kin,
This wheel shall explode!

If your mem'ry serves you well.
I was goin' to confiscate your lace,
And wrap it up in a sailor's knot
And hide it in your case.
If I knew for sure that it was yours . . .
But it was oh so hard to tell.
But you knew that we would meet again,
If your mem'ry serves you well.
This wheel's on fire,
Rolling down the road,
Best notify my next of kin,
This wheel shall explode!

If your mem'ry serves you well,
You'll remember you're the one
That called on me to call on them
To get you your favors done.
And after ev'ry plan had failed
And there was nothing more to tell,
You knew that we would meet again,
If your mem'ry serves you well.

This wheel's on fire,
Rolling down the road,
Best notify my next of kin,
This wheel shall explode!

# Sign on the Cross

Now, I try, oh for so awf'ly long
And I just try to be.
And now, oh it's a gold mine
But it's so fine.
Yes, but I know in my head
That we're all so misled,
And it's that ol' sign on the cross
That worries me.

Now, when I was just a bawlin' child,
I saw what I wanted to be,
And it's all for the sake
Of that picture I should see.
But I was lost on the moon
As I heard that front door slam,
And that old sign on the cross
Still worries me.

Well, it's that old sign on the cross,
Well, it's that old key to the kingdom,
Well, it's that old sign on the cross
Like you used to be.

But, when I hold my head so high
As I see my ol' friends go by,
And it's still that sign on the cross
That worries me.

Well, it seems to be the sign on the cross. Ev'ry day,
ev'ry night, see the sign on the cross just layin' up
on top of the hill. Yes, we thought it might have
disappeared long ago, but I'm here to tell you, friends,
that I'm afraid it's lyin' there still. Yes, just a
little time is all you need, you might say, but I don't

know 'bout that any more, because the bird is here and
you might want to enter it, but, of course, the door might
be closed. But I just would like to tell you one time,
if I don't see you again, that the thing is, that the sign
on the cross is the thing you might need the most.

Yes, the sign on the cross
Is just a sign on the cross.
Well, there is some on every chisel
And there is some in the championship, too.
Oh, when your, when your days are numbered
And your nights are long,
You might think you're weak
But I mean to say you're strong.
Yes you are, if that sign on the cross,
If it begins to worry you.
Well, that's all right because sing a song
And all your troubles will pass right on through.

# Quinn the Eskimo (The Mighty Quinn)

Ev'rybody's building the big ships and the boats,
Some are building monuments,
Others, jotting down notes,
Ev'rybody's in despair,
Ev'ry girl and boy
But when Quinn the Eskimo gets here,
Ev'rybody's gonna jump for joy.
Come all without, come all within,
You'll not see nothing like the mighty Quinn.

I like to do just like the rest, I like my sugar sweet,
But guarding fumes and making haste,
It ain't my cup of meat.
Ev'rybody's 'neath the trees,
Feeding pigeons on a limb
But when Quinn the Eskimo gets here,
All the pigeons gonna run to him.
Come all without, come all within,
You'll not see nothing like the mighty Quinn.

A cat's meow and a cow's moo, I can recite 'em all,
Just tell me where it hurts yuh, honey,
And I'll tell you who to call.
Nobody can get no sleep,
There's someone on ev'ryone's toes
But when Quinn the Eskimo gets here,
Ev'rybody's gonna wanna doze.
Come all without, come all within,
You'll not see nothing like the mighty Quinn.

# I Shall Be Released

They say ev'rything can be replaced,
Yet ev'ry distance is not near.
So I remember ev'ry face
Of ev'ry man who put me here.
I see my light come shining
From the west unto the east.
Any day now, any day now,
I shall be released.

They say ev'ry man needs protection,
They say ev'ry man must fall.
Yet I swear I see my reflection
Some place so high above this wall.
I see my light come shining
From the west unto the east.
Any day now, any day now,
I shall be released.

Standing next to me in this lonely crowd,
Is a man who swears he's not to blame.
All day long I hear him shout so loud,
Crying out that he was framed.
I see my light come shining
From the west unto the east.
Any day now, any day now,
I shall be released.

# Get Your Rocks Off!

You know, there's two ol' maids layin' in the bed,
One picked herself up an' the other one, she said:
'Get your rocks off!
Get your rocks off! (Get 'em off!)
Get your rocks off! (Get 'em off!)
Get your rocks off-a me! (Get 'em off!)'

Well, you know, there late one night up on Blueberry Hill,
One man turned to the other man and said, with a blood-
     curdlin' chill, he said:
'Get your rocks off! (Get 'em off!)
Get your rocks off! (Get 'em off!)
Get your rocks off! (Get 'em off!)
Get your rocks off-a me! (Get 'em off!)'

Well, you know, we was layin' down around Mink Muscle
     Creek,
One man said to the other man, he began to speak, he said:
'Get your rocks off! (Get 'em off!)
Get your rocks off! (Get 'em off!)
Get your rocks off! (Get 'em off!)
Get your rocks off-a me! (Get 'em off!)'

Well, you know, we was cruisin' down the highway in a
     Greyhound bus.
All kinds-a children in the side road, they was hollerin' at us,
     sayin':
'Get your rocks off! (Get 'em off!)
Get your rocks off! (Get 'em off!)
Get your rocks off! (Get 'em off!)
Get your rocks off-a me!

# Silent Weekend

Silent weekend,
My baby she gave it to me.
Silent weekend,
My baby she gave it to me.
She's actin' tough and hardy
She says it ain't my party
And she's leavin' me in misery.

Silent weekend,
My baby she took me by surprise.
Silent weekend,
My baby she took me by surprise.
She's rockin' and a-reelin'
Head up to ceiling
An' swinging with some other guys.

Silent weekend,
Oh Lord, I wish Monday would come.
Silent weekend,
Oh Lord, I sure wish Monday would come.
She's uppity, she's rollin',
She's in the groove, she's strolling
Over to the jukebox playin' deaf and dumb.

Well, I done a whole lotta thinkin' 'bout a whole lot of cheatin',
And I, maybe I did some just to please.
But I just walloped a lotta pizza after makin' our peace,
Puts ya down on bended knees.

Silent weekend,
Man alive, I'm burnin' up on my brain.
Silent weekend,

Man alive, I'm burnin' up on my brain.
She knows when I'm just teasin'
But it's not likely in the season
To open up a passenger train.

# Pat Garrett & Billy the Kid

**Billy**
**Knockin' on Heaven's Door**

# Billy

There's guns across the river aimin' at ya
Lawman on your trail, he'd like to catch ya
Bounty hunters, too, they'd like to get ya
Billy, they don't like you to be so free.

Campin' out all night on the berenda
Dealin' cards 'til dawn in the hacienda
Up to Boot Hill they'd like to send ya
Billy, don't you turn your back on me.

Playin' around with some sweet señorita
Into her dark hallway she will lead ya
In some lonesome shadows she will greet ya
Billy, you're so far away from home.

There's eyes behind the mirrors in empty places
Bullet holes and scars between the spaces
There's always one more notch and ten more paces
Billy, and you're walkin' all alone.

They say that Pat Garrett's got your number
So sleep with one eye open when you slumber
Every little sound just might be thunder
Thunder from the barrel of his gun.

Guitars will play your grand finale
Down in some Tularosa alley,
Maybe in the Rio Pecos valley
Billy, you're so far away from home.

There's always some new stranger sneakin' glances
Some trigger-happy fool willin' to take chances
And some old whore from San Pedro to make advances
Advances on your spirit and your soul.

The businessmen from Taos want you to go down
They've hired Pat Garrett to force a showdown.
Billy, don't it make ya feel so low-down
To be shot down by the man who was your friend?

Hang on to your woman if you got one
Remember in El Paso, once, you shot one.
She may have been a whore, but she was a hot one
Billy, you been runnin' for so long.

Guitars will play your grand finale
Down in some Tularosa alley,
Maybe in the Rio Pecos valley
Billy, you're so far away from home.

# Knockin'
# on Heaven's Door

Mama, take this badge off of me
I can't use it anymore.
It's gettin' dark, too dark for me to see
I feel like I'm knockin' on heaven's door.

Knock, knock, knockin' on heaven's door
Knock, knock, knockin' on heaven's door
Knock, knock, knockin' on heaven's door
Knock, knock, knockin' on heaven's door

Mama, put my guns in the ground
I can't shoot them anymore.
That long black cloud is comin' down
I feel like I'm knockin' on heaven's door.

Knock, knock, knockin' on heaven's door
Knock, knock, knockin' on heaven's door
Knock, knock, knockin' on heaven's door
Knock, knock, knockin' on heaven's door

# Planet Waves

**On a Night Like This**
**Going, Going, Gone**
**Tough Mama**
**Hazel**
**Something There Is About You**
**Forever Young**
**Dirge**
**You Angel You**
**Never Say Goodbye**
**Wedding Song**

Nobody 'Cept You

# On a Night Like This

On a night like this
So glad you came around,
Hold on to me so tight
And heat up some coffee grounds.
We got much to talk about
And much to reminisce,
It sure is right
On a night like this.

On a night like this
So glad you've come to stay
Hold on to me, pretty miss
Say you'll never go away to stray.
Run your fingers down my spine
Bring me a touch of bliss
It sure feels right
On a night like this.

On a night like this
I can't get any sleep,
The air is so cold outside
And the snow's so deep.
Build a fire, throw on logs
And listen to it hiss
And let it burn, burn, burn, burn
On a night like this.

Put your body next to mine
And keep me company,
There is plenty a room for all,
So please don't elbow me.

Let the four winds blow
Around this old cabin door,

If I'm not too far off
I think we did this once before.
There's more frost on the window glass
With each new tender kiss,
But it sure feels right
On a night like this.

# Going, Going, Gone

I've just reached a place
Where the willow don't bend.
There's not much more to be said
It's the top of the end.
I'm going,
I'm going,
I'm gone.

I'm closin' the book
On the pages and the text
And I don't really care
What happens next.
I'm just going,
I'm going,
I'm gone.

I been hangin' on threads,
I been playin' it straight,
Now, I've just got to cut loose
Before it gets late.
So I'm going,
I'm going,
I'm gone.

Grandma said, 'Boy, go and follow your heart
And you'll be fine at the end of the line.
All that's gold isn't meant to shine.
Don't you and your one true love ever part.'

I been walkin' the road,
I been livin' on the edge,
Now, I've just got to go
Before I get to the ledge.
So I'm going,

I'm just going,
I'm gone.

# Tough Mama

Tough Mama
Meat shakin' on your bones
I'm gonna go down to the river and get some stones.
Sister's on the highway with that steel-drivin' crew,
Papa's in the big house, his workin' days are through.
Tough Mama
Can I blow a little smoke on you?

Dark Beauty
Won't you move it on over and make some room?
It's my duty to bring you down to the field where the flowers
  bloom.
Ashes in the furnace, dust on the rise,
You came through it all the way, flyin' through the skies.
Dark Beauty
With that long night's journey in your eyes.

Sweet Goddess
Born of a blinding light and a changing wind,
Now, don't be modest, you know who you are and where
  you've been.
Jack the Cowboy went up north
He's buried in your past.
The Lone Wolf went out drinking
That was over pretty fast.
Sweet Goddess
Your perfect stranger's comin' in at last.

Silver Angel
With the badge of the lonesome road sewed in your sleeve,
I'd be grateful if this golden ring you would receive.
Today on the countryside it was a-hotter than a crotch,
I stood alone upon the ridge and all I did was watch.

Sweet Goddess
It must be time to carve another notch.

I'm crestfallen
The world of illusion is at my door,
I ain't a-haulin' any of my lambs to the marketplace anymore.
The prison walls are crumblin', there is no end in sight,
I've gained some recognition but I lost my appetite.
Dark Beauty
Meet me at the border late tonight.

# Hazel

Hazel, dirty-blonde hair
I wouldn't be ashamed to be seen with you anywhere.
You got something I want plenty of
Ooh, a little touch of your love.

Hazel, stardust in your eye
You're goin' somewhere and so am I.
I'd give you the sky high above
Ooh, for a little touch of your love.

Oh no, I don't need any reminder
To know how much I really care
But it's just making me blinder and blinder
Because I'm up on a hill and still you're not there.

Hazel, you called and I came,
Now don't make me play this waiting game.
You've got something I want plenty of
Ooh, a little touch of your love.

# Something There Is About You

Something there is about you that strikes a match in me
Is it the way your body moves or is it the way your hair blows
  free?
Or is it because you remind me of something that used to be
Somethin' that crossed over from another century?

Thought I'd shaken the wonder and the phantoms of my youth
Rainy days on the Great Lakes, walkin' the hills of old Duluth.
There was me and Danny Lopez, cold eyes, black night and
  then there was Ruth
Something there is about you that brings back a long-forgotten
  truth.

Suddenly I found you and the spirit in me sings
Don't have to look no further, you're the soul of many things.
I could say that I'd be faithful, I could say it in one sweet, easy
  breath
But to you that would be cruelty and to me it surely would be
  death.

Something there is about you that moves with style and grace
I was in a whirlwind, now I'm in some better place.
My hand's on the sabre and you've picked up the baton
Somethin' there is about you that I can't quite put my finger on.

# Forever Young

May God bless and keep you always,
May your wishes all come true,
May you always do for others
And let others do for you.
May you build a ladder to the stars
And climb on every rung,
May you stay forever young,
Forever young, forever young,
May you stay forever young.

May you grow up to be righteous,
May you grow up to be true,
May you always know the truth
And see the lights surrounding you.
May you always be courageous,
Stand upright and be strong,
May you stay forever young,
Forever young, forever young,
May you stay forever young.

May your hands always be busy,
May your feet always be swift,
May you have a strong foundation
When the winds of changes shift.
May your heart always be joyful,
May your song always be sung,
May you stay forever young,
Forever young, forever young,
May you stay forever young.

# Dirge

I hate myself for lovin' you and the weakness that it showed
You were just a painted face on a trip down Suicide Road.
The stage was set, the lights went out all around the old hotel,
I hate myself for lovin' you and I'm glad the curtain fell.

I hate that foolish game we played and the need that was
    expressed
And the mercy that you showed to me, who ever would have
    guessed?
I went out on Lower Broadway and I felt that place within,
That hollow place where martyrs weep and angels play with
    sin.

Heard your songs of freedom and man forever stripped,
Acting out his folly while his back is being whipped.
Like a slave in orbit, he's beaten 'til he's tame,
All for a moment's glory and it's a dirty, rotten shame.

There are those who worship loneliness, I'm not one of them,
In this age of fiberglass I'm searching for a gem.
The crystal ball up on the wall hasn't shown me nothing yet,
I've paid the price of solitude, but at last I'm out of debt.

Can't recall a useful thing you ever did for me
'Cept pat me on the back one time when I was on my knees.
We stared into each other's eyes 'til one of us would break,
No use to apologize, what diff'rence would it make?

So sing your praise of progress and of the Doom Machine,
The naked truth is still taboo whenever it can be seen.
Lady Luck, who shines on me, will tell you where I'm at,
I hate myself for lovin' you, but I should get over that.

494

# You Angel You

You angel you
You got me under your wing.
The way you walk and the way you talk
I feel I could almost sing.

You angel you
You're as fine as anything's fine.
The way you walk and the way you talk
It sure plays on my mind.

You know I can't sleep at night for trying,
Never did feel this way before.
I get up at night and walk the floor.
If this is love then gimme more
And more and more and more and more.

You angel you
You're as fine as can be.
The way you smile like a sweet baby child,
It just falls all over me.

You know I can't sleep at night for trying
Never did feel this way before.
Never did get up and walk the floor.
If this is love then gimme more
And more and more and more.

You angel you
You got me under your wing.
The way you walk and the way you talk
It says everything.

# Never Say Goodbye

Twilight on the frozen lake
North wind about to break
On footprints in the snow
Silence down below.

You're beautiful beyond words
You're beautiful to me
You can make me cry
Never say goodbye.

Time is all I have to give
You can have it if you choose
With me you can live
Never say goodbye.

My dreams are made of iron and steel
With a big bouquet
Of roses hanging down
From the heavens to the ground.

The crashing waves roll over me
As I stand upon the sand
Wait for you to come
And grab hold of my hand.

Oh, baby, baby, baby blue
You'll change your last name, too
You've turned your hair to brown
Love to see it hangin' down.

# Wedding Song

I love you more than ever, more than time and more than love,
I love you more than money and more than the stars above,
Love you more than madness, more than waves upon the sea,
Love you more than life itself, you mean that much to me.

Ever since you walked right in, the circle's been complete,
I've said goodbye to haunted rooms and faces in the street,
To the courtyard of the jester which is hidden from the sun,
I love you more than ever and I haven't yet begun.

You breathed on me and made my life a richer one to live,
When I was deep in poverty you taught me how to give,
Dried the tears up from my dreams and pulled me from the
      hole,
Quenched my thirst and satisfied the burning in my soul.

You gave me babies one, two, three, what is more, you saved
      my life,
Eye for eye and tooth for tooth, your love cuts like a knife,
My thoughts of you don't ever rest, they'd kill me if I lie,
I'd sacrifice the world for you and watch my senses die.

The tune that is yours and mine to play upon this earth,
We'll play it out the best we know, whatever it is worth,
What's lost is lost, we can't regain what went down in the
      flood,
But happiness to me is you and I love you more than blood.

It's never been my duty to remake the world at large,
Nor is it my intention to sound a battle charge,
'Cause I love you more than all of that with a love that doesn't
      bend,
And if there is eternity I'd love you there again.

497

Oh, can't you see that you were born to stand by my side
And I was born to be with you, you were born to be my bride,
You're the other half of what I am, you're the missing piece
And I love you more than ever with that love that doesn't
   cease.

You turn the tide on me each day and teach my eyes to see,
Just bein' next to you is a natural thing for me
And I could never let you go, no matter what goes on,
'Cause I love you more than ever now that the past is gone.

# Nobody 'Cept You

There's nothing 'round here I believe in
'Cept you, yeah you
And there's nothing to me that's sacred
'Cept you, yeah you

You're the one that reaches me
You're the one that I admire
Every time we meet together
My soul feels like it's on fire
Nothing matters to me
And there's nothing I desire
'Cept you, yeah you

Nothing 'round here I care to try for
'Cept you, yeah you
Got nothing left to live or die for
'Cept you, yeah you

There's a hymn I used to hear
In the churches all the time
Make me feel so good inside
So peaceful, so sublime
And there's nothing to remind me of that
Old familiar chime
'Cept you, uh huh you

Used to play in the cemetery
Dance and sing and run when I was a child
Never seemed strange
But now I just pass mournfully by
That place where the bones of life are piled
I know somethin' has changed
I'm a stranger here and no one sees me
'Cept you, yeah you

Nothing much matters or seems to please me
'Cept you, yeah you
Nothing hypnotizes me
Or holds me in a spell
Everything runs by me
Just like water from a well
Everybody wants my attention
Ev'rybody's got something to sell
'Cept you, yeah you

# Blood on the Tracks

**You're Gonna Make Me
   Lonesome When You Go**
**You're a Big Girl Now**
**Tangled Up in Blue**
**Simple Twist of Fate**
**Shelter from the Storm**
**Meet Me in the Morning**
**Lily, Rosemary
   and the Jack of Hearts**
**Idiot Wind**
**If You See Her, Say Hello**
**Buckets of Rain**

Up to Me

# You're Gonna Make Me
# Lonesome When You Go

I've seen love go by my door
It's never been this close before
Never been so easy or so slow.
Been shooting in the dark too long
When somethin' not right it's wrong
Yer gonna make me lonesome when you go.

Dragon clouds so high above
I've only known careless love,
It's always hit me from below.
This time around it's more correct
Right on target, so direct,
Yer gonna make me lonesome when you go.

Purple clover, Queen Anne lace,
Crimson hair across your face,
You could make me cry if you don't know.
Can't remember what I was thinkin' of
You might be spoilin' me too much, love,
Yer gonna make me lonesome when you go.

Flowers on the hillside, bloomin' crazy,
Crickets talkin' back and forth in rhyme,
Blue river runnin' slow and lazy,
I could stay with you forever
And never realize the time.

Situations have ended sad,
Relationships have all been bad.
Mine've been like Verlaine's and Rimbaud.
But there's no way I can compare
All those scenes to this affair,
Yer gonna make me lonesome when you go.

Yer gonna make me wonder what I'm doin',
Stayin' far behind without you.
Yer gonna make me wonder what I'm sayin',
Yer gonna make me give myself a good talkin' to.

I'll look for you in old Honolulu,
San Francisco, Ashtabula,
Yer gonna have to leave me now, I know.
But I'll see you in the sky above,
In the tall grass, in the ones I love,
Yer gonna make me lonesome when you go.

# You're a Big Girl Now

Our conversation was short and sweet
It nearly swept me off-a my feet.
And I'm back in the rain, oh, oh,
And you are on dry land.
You made it there somehow
You're a big girl now.

Bird on the horizon, sittin' on a fence,
He's singin' his song for me at his own expense.
And I'm just like that bird, oh, oh,
Singin' just for you.
I hope that you can hear,
Hear me singin' through these tears.

Time is a jet plane, it moves too fast
Oh, but what a shame if all we've shared can't last.
I can change, I swear, oh, oh,
See what you can do.
I can make it through,
You can make it too.

Love is so simple, to quote a phrase,
You've known it all the time, I'm learnin' it these days.
Oh, I know where I can find you, oh, oh,
In somebody's room.
It's a price I have to pay
You're a big girl all the way.

A change in the weather is known to be extreme
But what's the sense of changing horses in midstream?
I'm going out of my mind, oh, oh,
With a pain that stops and starts
Like a corkscrew to my heart
Ever since we've been apart.

# Tangled Up in Blue

Early one mornin' the sun was shinin',
I was layin' in bed
Wond'rin' if she'd changed at all
If her hair was still red.
Her folks they said our lives together
Sure was gonna be rough
They never did like Mama's homemade dress
Papa's bankbook wasn't big enough.
And I was standin' on the side of the road
Rain fallin' on my shoes
Heading out for the East Coast
Lord knows I've paid some dues gettin' through,
Tangled up in blue.

She was married when we first met
Soon to be divorced
I helped her out of a jam, I guess,
But I used a little too much force.
We drove that car as far as we could
Abandoned it out West
Split up on a dark sad night
Both agreeing it was best.
She turned around to look at me
As I was walkin' away
I heard her say over my shoulder,
'We'll meet again someday on the avenue,'
Tangled up in blue.

I had a job in the great north woods
Working as a cook for a spell
But I never did like it all that much
And one day the ax just fell.
So I drifted down to New Orleans
Where I happened to be employed

Workin' for a while on a fishin' boat
Right outside of Delacroix.
But all the while I was alone
The past was close behind,
I seen a lot of women
But she never escaped my mind, and I just grew
Tangled up in blue.

She was workin' in a topless place
And I stopped in for a beer,
I just kept lookin' at the side of her face
In the spotlight so clear.
And later on as the crowd thinned out
I's just about to do the same,
She was standing there in back of my chair
Said to me, 'Don't I know your name?'
I muttered somethin' underneath my breath,
She studied the lines on my face.
I must admit I felt a little uneasy
When she bent down to tie the laces of my shoe,
Tangled up in blue.

She lit a burner on the stove and offered me a pipe
'I thought you'd never say hello,' she said
'You look like the silent type.'
Then she opened up a book of poems
And handed it to me
Written by an Italian poet
From the thirteenth century.
And every one of them words rang true
And glowed like burnin' coal
Pourin' off of every page
Like it was written in my soul from me to you,
Tangled up in blue.

I lived with them on Montague Street
In a basement down the stairs,
There was music in the cafes at night
And revolution in the air.
Then he started into dealing with slaves
And something inside of him died.
She had to sell everything she owned
And froze up inside.
And when finally the bottom fell out
I became withdrawn,
The only thing I knew how to do
Was to keep on keepin' on like a bird that flew,
Tangled up in blue.

So now I'm goin' back again,
I got to get to her somehow.
All the people we used to know
They're an illusion to me now.
Some are mathematicians
Some are carpenter's wives.
Don't know how it all got started,
I don't what they're doin' with their lives.
But me, I'm still on the road
Headin' for another joint
We always did feel the same,
We just saw it from a different point of view,
Tangled up in blue.

# Simple Twist of Fate

They sat together in the park
As the evening sky grew dark,
She looked at him and he felt a spark tingle to his bones.
'Twas then he felt alone and wished that he'd gone straight
And watched out for a simple twist of fate.

They walked along by the old canal
A little confused, I remember well
And stopped into a strange hotel with a neon burnin' bright.
He felt the heat of the night hit him like a freight train
Moving with a simple twist of fate.

A saxophone someplace far off played
As she was walkin' by the arcade.
As the light bust through a beat-up shade where he was wakin'
    up,
She dropped a coin into the cup of a blind man at the gate
And forgot about a simple twist of fate.

He woke up, the room was bare
He didn't see her anywhere.
He told himself he didn't care, pushed the window open wide,
Felt an emptiness inside to which he just could not relate
Brought on by a simple twist of fate.

He hears the ticking of the clocks
And walks along with a parrot that talks,
Hunts her down by the waterfront docks where the sailers all
    come in.
Maybe she'll pick him out again, how long must he wait
Once more for a simple twist of fate.

People tell me it's a sin
To know and feel too much within.

I still believe she was my twin, but I lost the ring.
She was born in spring, but I was born too late
Blame it on a simple twist of fate.

# Shelter from the Storm

'Twas in another lifetime, one of toil and blood
When blackness was a virtue and the road was full of mud
I came in from the wilderness, a creature void of form.
'Come in,' she said,
'I'll give you shelter from the storm.'

And if I pass this way again, you can rest assured
I'll always do my best for her, on that I give my word
In a world of steel-eyed death, and men who are fighting to be
    warm.
'Come in,' she said,
'I'll give you shelter from the storm.'

Not a word was spoke between us, there was little risk involved
Everything up to that point had been left unresolved.
Try imagining a place where it's always safe and warm.
'Come in,' she said,
'I'll give you shelter from the storm.'

I was burned out from exhaustion, buried in the hail,
Poisoned in the bushes an' blown out on the trail,
Hunted like a crocodile, ravaged in the corn.
'Come in,' she said,
'I'll give you shelter from the storm.'

Suddenly I turned around and she was standin' there
With silver bracelets on her wrists and flowers in her hair.
She walked up to me so gracefully and took my crown of
    thorns.
'Come in,' she said,
'I'll give you shelter from the storm.'

Now there's a wall between us, somethin' there's been lost
I took too much for granted, got my signals crossed.

Just to think that it all began on a long-forgotten morn.
'Come in,' she said,
'I'll give you shelter from the storm.'

Well, the deputy walks on hard nails and the preacher rides a
    mount
But nothing really matters much, it's doom alone that counts
And the one-eyed undertaker, he blows a futile horn.
'Come in,' she said,
'I'll give you shelter from the storm.'

I've heard newborn babies wailin' like a mournin' dove
And old men with broken teeth stranded without love.
Do I understand your question, man, is it hopeless and forlorn?
'Come in,' she said,
'I'll give you shelter from the storm.'

In a little hilltop village, they gambled for my clothes
I bargained for salvation an' they gave me a lethal dose.
I offered up my innocence and got repaid with scorn.
'Come in,' she said,
'I'll give you shelter from the storm.'

Well, I'm livin' in a foreign country but I'm bound to cross the
    line
Beauty walks a razor's edge, someday I'll make it mine.
If I could only turn back the clock to when God and her were
    born.
'Come in,' she said,
'I'll give you shelter from the storm.'

# Meet Me in the Morning

Meet me in the morning, 56th and Wabasha
Meet me in the morning, 56th and Wabasha
Honey, we could be in Kansas
By time the snow begins to thaw.

They say the darkest hour is right before the dawn
They say the darkest hour is right before the dawn
But you wouldn't know it by me
Every day's been darkness since you been gone.

Little rooster crowin', there must be something on his mind
Little rooster crowin', there must be something on his mind
Well, I feel just like that rooster
Honey, ya treat me so unkind.

The birds are flyin' low babe, honey I feel so exposed
Well, the birds are flyin' low babe, honey I feel so exposed
Well now, I ain't got any matches
And the station doors are closed.

Well, I struggled through barbed wire, felt the hail fall from
    above
Well, I struggled through barbed wire, felt the hail fall from
    above
Well, you know I even outran the hound dogs
Honey, you know I've earned your love.

Look at the sun sinkin' like a ship
Look at the sun sinkin' like a ship
Ain't that just like my heart, babe
When you kissed my lips?

# Lily, Rosemary
# and the Jack of Hearts

The festival was over, the boys were all plannin' for a fall,
The cabaret was quiet except for the drillin' in the wall.
The curfew had been lifted and the gamblin' wheel shut down,
Anyone with any sense had already left town.
He was standin' in the doorway lookin' like the Jack of Hearts.

He moved across the mirrored room, 'Set it up for everyone,'
   he said,
Then everyone commenced to do what they were doin' before
   he turned their heads.
The he walked up to a stranger and he asked him with a grin,
'Could you kindly tell, me, friend, what time the show begins?'
Then he moved into the corner, face down like the Jack of
   Hearts.

Backstage the girls were playin' five-card stud by the stairs,
Lily had two queens, she was hopin' for a third to match her
   pair.
Outside the streets were fillin' up, the window was open wide,
A gentle breeze was blowin', you could feel it from inside.
Lily called another bet and drew up the Jack of Hearts.

Big Jim was no one's fool, he owned the town's only diamond
   mine,
He made his usual entrance lookin' so dandy and so fine.
With his bodyguards and silver cane and every hair in place,
He took whatever he wanted to and he laid it all to waste.
But his bodyguards and silver cane were no match for the Jack
   of Hearts.

Rosemary combed her hair and took a carriage into town,
She slipped in through the side door lookin' like a queen
   without a crown.

She fluttered her false eyelashes and whispered in his ear,
'Sorry, darlin', that I'm late,' but he didn't seem to hear.
He was starin' into space over at the Jack of Hearts.

'I know I've seen that face before,' Big Jim was thinkin' to
   himself,
'Maybe down in Mexico or a picture up on somebodys shelf.'
But then the crowd began to stamp their feet and the house
   lights did dim
And in the darkness of the room there was only Jim and him,
Starin' at the butterfly who just drew the Jack of Hearts.

Lily was a princess, she was fair-skinned and precious as a
   child,
She did whatever she had to do, she had that certain flash
   every time she smiled.
She'd come away from a broken home, had lots of strange
   affairs
With men in every walk of life which took her everywhere.
But she's never met anyone quite like the Jack of Hearts.

The hangin' judge came in unnoticed and was being wined and
   dined,
The drillin' in the wall kept up but no one seemed to pay it any
   mind.
It was known all around that Lily had Jim's ring
And nothing would ever come between Lily and the king.
No, nothin' ever would except maybe the Jack of Hearts.

Rosemary started drinkin' hard and seein' her reflection in the
   knife,
She was tired of the attention, tired of playin' the role of Big
   Jim's wife.
She had done a lot of bad things, even once tried suicide,

Was lookin' to do just one good deed before she died.
She was gazin' to the future, riding on the Jack of Hearts.

Lily washed her face, took her dress off and buried it away.
'Has your luck run out?' she laughed at him, 'Well, I guess you
　　must have known it would someday.
Be careful not to touch the wall, there's a brand-new coat of
　　paint,
I'm glad to see you're still alive, you're lookin' like a saint.'
Down the hallway footsteps were comin' for the Jack of Hearts.

The backstage manager was pacing all around by his chair.
'There's something funny going on,' he said, 'I can just feel it in
　　the air.'
He went to get the hangin' judge, but the hangin' judge was
　　drunk,
As the leading actor hurried by in the costume of a monk.
There was no actor anywhere better than the Jack of Hearts.

Lily's arms were locked around the man that she dearly loved
　　to touch,
She forgot all about the man she couldn't stand who hounded
　　her so much.
'I've missed you so,' she said to him, and he felt she was
　　sincere,
But just beyond the door he felt jealousy and fear.
Just another night in the life of the Jack of Hearts.

No one knew the circumstance but they say that it happened
　　pretty quick,
The door to the dressing room burst open and a cold revolver
　　clicked.
And Big Jim was standin' there, ya couldn't say surprised,

Rosemary right beside him, steady in her eyes.
She was with Big Jim but she was leanin' to the Jack of Hearts.

Two doors down the boys finally made it through the wall
And cleaned out the bank safe, it's said that they got off with
    quite a haul.
In the darkness by the riverbed they waited on the ground
For one more member who had business back in town.
But they couldn't go no further without the Jack of Hearts.

The next day was hangin' day, the sky was overcast and black,
Big Jim lay covered up, killed by a penknife in the back.
And Rosemary on the gallows, she didn't even blink,
The hangin' judge was sober, he hadn't had a drink.
The only person on the scene missin' was the Jack of Hearts.

The cabaret was empty now, a sign said, 'Closed for repair,'
Lily had already taken all of the dye out of her hair.
She was thinkin' 'bout her father, who she very rarely saw,
Thinkin' 'bout Rosemary and thinkin' about the law.
But most of all she was thinkin' 'bout the Jack of Hearts.

# Idiot Wind

Someone's got it in for me, they're planting stories in the press
Whoever it is I wish they'd cut it out but when they will I can
    only guess.
They say I shot a man named Gray and took his wife to Italy,
She inherited a million bucks and when she died it came to me.
I can't help it if I'm lucky.

People see me all the time and they just can't remember how to
    act
Their minds are filled with big ideas, images and distorted facts.
Even you, yesterday you had to ask me where it was at,
I couldn't believe after all these years, you didn't know me
    better than that
Sweet lady.

Idiot wind, blowing every time you move your mouth,
Blowing down the backroads headin' south.
Idiot wind, blowing every time you move your teeth,
You're an idiot, babe.
It's a wonder that you still know how to breathe.

I ran into the fortune-teller, who said beware of lightning that
    might strike
I haven't known peace and quiet for so long I can't remember
    what it's like.
There's a lone soldier on the cross, smoke pourin' out of a
    boxcar door,
You didn't know it, you didn't think it could be done, in the
    final end he won the wars
After losin' every battle.

I woke up on the roadside, daydreamin' 'bout the way things
    sometimes are

Visions of your chestnut mare shoot through my head and are
  makin' me see stars.
You hurt the ones that I love best and cover up the truth with
  lies.
One day you'll be in the ditch, flies buzzin' around your eyes,
Blood on your saddle.

Idiot wind, blowing through the flowers on your tomb,
Blowing through the curtains in your room.
Idiot wind, blowing every time you move your teeth,
You're an idiot, babe.
It's a wonder that you still know how to breathe.

It was gravity which pulled us down and destiny which broke
  us apart
You tamed the lion in my cage but it just wasn't enough to
  change my heart.
Now everything's a little upside down, as a matter of fact the
  wheels have stopped,
What's good is bad, what's bad is good, you'll find out when
  you reach the top
You're on the bottom.

I noticed at the ceremony, your corrupt ways had finally made
  you blind
I can't remember your face anymore, your mouth has changed,
  your eyes don't look into mine.
The priest wore black on the seventh day and sat stone-faced
  while the building burned.
I waited for you on the running boards, near the cypress trees,
  while the springtime turned
Slowly into autumn.

Idiot wind, blowing like a circle around my skull,
From the Grand Coulee Dam to the Capitol.
Idiot wind, blowing every time you move your teeth,
You're an idiot, babe.
It's a wonder that you still know how to breathe.

I can't feel you anymore, I can't even touch the books you've
　read
Every time I crawl past your door, I been wishin' I was
　somebody else instead.
Down the highway, down the tracks, down the road to ecstasy,
I followed you beneath the stars, hounded by your memory
And all your ragin' glory.

I been double-crossed now for the very last time and now I'm
　finally free,
I kissed goodbye the howling beast on the borderline which
　separated you from me.
You'll never know the hurt I suffered nor the pain I rise above,
And I'll never know the same about you, your holiness or your
　kind of love,
And it makes me feel so sorry.

Idiot wind, blowing through the buttons of our coats,
Blowing through the letters that we wrote.
Idiot wind, blowing through the dust upon our shelves,
We're idiots, babe.
It's a wonder we can even feed ourselves.

# If You See Her, Say Hello

If you see her, say hello, she might be in Tangier
She left here last early spring, is livin' there, I hear
Say for me that I'm all right though things get kind of slow
She might think that I've forgotten her, don't tell her it isn't so.

We had a falling-out, like lovers often will
And to think of how she left that night, it still brings me a chill
And though our separation, it pierced me to the heart
She still lives inside of me, we've never been apart.

If you get close to her, kiss her once for me
I always have respected her for busting out and gettin' free
Oh, whatever makes her happy, I won't stand in the way
Though the bitter taste still lingers on from the night I tried to
    make her stay.

I see a lot of people as I make the rounds
And I hear her name here and there as I go from town to town
And I've never gotten used to it, I've just learned to turn it off
Either I'm too sensitive or else I'm gettin' soft.

Sundown, yellow moon, I replay the past
I know every scene by heart, they all went by so fast
If she's passin' back this way, I'm not that hard to find
Tell her she can look me up if she's got the time.

# Buckets of Rain

Buckets of rain
Buckets of tears
Got all them buckets comin' out of my ears.
Buckets of moonbeams in my hand,
I got all the love, honey baby,
You can stand.

I been meek
And hard like an oak
I seen pretty people disappear like smoke.
Friends will arrive, friends will disappear,
If you want me, honey baby,
I'll be here.

Like your smile
And your fingertips
Like the way that you move your lips.
I like the cool way you look at me,
Everything about you is bringing me
Misery.

Little red wagon
Little red bike
I ain't no monkey but I know what I like.
I like the way you love me strong and slow,
I'm takin' you with me, honey baby,
When I go,

Life is sad
Life is a bust
All ya can do is do what you must.
You do what you must do and ya do it well,
I'll do it for you, honey baby,
Can't you tell?

# Up to Me

Everything went from bad to worse, money never changed a
  thing,
Death kept followin', trackin' us down, at least I heard your
  bluebird sing.
Now somebody's got to show their hand, time is an enemy,
I know you're long gone,
I guess it must be up to me.

If I'd thought about it I never would've done it, I guess I
  would've let it slide,
If I'd lived my life by what others were thinkin', the heart inside
  me would've died.
I was just too stubborn to ever be governed by enforced
  insanity,
Someone had to reach for the risin' star,
I guess it was up to me.

Oh, the Union Central is pullin' out and the orchids are in
  bloom,
I've only got me one good shirt left and it smells of stale
  perfume.
In fourteen months I've only smiled once and I didn't do it
  consciously,
Somebody's got to find your trail,
I guess it must be up to me.

It was like a revelation when you betrayed me with your touch,
I'd just about convinced myself that nothin' had changed that
  much.
The old Rounder in the iron mask slipped me the master key,
Somebody had to unlock your heart,
He said it was up to me.

Well, I watched you slowly disappear down into the officers'
    club,
I would've followed you in the door but I didn't have a ticket
    stub.
So I waited all night 'til the break of day, hopin' one of us could
    get free,
When the dawn came over the river bridge,
I knew it was up to me.

Oh, the only decent thing I did when I worked as a postal clerk
Was to haul your picture down off the wall near the cage where
    I used to work.
Was I a fool or not to try to protect your identity?
You looked a little burned out, my friend,
I thought it might be up to me.

Well, I met somebody face to face and I had to remove my hat,
She's everything I need and love but I can't be swayed by that.
It frightens me, the awful truth of how sweet life can be,
But she ain't a-gonna make me move,
I guess it must be up to me.

We heard the Sermon on the Mount and I knew it was too
    complex,
It didn't amount to anything more than what the broken glass
    reflects.
When you bite off more than you can chew you pay the
    penalty,
Somebody's got to tell the tale,
I guess it must be up to me.

Well, Dupree came in pimpin' tonight to the Thunderbird Cafe,
Crystal wanted to talk to him, I had to look the other way.
Well, I just can't rest without you, love, I need your company,

But you ain't a-gonna cross the line,
I guess it must be up to me.

There's a note left in the bottle, you can give it to Estelle,
She's the one you been wond'rin' about, but there's really
    nothin' much to tell.
We both heard voices for a while, now the rest is history,
Somebody's got to cry some tears,
I guess it must be up to me.

So go on, boys, and play your hands, life is a pantomime,
The ringleaders from the county seat say you don't have all that
    much time.
And the girl with me behind the shades, she ain't my property,
One of us has got to hit the road,
I guess it must be up to me.

And if we never meet again, baby, remember me,
How my lone guitar played sweet for you that old-time melody.
And the harmonica around my neck, I blew it for you, free,
No one else could play that tune,
You know it was up to me.

# Desire

**Hurricane**
**Isis**
**Mozambique**
**One More Cup of Coffee (Valley Below)**
**Oh, Sister**
**Joey**
**Romance in Durango**
**Black Diamond Bay**
**Sara**

Desire (liner notes)
Abandoned Love
Catfish
Golden Loom
Rita May
Seven Days
Sign Language
Money Blues

# Hurricane <small>(with Jacques Levy)</small>

Pistol shots ring out in the barroom night
Enter Patty Valentine from the upper hall.
She sees the bartender in a pool of blood,
Cries out, 'My God, they killed them all!'
Here comes the story of the Hurricane,
The man the authorities came to blame
For somethin' that he never done.
Put in a prison cell, but one time he could-a been
The champion of the world.

Three bodies lyin' there does Patty see
And another man named Bello, movin' around mysteriously.
'I didn't do it,' he says, and he throws up his hands
'I was only robbin' the register, I hope you understand.
I saw them leavin',' he says, and he stops
'One of us had better call up the cops.'
And so Patty calls the cops
And they arrive on the scene with their red lights flashin'
In the hot New Jersey night.

Meanwhile, far away in another part of town
Rubin Carter and a couple of friends are drivin' around.
Number one contender for the middleweight crown
Had no idea what kinda shit was about to go down
When a cop pulled him over to the side of the road
Just like the time before and the time before that.
In Paterson that's just the way things go.
If you're black you might as well not show up on the street
'Less you wanna draw the heat.

Alfred Bello had a partner and he had a rap for the cops.
Him and Arthur Dexter Bradley were just out prowlin' around
He said, 'I saw two men runnin' out, they looked like
    middleweights

They jumped into a white car with out-of-state plates.'
And Miss Patty Valentine just nodded her head.
Cop said, 'Wait a minute, boys, this one's not dead'
So they took him to the infirmary
And though this man could hardly see
They told him that he could identify the guilty men.

Four in the mornin' and they haul Rubin in,
Take him to the hospital and they bring him upstairs.
The wounded man looks up through his one dyin' eye
Says, 'Wha'd you bring him in here for? He ain't the guy!'
Yes, here's the story of the Hurricane,
The man the authorities came to blame
For somethin' that he never done.
Put in a prison cell, but one time he could-a been
The champion of the world.

Four months later, the ghettos are in flame,
Rubin's in South America, fightin' for his name
While Arthur Dexter Bradley's still in the robbery game
And the cops are puttin' the screws to him, lookin' for
    somebody to blame.
'Remember that murder that happened in a bar?'
'Remember you said you saw the getaway car?'
'You think you'd like to play ball with the law?'
'Think it might-a been that fighter that you saw runnin' that
    night?'
'Don't forget that you are white.'

Arthur Dexter Bradley said, 'I'm really not sure.'
Cops said, 'A boy like you could use a break
We got you for the motel job and we're talkin' to your friend
    Bello
Now you don't wanta have to go back to jail, be a nice fellow.

You'll be doin' society a favor.
That sonofabitch is brave and gettin' braver.
We want to put his ass in stir
We want to pin this triple murder on him
He ain't no Gentleman Jim.'

Rubin could take a man out with just one pouch
But he never did like to talk about it all that much.
It's my work, he'd say, and I do it for pay
And when it's over I'd just as soon go on my way
Up to some paradise
Where the trout streams flow and the air is nice
And ride a horse along a trail.
But then they took him to the jailhouse
Where they try to turn a man into a mouse.

All of Rubin's cards were marked in advance
The trial was a pig-circus, he never had a chance.
The judge made Rubin's witnesses drunkards from the slums
To the white folks who watched he was a revolutionary bum
And to the black folks he was just a crazy nigger.
No one doubted that he pulled the trigger.
And though they could not produce the gun,
The DA said he was the one who did the deed
And the all-white jury agreed.

Rubin Carter was falsely tried.
The crime was murder 'one,' guess who testified?
Bello and Bradley and they both baldly lied
And the newspapers, they all went along for the ride.
How can the life of such a man
Be in the palm of some fool's hand?
To see him obviously framed

Couldn't help but make me feel ashamed to live in a land
Where justice is a game.

Now all the criminals in their coats and their ties
Are free to drink martinis and watch the sun rise
While Rubin sits like Buddha in a ten-foot cell
An innocent man in a living hell.
That's the story of the Hurricane,
But it won't be over till they clear his name
And give him back the time he's done.
Put in a prison cell, but one time he could-a been
The champion of the world.

# Isis <small>(with Jacques Levy)</small>

I married Isis on the fifth day of May,
But I could not hold on to her very long
So I cut off my hair and I rode straight away
For the wild unknown country where I could not go wrong.

I came to a high place of darkness and light.
The dividing line ran through the center of town.
I hitched up my pony to a post on the right,
Went in to a laundry to wash my clothes down.

A man in the corner approached me for a match.
I knew right away he was not ordinary.
He said, 'Are you lookin' for somethin' easy to catch?'
I said, 'I got no money.' He said, 'That ain't necessary.'

We set out that night for the cold in the North.
I gave him my blanket, he gave me his word.
I said, 'Where are we goin'?' He said we'd be back by the
   fourth.
I said, 'That's the best news that I've ever heard.'

I was thinkin' about turquoise, I was thinkin' about gold,
I was thinkin' about diamonds and the world's biggest
   necklace.
As we rode through the canyons, through the devilish cold,
I was thinkin' about Isis, how she thought I was so reckless.

How she told me that one day we would meet up again,
And things would be different the next time we wed,
If I only could hang on and just be her friend.
I still can't remember all the best things she said.

We came to the pyramids all embedded in ice.
He said, 'There's a body I'm tryin' to find.

If I carry it out it'll bring a good price.'
'Twas then that I knew what he had on his mind.

The wind it was howlin' and the snow was outrageous.
We chopped through the night and we chopped through the
    dawn.
When he died I was hopin' that it wasn't contagious,
But I made up my mind that I had to go on.

I broke into the tomb, but the casket was empty.
There was no jewels, no nothin', I felt I'd been had.
When I saw that my partner was just bein' friendly,
When I took up his offer I must-a been mad.

I picked up his body and I dragged him inside,
Threw him down in the hole and I put back the cover.
I said a quick prayer and I felt satisfied.
Then I rode back to find Isis just to tell her I love her.

She was there in the meadow where the creek used to rise.
Blinded by sleep and in need of a bed,
I came in from the East with the sun in my eyes.
I cursed her one time then I rode on ahead.

She said, 'Where ya been?' I said, 'No place special.'
She said, 'You look different.' I said, 'Well, not quite.'
She said, 'You been gone.' I said, 'That's only natural.'
She said, 'You gonna stay?' I said, 'Yeah, I jes might.'

Isis, oh, Isis, you mystical child.
What drives me to you is what drives me insane.
I still can remember the way that you smiled
On the fifth day of May in the drizzlin' rain.

# Mozambique (with Jacques Levy)

I like to spend some time in Mozambique
The sunny sky is aqua blue
And all the couples dancing cheek to cheek.
It's very nice to stay a week or two.

There's lots of pretty girls in Mozambique
And plenty time for good romance
And everybody likes to stop and speak
To give the special one you seek a chance
Or maybe say hello with just a glance.

Lying next to her by the ocean
Reaching out and touching her hand,
Whispering your secret emotion
Magic in a magical land.

And when it's time for leaving Mozambique,
To say goodbye to sand and sea,
You turn around to take a final peek
And you see why it's so unique to be
Among the lovely people living free
Upon the beach of sunny Mozambique.

# One More Cup of Coffee
# (Valley Below)

Your breath is sweet
Your eyes are like two jewels in the sky.
Your back is straight, your hair is smooth
On the pillow where you lie.
But I don't sense affection
No gratitude or love
Your loyalty in not to me
But to the stars above.

One more cup of coffee for the road,
One more cup of coffee 'fore I go
To the valley below.

Your daddy he's an outlaw
And a wanderer by trade
He'll teach you how to pick and choose
And how to throw the blade.
He oversees his kingdom
So no stranger does intrude
His voice it trembles as he calls out
For another plate of food.

One more cup of coffee for the road,
One more cup of coffee 'fore I go
To the valley below.

Your sister sees the future
Like you mama and yourself.
You've never learned to read or write
There's no books upon your shelf.
And your pleasure knows no limits
Your voice is like a meadowlark
But your heart is like an ocean
Mysterious and dark.

One more cup of coffee for the road,
One more cup of coffee 'fore I go
To the valley below.

# Oh, Sister (with Jacques Levy)

Oh, sister, when I come to lie in your arms
You should not treat me like a stranger.
Our Father would not like the way that you act
And you must realize the danger.

Oh, sister, am I not a brother to you
And one deserving of affection?
And is our purpose not the same on this earth,
To love and follow His direction?

We grew up together
From the cradle to the grave
We died and were reborn
And then mysteriously saved.

Oh, sister, when I come to knock on your door,
Don't turn away, you'll create sorrow.
Time is an ocean but it ends at the shore
You may not see me tomorrow.

# Joey (with Jacques Levy)

Born in Red Hook, Brooklyn, in the year of who knows when
Opened up his eyes to the tune of an accordion
Always on the outside of whatever side there was
When they asked him why it had to be that way, 'Well,' he
    answered, 'just because.'

Larry was the oldest, Joey was next to last.
They called Joe 'Crazy,' the baby they called 'Kid Blast.'
Some say they lived off gambling and runnin' numbers too.
It always seemed they got caught between the mob and the
    men in blue.

Joey, Joey,
King of the streets, child of clay.
Joey, Joey,
What made them want to come and blow you away?

There was talk they killed their rivals, but the truth was far from
    that
No one ever knew for sure where they were really at.
When they tried to strangle Larry, Joey almost hit the roof.
He went out that night to seek revenge, thinkin' he was
    bulletproof.

The war broke out at the break of dawn, it emptied out the
    streets
Joey and his brothers suffered terrible defeats
Till they ventured out behind the lines and took five prisoners.
They stashed them away in a basement, called them amateurs.

The hostages were tremblin' when they heard a man exclaim,
'Let's blow this place to kingdom come, let Con Edison take the
    blame.'

But Joey stepped up, he raised his hand, said, 'We're not those
kind of men.
It's peace and quiet that we need to go back to work again.'


Joey, Joey,
King of the streets, child of clay.
Joey, Joey,
What made them want to come and blow you away?


The police department hounded him, they called him Mr Smith
They got him on conspiracy, they were never sure who with.
'What time is it?' said the judge to Joey when they met
'Five to ten,' said Joey. The judge says, 'That's exactly what you
get.'


He did ten years in Attica, reading Nietzsche and Wilhelm
Reich
They threw him in the hole one time for tryin' to stop a strike.
His closest friends were black men 'cause they seemed to
understand
What it's like to be in society with a shackle on your hand.


When they let him out in '71 he'd lost a little weight
But he dressed like Jimmy Cagney and I swear he did look
great.
He tried to find the way back into the life he left behind
To the boss he said, 'I have returned and now I want what's
mine.'


Joey, Joey,
King of the streets, child of clay.
Joey, Joey,
Why did they have to come and blow you away?

It was true that in his later years he would not carry a gun
'I'm around too many children,' he'd say, 'they should never
　　know of one.'
Yet he walked right into the clubhouse of his lifelong deadly
　　foe,
Emptied out the register, said, 'Tell 'em it was Crazy Joe.'

One day they blew him down in a clam bar in New York
He could see it comin' through the door as he lifted up his fork.
He pushed the table over to protect his family
Then he staggered out into the streets of Little Italy

Joey, Joey,
King of the streets, child of clay.
Joey, Joey,
What made them want to come and blow you away?

Sister Jacqueline and Carmela and mother Mary all did weep.
I heard his best friend Frankie say, 'He ain't dead, he's just
　　asleep.'
Then I saw the old man's limousine head back towards the
　　grave
I guess he had to say one last goodbye to the son that he could
　　not save.

The sun turned cold over President Street and the town of
　　Brooklyn mourned
They said a mass in the old church near the house where he
　　was born.
And someday if God's in heaven overlookin' His preserve
I know the men that shot him down will get what they deserve.

Joey, Joey,
King of the streets, child of clay.

Joey, Joey,
What made them want to come and blow you away?

# Romance in Durango (with Jacques Levy)

Hot chili peppers in the blistering sun
Dust on my face and my cape,
Me and Magdalena on the run
I think this time we shall escape.

Sold my guitar to the baker's son
For a few crumbs and a place to hide,
But I can get another one
And I'll play for Magdalena as we ride.

No llores, mi querida
Dios nos vigila
Soon the horse will take us to Durango.
Agarrame, mi vida
Soon the desert will be gone
Soon you will be dancing the fandango.

Past the Aztec ruins and the ghosts of our people
Hoofbeats like castanets on stone.
At night I dream of bells in the village steeple
Then I see the bloody face of Ramon.

Was it me that shot him down in the cantina
Was it my hand that held the gun?
Come, let us fly, my Magdalena
The dogs are barking and what's done is done.

No llores, mi querida
Dios nos vigila
Soon the horse will take us to Durango.
Agarrame, mi vida
Soon the desert will be gone
Soon you will be dancing the fandango.

At the corrida we'll sit in the shade
And watch the young torero stand alone.
We'll drink tequila where our grandfathers stayed
When they rode with Villa into Torreón.

Then the padre will recite the prayers of old
In the little church this side of town.
I will wear new boots and an earring of gold
You'll shine with diamonds in your wedding gown.

The way is long but the end is near
Already the fiesta has begun.
The face of God will appear
With His serpent eyes of obsidian.

No llores, mi querida
Dios nos vigila
Soon the horse will take us to Durango.
Agarrame, mi vida
Soon the desert will be gone
Soon you will be dancing the fandango.

Was that the thunder that I heard?
My head is vibrating, I feel a sharp pain.
Come sit by me, don't say a word
Oh, can it be that I am slain?

Quick, Magdalena, take my gun
Look up in the hills, that flash of light.
Aim well my little one
We may not make it through the night.

No llores, mi querida
Dios nos vigila

Soon the horse will take us to Durango.
Agarrame, mi vida
Soon the desert will be gone
Soon you will be dancing the fandango.

# Black Diamond Bay (with Jacques Levy)

Up on the white veranda
She wears a necktie and a Panama hat.
Her passport shows a face
From another time and place
She looks nothin' like that.
And all the remnants of her recent past
Are scattered in the wild wind.
She walks across the marble floor
Where a voice from the gambling room is callin' her to come
   on in.
She smiles, walks the other way
As the last ship sails and the moon fades away
From Black Diamond Bay.

As the mornin' light breaks open, the Greek comes down
And he asks for a rope and a pen that will write.
'Pardon, monsieur,' the desk clerk says,
Carefully removes his fez,
'Am I hearin' you right?'
And as the yellow fog is liftin'
The Greek is quickly headin' for the second floor.
She passes him on the spiral staircase
Thinkin' he's the Soviet Ambassador,
She starts to speak, but he walks away
As the storm clouds rise and the palm branches sway
On Black Diamond Bay.

A soldier sits beneath the fan
Doin' business with a tiny man who sells him a ring.
Lightning strikes, the lights blow out.
The desk clerk wakes and begins to shout,
'Can you see anything?'
Then the Greek appears on the second floor
In his bare feet with a rope around his neck,

546

While a loser in the gambling room lights up a candle,
Says, 'Open up another deck.'
But the dealer says, 'Attendez-vous, s'il vous plaît,'
As the rain beats down and the cranes fly away
From Black Diamond Bay.

The desk clerk heard the woman laugh
As he looked around the aftermath and the soldier got tough.
He tried to grab the woman's hand,
Said, 'Here's a ring, it cost a grand.'
She said, 'That ain't enough.'
Then she ran upstairs to pack her bags
While a horse-drawn taxi waited at the curb.
She passed the door that the Greek had locked,
Where a handwritten sign read, 'Do Not Disturb.'
She knocked upon it anyway
As the sun went down and the music did play
On Black Diamond Bay.

'I've got to talk to someone quick!'
But the Greek said, 'Go away,' and he kicked the chair to the
    floor.
He hung there from the chandelier.
She cried, 'Help, there's danger near
Please open up the door!'
Then the volcano erupted
And the lava flowed down from the mountain high above.
The soldier and the tiny man were crouched in the corner
Thinking of forbidden love.
But the desk clerk said, 'It happens every day.'
As the stars fell down and the fields burned away
On Black Diamond Bay.

As the island slowly sank
The loser finally broke the bank in the gambling room.

The dealer said, 'It's too late now.
You can take your money, but I don't know how
You'll spend it in the tomb.'
The tiny man bit the soldier's ear
As the floor caved in and the boiler in the basement blew,
While she's out on the balcony, where a stranger tells her,
'My darling, je vous aime beaucoup.'
She sheds a tear and then begins to pray
As the fire burns on and the smoke drifts away
From Black Diamond Bay.

I was sittin' alone one night in LA,
Watchin' old Cronkite on the seven o'clock news.
It seems there was an earthquake that
Left nothin' but a Panama hat
And a pair of old Greek shoes.
Didn't seem like much was happenin',
So I turned it off and went to grab another beer.
Seems like every time you turn around
There's another hard-luck story that you're gonna hear
And there's really nothin' anyone can say
And I never did plan to go anyway
To Black Diamond Bay.

# Sara

I laid on a dune, I looked at the sky,
When the children were babies and played on the beach.
You came up behind me, I saw you go by,
You were always so close and still within reach.

Sara, Sara,
Whatever made you want to change your mind?
Sara, Sara,
So easy to look at, so hard to define.

I can still see them playin' with their pails in the sand,
They run to the water their buckets to fill.
I can still see the shells fallin' out of their hands
As they follow each other back up the hill.

Sara, Sara,
Sweet virgin angel, sweet love of my life,
Sara, Sara,
Radiant jewel, mystical wife.

Sleepin' in the woods by a fire in the night,
Drinkin' white rum in a Portugal bar,
Them playin' leapfrog and hearin' about Snow White,
You in the marketplace in Savanna-la-Mar.

Sara, Sara,
It's all so clear, I could never forget,
Sara, Sara,
Lovin' you is the one thing I'll never regret.

I can still hear the sounds of those Methodist bells,
I'd taken the cure and had just gotten through,
Stayin' up for days in the Chelsea Hotel,
Writin' 'Sad-Eyed Lady of the Lowlands' for you.

Sara, Sara,
Wherever we travel we're never apart.
Sara, oh Sara,
Beautiful lady, so dear to my heart.

How did I meet you? I don't know.
A messenger sent me in a tropical storm.
You were there in the winter, moonlight on the snow
And on Lily Pond Lane when the weather was warm.

Sara, Sara,
Scorpio Sphinx in a calico dress,
Sara, Sara,
You must forgive me my unworthiness.

Now the beach is deserted except for some kelp
And a piece of an old ship that lies on the shore.
You always responded when I needed your help,
You gimme a map and a key to your door.

Sara, oh Sara,
Glamorous nymph with an arrow and bow,
Sara, oh Sara,
Don't ever leave me, don't ever go.

# Desire (liner notes)

Where do I begin . . . on the heels of Rimbaud moving like a
dancing bullet thru the secret streets of a hot New Jersey night
filled with venom and wonder. Meeting the Queen Angel in the
reeds of Babylon and then to the fountain of sorrow to drift
away in the hot mass of the deluge . . . to sing praise to the king
of those dead streets, to grasp and let go in a heavenly way . . .
streaming into the lost belly of civilization at a standstill.
Romance is taking over. Tolstoy was right. These notes are
being written in a bathtub in Maine under ideal conditions, in
every curio lounge from Brooklyn to Guam, from Lowell to
Durango oh sister, when I fall into your spacy arms, can not ya
feel the weight of oblivion and the songs of redemption on your
backside we surface alongside Miles Standish and take the rock.
We have relations in Mozambique. I have a brother or two and
a whole lot of karma to burn . . . Isis and the moon shine on
me. When Rubin gets out of jail, we celebrate in the historical
parking lot in sunburned California . . .

# Abandoned Love

I can hear the turning of the key
I've been deceived by the clown inside of me.
I thought that he was righteous but he's vain
Oh, something's a-telling me I wear the ball and chain.

My patron saint is a-fighting with a ghost
He's always off somewhere when I need him most.
The Spanish moon is rising on the hill
But my heart is a-tellin' me I love ya still.

I come back to the town from the flaming moon
I see you in the streets, I begin to swoon.
I love to see you dress before the mirror
Won't you let me in your room one time 'fore I finally
    disappear?

Everybody's wearing a disguise
To hide what they've got left behind their eyes.
But me, I can't cover what I am
Wherever the children go I'll follow them.

I march in the parade of liberty
But as long as I love you I'm not free.
How long must I suffer such abuse
Won't you let me see you smile one time before I turn you
    loose?

I've given up the game, I've got to leave,
The pot of gold is only make-believe.
The treasure can't be found by men who search
Whose gods are dead and whose queens are in the church.

We sat in an empty theater and we kissed,
I asked ya please to cross me off-a your list.

My head tells me it's time to make a change
But my heart is telling me I love ya but you're strange.

One more time at midnight, near the wall
Take off your heavy make-up and your shawl.
Won't you descend from the throne, from where you sit?
Let me feel your love one more time before I abandon it.

# Catfish (with Jacques Levy)

Lazy stadium night
Catfish on the mound.
'Strike three,' the umpire said,
Batter have to go back and sit down.

Catfish, million-dollar-man,
Nobody can throw the ball like Catfish can.

Used to work on Mr Finley's farm
But the old man wouldn't pay
So he packed his glove and took his arm
An' one day he just ran away.

Catfish, million-dollar-man,
Nobody can throw the ball like Catfish can.

Come up where the Yankees are,
Dress up in a pinstripe suit,
Smoke a custom-made cigar,
Wear an alligator boot.

Catfish, million-dollar-man,
Nobody can throw the ball like Catfish can.

Carolina born and bred,
Love to hunt the little quail.
Got a hundred-acre spread,
Got some huntin' dogs for sale.

Catfish, million-dollar-man,
Nobody can throw the ball like Catfish can.

Reggie Jackson at the plate
Seein' nothin' but the curve,

Swing too early or too late
Got to eat what Catfish serve.

Catfish, million-dollar-man,
Nobody can throw the ball like Catfish can.

Even Billy Martin grins
When the Fish is in the game.
Every season twenty wins
Gonna make the Hall of Fame.

Catfish, million-dollar-man,
Nobody can throw the ball like Catfish can.

# Golden Loom

Smoky autumn night, stars up in the sky,
I see the sailin' boats across the bay go by.
Eucalyptus trees hang above the street
And then I turn my head, for you're approachin' me.
Moonlight on the water, fisherman's daughter, floatin' in to my
   room
With a golden loom.

First we wash our feet near the immortal shrine
And then our shadows meet and then we drink the wine.
I see the hungry clouds up above your face
And then the tears roll down, what a bitter taste.
And then you drift away on a summer's day where the
   wildflowers bloom
With your golden loom.

I walk across the bridge in the dismal light
Where all the cars are stripped between the gates of night.
I see the trembling lion with the lotus flower tail
And then I kiss your lips as I lift your veil.
But you're gone and then all I seem to recall is the smell of
   perfume
And your golden loom.

# Rita May (with Jacques Levy)

Rita May, Rita May,
You got your body in the way.
You're so damn nonchalant
But it's your mind that I want.
You got me huffin' and a-puffin',
Next to you I feel like nothin',
Rita May.

Rita May, Rita May,
How'd you ever get that way?
When do you ever see the light?
Don't you ever feel a fright?
You got me burnin' and I'm turnin'
But I know I must be learnin',
Rita May.

All my friends have told me
If I hang around with you
That I'll go blind
But I know that when you hold me
That there really must be somethin'
On your mind.

Rita May, Rita May,
Laying in a stack of hay,
Do you remember where you been?
What's that crazy place you're in?
I'm gonna have to go to college
'Cause you are the book of knowledge,
Rita May.

# Seven Days

Seven days, seven more days she'll be comin'
I'll be waiting at the station for her to arrive
Seven more days, all I gotta do is survive.

She been gone ever since I been a child
Ever since I seen her smile, I ain't forgotten her eyes.
She had a face that could outshine the sun in the skies.

I been good, I been good while I been waitin'
Maybe guilty of hesitatin', I just been holdin' on
Seven more days, all that'll be gone.

There's kissing in the valley,
Thieving in the alley,
Fighting every inch of the way.
Trying to be tender
With somebody I remember
In a night that's always brighter'n the day.

Seven days, seven more days that are connected
Just like I expected, she'll be comin' on forth,
My beautiful comrade from the north.

There's kissing in the valley,
Thieving in the alley,
Fighting every inch of the way.
Trying to be tender
With somebody I remember
In a night that's always brighter'n the day.

# Sign Language

You speak to me
In sign language
As I'm eating a sandwich
In a small cafe
At a quarter to three
But I can't respond
To your sign language.
You're taking advantage,
Bringing me down.
Can't you make any sound?

'Twas there by the bakery
Surrounded by fakery
Tell her my story
Still I'm still there.
Does she know I still care?

Link Wray was playin'
On a jukebox I was payin'
For the words I was sayin'
So misunderstood
He didn't do me no good.

You speak to me
In sign language
As I'm eating a sandwich
In a small cafe
At a quarter to three
But I can't respond
To your sign language.
You're taking advantage,
Bringing me down.
Can't you make any sound?

# Money Blues (with Jacques Levy)


Sittin' here thinkin'
Where does the money go,
Sittin' here thinkin'
Where does the money go.
Well, I give it to my woman
She ain't got it no more.

Went out last night
Bought two eggs and a slice of ham,
Went out last night
Bought two eggs and a slice of ham.
Bill came to three dollars and ten cents
And I didn't even get no jam.

Man came around
Askin' for the rent,
Man came around
Askin' for the rent.
Well, I looked into the drawer
But the money's all been spent.

Well, well
Ain't got no bank account,
Well, well
Ain't got no bank account.
Went down to start one
But I didn't have the right amount.

Everything's inflated
Like a tire on a car,
Everything's inflated
Like a tire on a car.
Well, the man came and took my Chevy back
I'm glad I hid my old guitar.

Come to me, mama
Ease my money crisis now,
Come to me, mama
Ease my money crisis now.
I need something to support me
And only you know how.

# Street Legal

**Changing of the Guards**
**New Pony**
**No Time to Think**
**Baby, Stop Crying**
**Is Your Love in Vain?**
**Señor (Tales of Yankee Power)**
**True Love Tends to Forget**
**We Better Talk This Over**
**Where Are You Tonight?**
   **(Journey Through Dark Heat)**

Coming from the Heart (The Road Is Long)
If I Don't Be There by Morning
Legionnaire's Disease
Love You Too Much
Walk Out in the Rain

# Changing of the Guards

Sixteen years,
Sixteen banners united over the field
Where the good shepherd grieves.
Desperate men, desperate women divided,
Spreading their wings 'neath the falling leaves.

Fortune calls.
I stepped forth from the shadows, to the marketplace,
Merchants and thieves, hungry for power, my last deal gone
   down.
She's smelling sweet like the meadows where she was born,
On midsummer's eve, near the tower.

The cold-blooded moon.
The captain waits above the celebration
Sending his thoughts to a beloved maid
Whose ebony face is beyond communication.
The captain is down but still believing that his love will be
   repaid.

They shaved her head.
She was torn between Jupiter and Apollo.
A messenger arrived with a black nightingale.
I seen her on the stairs and I couldn't help but follow,
Follow her down past the fountain where they lifted her veil.

I stumbled to my feet.
I rode past destruction in the ditches
With the stitches still mending 'neath a heart-shaped tattoo.
Renegade priests and treacherous young witches
Were handing out the flowers that I'd given to you.

The palace of mirrors
Where dog soldiers are reflected,

The endless road and the wailing of chimes,
The empty rooms where her memory is protected,
Where the angels' voices whisper to the souls of previous times.

She wakes him up
Forty-eight hours later, the sun is breaking
Near broken chains, mountain laurel and rolling rocks.
She's begging to know what measures he now will be taking.
He's pulling her down and she's clutching on to his long golden
   locks.

Gentlemen, he said,
I don't need your organization, I've shined your shoes,
I've moved your mountains and marked your cards
But Eden is burning, either brace yourself for elimination
Or else your hearts must have the courage for the changing of
   the guards.

Peace will come
With tranquillity and splendor on the wheels of fire
But will bring us no reward when her false idols fall
And cruel death surrenders with its pale ghost retreating
Between the King and the Queen of Swords.

# New Pony

Once I had a pony, her name was Lucifer
I had a pony, her name was Lucifer
She broke her leg and she needed shooting
I swear it hurt me more than it could ever have hurted her

Sometimes I wonder what's going on in the mind of Miss X
Sometimes I wonder what's going on in the mind of Miss X
You know she got such a sweet disposition
I never know what the poor girl's gonna do to me next

I got a new pony, she knows how to fox-trot, lope and pace
Well, I got a new pony, she knows how to fox-trot, lope and
    pace
She got great big hind legs
And long black shaggy hair above her face

Well now, it was early in the mornin', I seen your shadow in
    the door
It was early in the mornin', I seen your shadow in the door
Now, I don't have to ask nobody
I know what you come here for

They say you're usin' voodoo, your feet walk by themselves
They say you're usin' voodoo, I seen your feet walk by
    themselves
Oh, baby, that god you been prayin' to
Is gonna give ya back what you're wishin' on someone else

Come over here pony, I, I wanna climb up one time on you
Come over here pony, I, I wanna climb up one time on you
Well, you're so bad and nasty
But I love you, yes I do

# No Time to Think

In death, you face life with a child and a wife
Who sleep-walks through your dreams into walls.
You're a soldier of mercy, you're cold and you curse,
'He who cannot be trusted must fall.'

Loneliness, tenderness, high society, notoriety.
You fight for the throne and you travel alone
Unknown as you slowly sink
And there's no time to think.

In the Federal City you been blown and shown pity,
In secret, for pieces of change.
The empress attracts you but oppression distracts you
And it makes you feel violent and strange.

Memory, ecstasy, tyranny, hypocrisy
Betrayed by a kiss on a cool night of bliss
In the valley of the missing link
And you have no time to think.

Judges will haunt you, the country priestess will want you
Her worst is better than best.
I've seen all these decoys through a set of deep turquoise eyes
And I feel so depressed.

China doll, alcohol, duality, mortality.
Mercury rules you and destiny fools you
Like the plague, with a dangerous wink
And there's no time to think.

Your conscience betrayed you when some tyrant waylaid you
Where the lion lies down with the lamb.
I'd have paid off the traitor and killed him much later
But that's just the way that I am.

Paradise, sacrifice, mortality, reality.
But the magician is quicker and his game
Is much thicker than blood and blacker than ink
And there's no time to think.

Anger and jealousy's all that he sells us,
He's content when you're under his thumb.
Madmen oppose him, but your kindness throws him
To survive it you play deaf and dumb

Equality, liberty, humility, simplicity.
You glance through the mirror and there's eyes staring clear
At the back of your head as you drink
And there's no time to think.

Warlords of sorrow and queens of tomorrow
Will offer their heads for a prayer.
You can't find no salvation, you have no expectations
Anytime, anyplace, anywhere.

Mercury, gravity, nobility, humility.
You know you can't keep her and the water gets deeper
That is leading you onto the brink
But there's no time to think.

You've murdered your vanity, buried your sanity
For pleasure you must now resist.
Lovers obey you but they cannot sway you
They're not even sure you exist.

Socialism, hypnotism, patriotism, materialism.
Fools making laws for the breaking of jaws
And the sound of the keys as they clink
But there's no time to think.

The bridge that you travel on goes to the Babylon girl
With the rose in her hair.
Starlight in the East and you're finally released
You're stranded but with nothing to share.

Loyality, unity, epitome, rigidity.
You turn around for one real last glimpse of Camille
'Neath the moon shinin' bloody and pink
And there's no time to think.

Bullets can harm you and death can disarm you
But no, you will not be deceived.
Stripped of all virtue as you crawl through the dirt,
You can give but you cannot receive.

No time to choose when the truth must die,
No time to lose or say goodbye,
No time to prepare for the victim that's there,
No time to suffer or blink
And no time to think.

# Baby, Stop Crying

You been down to the bottom with a bad man, babe,
But you're back where you belong.
Go get me my pistol, babe,
Honey, I can't tell right from wrong.

Baby, please stop crying, stop crying, stop crying
Baby, please stop crying, stop crying, stop crying
Baby, please stop crying.
You know, I know, the sun will always shine
So baby, please stop crying 'cause it's tearing up my mind.

Go down to the river, babe,
Honey, I will meet you there.
Go down to the river, babe,
Honey, I will pay your fare.

Baby, please stop crying, stop crying, stop crying
Baby, please stop crying, stop crying, stop crying
Baby, please stop crying.
You know, I know, the sun will always shine
So baby, please stop crying 'cause it's tearing up my mind.

If you're looking for assistance, babe,
Or if you just want some company
Or if you just want a friend you can talk to,
Honey, come and see about me.

Baby, please stop crying, stop crying, stop crying
Baby, please stop crying, stop crying, stop crying
Baby, please stop crying.
You know, I know, the sun will always shine
So baby, please stop crying 'cause it's tearing up my mind.

You been hurt so many times
And I know what you're thinking of.
Well, I don't have to be no doctor, babe,
To see that you're madly in love.

Baby, please stop crying, stop crying, stop crying
Baby, please stop crying, stop crying, stop crying
Baby, please stop crying.
You know, I know, the sun will always shine
So baby, please stop crying 'cause it's tearing up my mind.

# Is Your Love in Vain?

Do you love me, or are you just extending goodwill?
Do you need me half as bad as you say, or are you just feeling
   guilt?
I've been burned before and I know the score
So you won't hear me complain.
Will I be able to count on you
Or is your love in vain?

Are you so fast that you cannot see that I must have solitude?
When I am in the darkness, why do you intrude?
Do you know my world, do you know my kind
Or must I explain?
Will you let me be myself
Or is your love in vain?

Well I've been to the mountain and I've been in the wind,
I've been in and out of happiness.
I have dined with kings, I've been offered wings
And I've never been too impressed.

All right, I'll take a chance, I will fall in love with you
If I'm a fool you can have the night, you can have the morning
   too.
Can you cook and sew, make flowers grow,
Do you understand my pain?
Are you willing to risk it all
Or is your love in vain?

# Señor
# (Tales of Yankee Power)

Señor, señor, do you know where we're headin'?
Lincoln County Road or Armageddon?
Seems like I been down this way before.
Is there any truth in that, señor?

Señor, señor, do you know where she is hidin'?
How long are we gonna be ridin'?
How long must I keep my eyes glued to the door?
Will there be any comfort there, señor?

There's a wicked wind still blowin' on that upper deck,
There's an iron cross still hanging down from around her neck.
There's a marchin' band still playin' in that vacant lot
Where she held me in her arms one time and said, 'Forget me
    not.'

Señor, señor, I can see that painted wagon,
I can smell the tail of the dragon.
Can't stand the suspense anymore.
Can you tell me who to contact here, señor?

Well, the last thing I remember before I stripped and kneeled
Was that trainload of fools bogged down in a magnetic field.
A gypsy with a broken flag and a flashing ring
Said, 'Son, this ain't a dream no more, it's the real thing.'

Señor, señor, you know their hearts is as hard as leather.
Well, give me a minute, let me get it together.
I just gotta pick myself up off the floor.
I'm ready when you are, señor.

Señor, señor, let's disconnect these cables,
Overturn these tables.

This place don't make sense to me no more.
Can you tell me what we're waiting for, señor?

# True Love
# Tends to Forget

I'm getting weary looking in my baby's eyes
When she's near me she's so hard to recognize.
I finally realize there's no room for regret,
True love, true love, true love tends to forget.

Hold me, baby be near,
You told me that you'd be sincere.
Every day of the year's like playin' Russian roulette,
True love, true love, true love tends to forget.

I was lyin' down in the reeds without any oxygen
I saw you in the wilderness among the men.
Saw you drift into infinity and come back again
All you got to do is wait and I'll tell you when.

You're a tearjerker, baby, but I'm under your spell,
You're a hard worker, baby, and I know you well.
But this weekend in hell is making me sweat,
True love, true love, true love tends to forget,
True love, true love, true love tends to forget.

I was lyin' down in the reeds without any oxygen
I saw you in the wilderness among the men.
Saw you drift into infinity and come back again
All you got to do is wait and I'll tell you when.

You belong to me, baby, without any doubt,
Don't forsake me, baby, don't sell me out.
Don't keep me knockin' about from Mexico to Tibet,
True love, true love, true love tends to forget.

# We Better Talk This Over

I think we better talk this over
Maybe when we both get sober
You'll understand I'm only a man
Doin' the best that I can.

This situation can only get rougher.
Why should we needlessly suffer?
Let's call it a day, go our own different ways
Before we decay.

You don't have to be afraid of looking into my face,
We've done nothing to each other time will not erase.

I feel displaced, I got a low-down feeling
You been two-faced, you been double-dealing.
I took a chance, got caught in the trance
Of a downhill dance.

Oh, child, why you wanna hurt me?
I'm exiled, you can't convert me.
I'm lost in the haze of your delicate ways
With both eyes glazed.

You don't have to yearn for love, you don't have to be alone,
Somewhere in the universe there's a place that you can call
    home.

I guess I'll be leaving tomorrow
If I have to beg, steal or borrow.
It'd be great to cross paths in a day and a half
Look at each other and laugh.

But I don't think it's liable to happen
Like the sound of one hand clappin'.

The vows that we kept are now broken and swept
'Neath the bed where we slept.

Don't think of me and fantasize on what we never had,
Be grateful for what we've shared together and be glad.

Why should we go on watching each other through a
    telescope?
Eventually we'll hang ourselves on all this tangled rope.

Oh, babe, time for a new transition
I wish I was a magician.
I would wave a wand and tie back the bond
That we've both gone beyond.

# Where Are You Tonight?
# (Journey Through Dark Heat)

There's a long-distance train rolling through the rain, tears on
the letter I write.
There's a woman I long to touch and I miss her so much but
she's drifting like a satellite.
There's a neon light ablaze in this green smoky haze, laughter
down on Elizabeth Street
And a lonesome bell tone in that valley of stone where she
bathed in a stream of pure heat.
Her father would emphasize you got to be more than street-
wise but he practiced what he preached from the heart.
A full-blooded Cherokee, he predicted to me the time and the
place that the trouble would start.

There's a babe in the arms of a woman in a rage
And a longtime golden-haired stripper onstage
And she winds back the clock and she turns back the page
Of a book that no one can write.
Oh, where are you tonight?

The truth was obscure, too profound and too pure, to live it
you have to explode.
In that last hour of need, we entirely agreed, sacrifice was the
code of the road.
I left town at dawn, with Marcel and St John, strong men
belittled by doubt.
I couldn't tell her what my private thoughts were but she had
some way of finding them out.
He took dead-center aim but he missed just the same, she was
waiting, putting flowers on the shelf.
She could feel my despair as I climbed up her hair and
discovered her invisible self.

There's a lion in the road, there's a demon escaped,
There's a million dreams gone, there's a landscape being raped,

As her beauty fades and I watch her undrape,
I won't, but then again, maybe I might.
Oh, if I could just find you tonight.

I fought with my twin, that enemy within, 'til both of us fell by
   the way.
Horseplay and disease is killing me by degrees while the law
   looks the other way.
Your partners in crime hit me up for nickels and dimes, the guy
   you were lovin' couldn't stay clean.
It felt outa place, my foot in his face, but he should-a stayed
   where his money was green.
I bit into the root of forbidden fruit with the juice running down
   my leg.
Then I dealt with your boss, who'd never known about loss and
   who always was too proud to beg.
There's a white diamond gloom on the dark side of this room
   and a pathway that leads up to the stars.
If you don't believe there's a price for this sweet paradise,
   remind me to show you the scars.

There's a new day at dawn and I've finally arrived.
If I'm there in the morning, baby, you'll know I've survived.
I can't believe it, I can't believe I'm alive,
But without you it just doesn't seem right.
Oh, where are you tonight?

# Coming from the Heart
# (The Road Is Long) (with Helena Springs)

We have got to come together
How long can we stay apart?
You may get it maybe never
But it's coming from the heart.

Your life is full of indecision
You can't make up your mind.
We must get it in position
And move it on down the line.

'Cause the road it long, it's a long hard climb
I been on that road too long of a time
Yes the road is long, and it winds and winds
When I think of the love that I left behind.

Make me up a bed of roses
And hang them down from the vine
Of all my loves you've been the closest
That's ever been on my mind.

Please don't talk about tomorrow
I'm really not one to care
This world is filled with too much sorrow
That nobody's heart should bear.

'Cause the road is long, it's a long hard climb
I been on that road too long of a time
Yes the road is long, and it winds and winds
When I think of the love that I left behind.

Please, please give me indication
Stop and talk to me
Like a river that is flowing
My love will never cease to be.

You will always be my honey
No one could take your part
Our love can't be bought with money
'Cause it's coming from the heart.

'Cause the road is long, it's a long hard climb
I been on that road too long of a time
Yes the road is long, and it winds and winds
When I think of the love that I left behind.

# If I Don't Be There
# by Morning (with Helena Springs)


Blue sky upon the horizon,
Private eye on my trail,
And if I don't be there by morning
She'll know that I must've spent the night in jail.


I been runnin' from Memphis to LA,
Had an appointment set sometime for today
And if I don't be there by morning
She'll know that I must have gone the other way.


Finding my way home to you, girl, lonely and blue, mistreated
   too,
Sometimes I think about you, girl, is it true that you think of me
   too?


I got a woman living in LA,
I got a woman waiting for my pay,
And if I don't be there by morning
Pack my clothes, get down on your knees and pray.


I left my woman with a twenty-dollar bill,
Left her waiting, hope she's waiting for me still.
But if I don't be there by morning
I guess that I never will.


Finding my way home to you, girl, lonely and blue, mistreated
   too,
Sometimes I think about you, girl, is it true that you think of me
   too?

I left my woman with a twenty-dollar bill,
Left her waiting, hope she's waiting for me still.
Well, if I don't be there by morning
I guess that I never will.

# Legionnaire's Disease

Some say it was radiation, some say there was acid on the
   microphone,
Some say a combination that turned their hearts to stone,
But whatever it was, it drove them to their knees
Oh, Legionnaire's disease.

I wish I had a dollar for everyone that died within that year,
Got 'em hot by the collar, plenty an old maid shed a tear,
Now within my heart, it sure put on a squeeze.
Oh, Legionnaire's disease.

Granddad fought in a revolutionary war, father in the War of
   1812,
Uncle fought in Vietnam and then he fought a war all by
   himself,
But whatever it was, it came out of the trees.
Oh, Legionnaire's disease.

# Love You Too Much (with Helena Springs and Greg Lake)

My momma told me you were bad news, honey,
She said you're gonna ruin my life
'Cause I love you too much,
Yeah, I love you too much.

I wanna leave you, there's no denying.
I must have tried a million times
But I love you too much
I just love you too much.

I stand convicted behind the bars of love,
For me there is no escape, not even mercy from heaven above.

You've got me fallin' this way and that way,
Anyway you just ain't here
And I love you too much,
Yeah, I love you too much.

Well you can take me honey, you can steal my money,
You can step on my blue suede shoes
'Cause I love you too much,
Yeah, I love you too much.

I've been neglected, but I feel no pain
'Cause my line's been connected and I can ring it again and
    again.

So think of what you're doing, leading me to ruin.
Don't be cruel baby, can't you see
That I love you too much?
You know I love you too much.

Well, even if you hurt me, abuse me and desert me,
You know that I would go down in flames

'Cause I love you too much,
Yeah, I love you too much.

I'm declaring a state of emergency baby, dial 999.
You gotta help me, I'm falling, I just don't know if I can make it
    this time
'Cause I love you too much,
You know I love you too much.

So baby, why do you hate me and humiliate me?
I wish you'd get out of my life
'Cause I love you too much,
You know I love you too much.

I feel frustrated like a tiger in a cage.
You gotta release me before I fly into a screaming rage.

You know I really ought to put you down
Before you make a fool out of me
But I love you too much,
Yeah, I love you too much.

So think of what you're doing, leading me to ruin,
Don't be cruel baby, can't you see
That I love you too much?
Yeah, I love you too much.

You got me fallin' this way and that way
Anyway you just ain't here
And I love you too much,
Yeah, I love you too much.

Well you can take me honey, you can steal my money,
You can step on my blue suede boots

587

'Cause I love you too much,
Yeah, I love you too much.

Well, and even if you hurt me, abuse me and desert me,
Baby, I'd go down in flames
'Cause I love you too much,
Yeah, I love you too much.

# Walk Out
# in the Rain (with Helena Springs)

Walk out if it doesn't feel right,
I can tell you're only lying.
If you got something better tonight,
Don't mess up my mind with your crying.

Walk out in the rain,
Walk out with your dreams,
Walk out of my life
If it doesn't feel right
And catch the next train.
Oh, darling, walk out in the rain.

I have come from so far away
Just to put a ring on your finger.
You've said all that you've got to say,
So please don't feel the need to linger.

Walk out in the rain,
Walk out with your dreams,
Walk out of my life
If it doesn't feel right
And catch the next train.
Oh, darling, walk out in the rain.

It's rainin' inside of the city,
My poor feet have walked 'til they're sore.
If you don't want my love, it's a pity,
I guess I can't see you no more.

Walk out in the rain,
Walk out with your dreams,
Walk out of my life
If it doesn't feel right
And catch the next train.
Oh, darling, walk out in the rain.

# Slow Train Coming

**Gotta Serve Somebody**
**I Believe in You**
**Precious Angel**
**Gonna Change My Way of Thinking**
**Do Right to Me Baby (Do Unto Others)**
**When You Gonna Wake Up?**
**Man Gave Names to All the Animals**
**Slow Train**
**When He Returns**

Ain't No Man Righteous, No Not One
Trouble in Mind

# Gotta Serve Somebody

You may be an ambassador to England or France,
You may like to gamble, you might like to dance,
You may be the heavyweight champion of the world,
You may be a socialite with a long string of pearls

But you're gonna have to serve somebody, yes indeed
You're gonna have to serve somebody,
Well, it may be the devil or it may be the Lord
But you're gonna have to serve somebody.

You might be a rock 'n' roll addict prancing on the stage,
You might have drugs at your command, women in a cage,
You may be a business man or some high degree thief,
They may call you Doctor or they may call you Chief

But you're gonna have to serve somebody, yes indeed
You're gonna have to serve somebody,
Well, it may be the devil or it may be the Lord
But you're gonna have to serve somebody.

You may be a state trooper, you might be a young Turk,
You may be the head of some big TV network,
You may be rich or poor, you may be blind or lame,
You may be living in another country under another name

But you're gonna have to serve somebody, yes indeed
You're gonna have to serve somebody,
Well, it may be the devil or it may be the Lord
But you're gonna have to serve somebody.

You may be a construction worker working on a home,
You may be living in a mansion or you might live in a dome,
You might own guns and you might even own tanks,
You might be somebody's landlord, you might even own banks

But you're gonna have to serve somebody, yes indeed
You're gonna have to serve somebody,
Well, it may be the devil or it may be the Lord
But you're gonna have to serve somebody.

You may be a preacher with your spiritual pride,
You may be a city councilman taking bribes on the side,
You may be workin' in a barbershop, you may know how to
    cut hair,
You may be somebody's mistress, may be somebody's heir

But you're gonna have to serve somebody, yes indeed
You're gonna have to serve somebody,
Well, it may be the devil or it may be the Lord
But you're gonna have to serve somebody.

Might like to wear cotton, might like to wear silk,
Might like to drink whiskey, might like to drink milk,
You might like to eat caviar, you might like to eat bread,
You may be sleeping on the floor, sleeping in a king-sized bed

But you're gonna have to serve somebody, yes indeed
You're gonna have to serve somebody,
Well, it may be the devil or it may be the Lord
But you're gonna have to serve somebody.

You may call me Terry, you may call me Timmy,
You may call me Bobby, you may call me Zimmy,
You may call me R.J., you may call me Ray,
You may call me anything but no matter what you say

You're gonna have to serve somebody, yes indeed
You're gonna have to serve somebody,
Well, it may be the devil or it may be the Lord
But you're gonna have to serve somebody.

# I Believe in You

They ask me how I feel
And if my love is real
And how I know I'll make it through.
And they, they look at me and frown,
They'd like to drive me from this town,
They don't want me around
'Cause I believe in you.

They show me to the door,
They say don't come back no more
'Cause I don't be like they'd like me to,
And I walk out on my own
A thousand miles from home
But I don't feel alone
'Cause I believe in you.

I believe in you even through the tears and the laughter,
I believe in you even though we be apart.
I believe in you even on the morning after.
Oh, when the dawn is nearing
Oh, when the night is disappearing
Oh, this feeling is still here in my heart.

Don't let me drift too far,
Keep me where you are
Where I will always be renewed.
And that which you've given me today
Is worth more than I could pay
And no matter what they say
I believe in you.

I believe in you when winter turn to summer,
I believe in you when white turn to black,
I believe in you even though I be outnumbered.

Oh, though the earth may shake me
Oh, though my friends forsake me
Oh, even that couldn't make me go back.

Don't let me change my heart,
Keep me set apart
From all the plans they do pursue.
And I, I don't mind the pain
Don't mind the driving rain
I know I will sustain
'Cause I believe in you.

# Precious Angel

Precious angel, under the sun,
How was I to know you'd be the one
To show me I was blinded, to show me I was gone
How weak was the foundation I was standing upon?

Now there's spiritual warfare and flesh and blood breaking
    down.
Ya either got faith or ya got unbelief and there ain't no neutral
    ground.
The enemy is subtle, how be it we are so deceived
When the truth's in our hearts and we still don't believe?

Shine you light, shine your light on me
Shine your light, shine your light on me
Shine your light, shine your light on me
Ya know I just couldn't make it by myself.
I'm a little too blind to see.

My so-called friends have fallen under a spell.
They look me squarely in the eye and they say, 'All is well.'
Can they imagine the darkness that will fall from on high
When men will beg God to kill them and they won't be able to
    die?

Sister, lemme tell you about a vision I saw.
You were drawing water for your husband, you were suffering
    under the law.
You were telling him about Buddha, you were telling him about
    Mohammed in the same breath.
You never mentioned one time the Man who came and died a
    criminal's death.

Shine your light, shine your light on me
Shine your light, shine your light on me

Shine your light, shine your light on me
Ya know I just couldn't make it by myself.
I'm a little too blind to see.

Precious angel, you believe me when I say
What God has given to us no man can take away.
We are covered in blood, girl, you know our forefathers were
    slaves.
Let us hope they've found mercy in their bone-filled graves.

You're the queen of my flesh, girl, you're my woman, you're
    my delight,
You're the lamp of my soul, girl, and you touch up the night.
But there's violence in the eyes, girl, so let us not be enticed
On the way out of Egypt, through Ethiopia, to the judgment hall
    of Christ.

Shine your light, shine your light on me
Shine your light, shine your light on me
Shine your light, shine your light on me
Ya know I just couldn't make it by myself.
I'm a little too blind to see.

# Gonna Change
# My Way of Thinking

Gonna change my way of thinking,
Make myself a different set of rules.
Gonna change my way of thinking,
Make myself a different set of rules.
Gonna put my good foot forward,
And stop being influenced by fools.

So much oppression,
Can't keep track of it no more.
So much oppression,
Can't keep track of it no more.
Sons becoming husbands to their mothers,
And old men turning young daughters into whores.

Stripes on your shoulders,
Stripes on your back and on your hands.
Stripes on your shoulders,
Stripes on your back and on your hands.
Swords piercing your side,
Blood and water flowing through the land.

Well don't know which one is worse,
Doing your own thing or just being cool.
Well don't know which one is worse,
Doing your own thing or just being cool.
You remember only about the brass ring,
You forget all about the golden rule.

You can mislead a man,
You can take ahold of his heart with your eyes.
You can mislead a man,
You can take ahold of his heart with your eyes.
But there's only one authority,
And that's the authority on high.

I got a God-fearing woman,
One I can easily afford.
I got a God-fearing woman,
One I can easily afford.
She can do the Georgia crawl,
She can walk in the spirit of the Lord.

Jesus said. 'Be ready,
For you know not the hour in which I come.'
Jesus said, 'Be ready,
For you know not the hour in which I come.'
He said, 'He who is not for Me is against Me,'
Just so you know where He's coming from.

There's a kingdom called Heaven,
A place where there is no pain of birth.
There's a kingdom called Heaven,
A place where there is no pain of birth.
Well the Lord created it, mister,
About the same time He made the earth.

# Do Right to Me Baby
## (Do Unto Others)

Don't wanna judge nobody, don't wanna be judged,
Don't wanna touch nobody, don't wanna be touched.
Don't wanna hurt nobody, don't wanna be hurt,
Don't wanna treat nobody like they was dirt.

But if you do right to me, baby,
I'll do right to you, too.
Ya got to do unto others
Like you'd have them, like you'd have them, do unto you.

Don't wanna shoot nobody, don't wanna be shot,
Don't wanna buy nobody, don't wanna be bought.
Don't wanna bury nobody, don't wanna be buried,
Don't wanna marry nobody if they're already married.

But if you do right to me, baby,
I'll do right to you, too.
Ya got to do unto others
Like you'd have them, like you'd have them, do unto you.

Don't wanna burn bobody, don't wanna be be burned,
Don't wanna learn from nobody what I gotta unlearn.
Don't wanna cheat nobody, don't wanna be cheated,
Don't wanna defeat nobody if they already been defeated.

But if you do right to me, baby,
I'll do right to you, too.
Ya got to do unto others
Like you'd have them, like you'd have them, do unto you.

Don't wanna wink at nobody, don't wanna be winked at,
Don't wanna be used by nobody for a doormat.
Don't wanna confuse nobody, don't wanna be confused,
Don't wanna amuse nobody, don't wanna be amused.

But if you do right to me, baby,
I'll do right to you, too.
Ya got to do unto others
Like you'd have them, like you'd have them, do unto you.

Don't wanna betray nobody, don't wanna be betrayed,
Don't wanna play with nobody, don't wanna be waylaid.
Don't wanna miss nobody, don't wanna be missed,
Don't put my faith in nobody, not even a scientist.

But if you do right to me, baby,
I'll do right to you, too.
Ya got to do unto others
Like you'd have them, like you'd have them, do unto you.

# When You Gonna Wake Up?

God don't make no promises that He don't keep.
You got some big dreams, baby, but in order to dream you
   gotta still be asleep.

When you gonna wake up, when you gonna wake up
When you gonna wake up and strengthen the things that
   remain?

Counterfeit philosophies have polluted all of your thoughts.
Karl Marx has got ya by the throat, Henry Kissinger's got you
   tied up in knots.

When you gonna wake up, when you gonna wake up
When you gonna wake up and strengthen the things that
   remain?

You got innocent men in jail, your insane asylums are filled,
You got unrighteous doctors dealing drugs that'll never cure
   your ills.

When you gonna wake up, when you gonna wake up
When you gonna wake up and strengthen the things that
   remain?

You got men who can't hold their peace and women who can't
   control their tongues,
The rich seduce the poor and the old are seduced by the
   young.

When you gonna wake up, when you gonna wake up
When you gonna wake up and strengthen the things that
   remain?

Adulterers in churches and pornography in the schools,
You got gangsters in power and lawbreakers making rules.

When you gonna wake up, when you gonna wake up
When you gonna wake up and strengthen the things that
    remain?

Spiritual advisors and gurus to guide your every move,
Instant inner peace and every step you take has got to be
    approved.

When you gonna wake up, when you gonna wake up
When you gonna wake up and strengthen the things that
    remain?

Do you ever wonder just what God requires?
You think He's just an errand boy to satisfy your wandering
    desires.

When you gonna wake up, when you gonna wake up
When you gonna wake up and strengthen the things that
    remain?

You can't take it with you and you know that it's too worthless
    to be sold,
They tell you, 'Time is money' as if your life was worth its
    weight in gold.

When you gonna wake up, when you gonna wake up
When you gonna wake up and strengthen the things that
    remain?

There's a Man up on a cross and He's been crucified.
Do you have any idea why or for who He died?

When you gonna wake up, when you gonna wake up
When you gonna wake up and strengthen the things that
   remain?

# Man Gave Names
# All the Animals

Man gave names to all the animals
In the beginning, in the beginning.
Man gave names to all the animals
In the beginning, long time ago.

He saw an animal that liked to growl,
Big furry paws and he liked to howl,
Great big furry back and furry hair.
'Ah, think I'll call it a bear.'

Man gave names to all the animals
In the beginning, in the beginning.
Man gave names to all the animals
In the beginning, long time ago.

He saw an animal up on a hill
Chewing up so much grass until she was filled.
He saw milk comin' out but he didn't know how.
'Ah, think I'll call it a cow.'

Man gave names to all the animals
In the beginning, in the beginning.
Man gave names to all the animals
In the beginning, long time ago.

He saw an animal that liked to snort,
Horns on his head and they weren't too short.
It looked like there wasn't nothin' that he couldn't pull.
'Ah, think I'll call it a bull.'

Man gave names to all the animals
In the beginning, in the beginning.
Man gave names to all the animals
In the beginning, long time ago.

He saw an animal leavin' a muddy trail,
Real dirty face and a curly tail.
He wasn't too small and he wasn't too big.
'Ah, think I'll call it a pig.'

Man gave names to all the animals
In the beginning, in the beginning.
Man gave names to all the animals
In the beginning, long time ago.

Next animal that he did meet
Had wool on his back and hooves on his feet,
Eating grass on a mountainside so steep.
'Ah, think I'll call it a sheep.'

Man gave names to all the animals
In the beginning, in the beginning.
Man gave names to all the animals
In the beginning, long time ago.

He saw an animal as smooth as glass
Slithering his way through the grass.
Saw him disappear by a tree near a lake . . .

# Slow Train

Sometimes I feel so low-down and disgusted
Can't help but wonder what's happenin' to my companions,
Are they lost or are they found, have they counted the cost it'll
    take to bring down
All their earthly principles they're gonna have to abandon?
There's a slow, slow train comin' up around the bend.

I had a woman down in Alabama,
She was a backwoods girl, but she sure was realistic,
She said, 'Boy, without a doubt, have to quit your mess and
    straighten out,
You could die down here, be just another accident statistic.'
There's a slow, slow train comin' up around the bend.

All that foreign oil controlling American soil,
Look around you, it's just bound to make you embarrassed.
Sheiks walkin' around like kings, wearing fancy jewels and nose
    rings,
Deciding America's future from Amsterdam and to Paris
And there's a slow, slow train comin' up around the bend.

Man's ego is inflated, his laws are outdated, they don't apply no
    more,
You can' rely no more to be standin' around waitin'
In the home of the brave, Jefferson turnin' over in his grave,
Fools glorifying themselves, trying to manipulate Satan
And there's a slow, slow train comin' up around the bend.

Big-time negotiators, false healers and woman haters,
Masters of the bluff and masters of the proposition
But the enemy I see wears a cloak of decency,
All non-believers and men stealers talkin' in the name of
    religion
And there's a slow, slow train comin' up around the bend.

People starving and thirsting, grain elevators are bursting
Oh, you know it costs more to store the food than it do to give
   it.
They say lose your inhibitions, follow your own ambitions,
They talk about a life of brotherly love, show me someone who
   knows how to live it.
There's a slow, slow train comin' up around the bend.

Well, my baby went to Illinois with some bad-talkin' boy she
   could destroy
A real suicide case, but there was nothin' I could do to stop it,
I don't care about economy, I don't care about astronomy
But it sure do bother me to see my loved ones turning into
   puppets,
There's a slow, slow train comin' up around the bend.

# When He Returns

The iron hand it ain't no match for the iron rod,
The strongest wall will crumble and fall to a mighty God.
For all those who have eyes and all those who have ears
It is only He who can reduce me to tears.
Don't you cry and don't you die and don't you burn
For like a thief in the night, He'll replace wrong with right
When He returns.

Truth is an arrow and the gate is narrow that it passes through,
He unleashed His power at an unknown hour that no one
    knew.
How long can I listen to the lies of prejudice?
How long can I stay drunk on fear out in the wilderness?
Can I cast it aside, all this loyalty and this pride?
Will I ever learn that there'll be no peace, that the war won't
    cease
Until He returns?

Surrender your crown on this blood-stained ground, take off
    your mask,
He sees your deeds, He knows your needs even before you
    ask.
How long can you falsify and deny what is real?
How long can you hate yourself for the weakness you conceal?
Of every earthly plan that be known to man, He is
    unconcerned,
He's got plans of His own to set up His throne
When He returns.

# Ain't No Man Righteous,
# No Not One

When a man he serves the Lord, it makes his life worthwhile.
It don't matter 'bout his position, it don't matter 'bout his
    lifestyle.
Talk about perfection, I ain't never seen none
And there ain't no man righteous, no not one.

Sometimes the devil likes to drive you from the neighborhood.
He'll even work his ways through those whose intentions are
    good.
Some like to worship on the moon, others are worshipping the
    sun
And there ain't no man righteous, no not one.

Look around, ya see so many social hypocrites
Like to make rules for others while they do just the opposite.

You can't get to glory by the raising and the lowering of no flag.
Put your goodness next to God's and it comes out like a filthy
    rag.
In a city of darkness there's no need of the sun
And there ain't no man righteous, no not one.

Done so many evil things in the name of love, it's a crying
    shame
I never did see no fire that could put out a flame.

Pull your hat down, baby, pull the wool down over your eyes,
Keep a-talking, baby, 'til you run right out of alibis.
Someday you'll account for all the deeds that you done.
Well, there ain't no man righteous, no not one.

God got the power, man has got his vanity,
Man gotta choose before God can set him free.

Don't you know there's nothing new that's under the sun?
Well, there ain't no man righteous, no not one.

When I'm gone don't wonder where I be.
Just say that I trusted in God and that Christ was in me.
Say He defeated the devil, He was God's chosen Son
And that there ain't no man righteous, no not one.

# Trouble in Mind

I got to know, Lord, when to pull back on the reins,
Death can be the result of the most underrated pain.
Satan whispers to ya, 'Well, I don't want to bore ya,
But when ya get tired of the Miss So-and-so I got another
    woman for ya.'

Trouble in mind, Lord, trouble in mind,
Lord, take away this trouble in mind.

When the deeds that you do don't add up to zero,
It's what's inside that counts, ask any war hero.
You think you can hide but you're never alone,
Ask Lot what he thought when his wife turned to stone.

Trouble in mind, Lord, trouble in mind,
Lord, take away this trouble in mind.

Here comes Satan, prince of the power of the air,
He's gonna make you a law unto yourself, gonna build a bird's
    nest in your hair.
He's gonna deaden your conscience 'til you worship the work
    of your own hands,
You'll be serving strangers in a strange, forsaken land.

Trouble in mind, Lord, trouble in mind,
Lord, take away this trouble in mind.

Well, your true love has caught you where you don't belong,
You say, 'Baby, everybody's doing it so I guess it can't be
    wrong.'
The truth is far from you, so you know you got to lie,
Then you're all the time defending what you can never justify.

Trouble in mind, Lord, trouble in mind,
Lord, take away this trouble in mind.

So many of my brothers, they still want to be the boss,
They can't relate to the Lord's kingdom, they can't relate to the
    cross.
They self-inflict punishment on their own broken lives,
Put their faith in their possessions, in their jobs or their wives.

Trouble in mind, Lord, trouble in mind,
Lord, take away this trouble in mind.

When my life is over, it'll be like a puff of smoke,
How long must I suffer, Lord, how long must I be provoked?
Satan will give you a little taste, then he'll move in with rapid
    speed,
Lord, keep my blind side covered and see that I don't bleed.

# Saved

**Saved**
**Covenant Woman**
**What Can I Do for You?**
**Solid Rock**
**Pressing On**
**In the Garden**
**Saving Grace**
**Are You Ready?**

# Saved


I was blinded by the devil,
Born already ruined,
Stone-cold dead
As I stepped out of the womb.
By His grace I have been touched,
By His word I have been healed,
By His hand I've been delivered,
By His spirit I've been sealed.

I've been saved
By the blood of the lamb,
Saved
By the blood of the lamb,
Saved,
Saved,
And I'm so glad.
Yes, I'm so glad,
I'm so glad,
So glad,
I want to thank You, Lord,
I just want to thank You, Lord,
Thank You, Lord.

By His truth I can be upright,
By His strength I do endure,
By His power I've been lifted,
In His love I am secure.
He bought me with a price,
Freed me from the pit,
Full of emptiness and wrath
And the fire that burns in it.

I've been saved
By the blood of the lamb,

Saved
By the blood of the lamb,
Saved,
Saved,
And I'm so glad.
Yes, I'm so glad,
I'm so glad,
So glad,
I want to thank You, Lord,
I just want to thank You, Lord,
Thank You, Lord.

Nobody to rescue me,
Nobody would dare,
I was going down for the last time,
But by His mercy I've been spared.
Not by works,
But by faith in Him who called,
For so long I've been hindered,
For so long I've been stalled.

I've been saved
By the blood of the lamb,
Saved
By the blood of the lamb,
Saved,
Saved,
And I'm so glad.
Yes, I'm so glad,
I'm so glad,
So glad,
I want to thank You, Lord,
I just want to thank You, Lord,
Thank You, Lord.

# Covenant Woman

Covenant woman got a contract with the Lord
Way up yonder, great will be her reward.
Covenant woman, shining like a morning star,
I know I can trust you to stay where you are.

And I just got to tell you
I do intend
To stay closer than any friend.
I just got to thank you
Once again
For making your prayers known
Unto heaven for me
And to you, always, so grateful
I will forever be.

I've been broken, shattered like an empty cup.
I'm just waiting on the Lord to rebuild and fill me up
And I know He will do it 'cause He's faithful and He's true,
He must have loved me so much to send me someone as fine
    as you.

And I just got to tell you
I do intend
To stay closer than any friend.
I just got to thank you
Once again
For making your prayers known
Unto heaven for me
And to you, always, so grateful
I will forever be.

Covenant woman, intimate little girl
Who knows those most secret things of me that are hidden
    from the world.

621

You know we are strangers in a land we're passing through.
I'll always be right by your side, I've got a covenant too.

And I just got to tell you
I do intend
To stay closer than any friend.
I just got to thank you
Once again
For making your prayers known
Unto heaven for me
And to you, always, so grateful
I will forever be.

# What Can I Do for You?

You have given everything to me.
What can I do for You?
You have given me eyes to see.
What can I do for You?

Pulled me out of bondage and You made me renewed inside,
Filled up a hunger that had always been denied,
Opened up a door no man can shut and You opened it up so
  wide
And You've chosen me to be among the few.
What can I do for You?

You have laid down Your life for me.
What can I do for You?
You have explained every mystery.
What can I do for You?

Soon as a man is born, you know the sparks begin to fly,
He gets wise in his own eyes and he's made to believe a lie.
Who would deliver him from the death he's bound to die?
Well, You've done it all and there's no more anyone can
  pretend to do.
What can I do for You?

You have given all there is to give.
What can I do for You?
You have given me life to live.
How can I live for You?

I know all about poison, I know all about fiery darts,
I don't care how rough the road is, show me where it starts,
Whatever pleases You, tell it to my heart.
Well, I don't deserve it but I sure did make it through.
What can I do for You?

# Solid Rock

Well, I'm hangin' on to a solid rock
Made before the foundation of the world
And I won't let go, and I can't let go, won't let go
And I can't let go, won't let go, and I can't let go no more.

For me He was chastised, for me He was hated,
For me He was rejected by a world that He created.
Nations are angry, cursed are some,
People are expecting a false peace to come.

Well, I'm hangin' on to a solid rock
Made before the foundation of the world
And I won't let go, and I can't let go, won't let go
And I can't let go, won't let go, and I can't let go no more.

It's the ways of the flesh to war against the spirit
Twenty-four hours a day you can feel it and you can hear it
Using all the devices under the sun.
And He never give up 'til the battle's lost or won.

Well, I'm hangin' on to a solid rock
Made before the foundation of the world
And I won't let go, and I can't let go, won't let go
And I can't let go, won't let go, and I can't let go no more.

# Pressing On

Well I'm pressing on
Yes, I'm pressing on
Well I'm pressing on
To the higher calling of my Lord.

Many try to stop me, shake me up in my mind,
Say, 'Prove to me that He is Lord, show me a sign.'
What kind of sign they need when it all come from within,
When what's lost has been found, what's to come has already
     been?

Well I'm pressing on
Yes, I'm pressing on
Well I'm pressing on
To the higher calling of my Lord.

Shake the dust off of your feet, don't look back.
Nothing now can hold you down, nothing that you lack.
Temptation's not an easy thing, Adam given the devil reign
Because he sinned I got no choice, it run in my vein.

Well I'm pressing on
Yes, I'm pressing on
Well I'm pressing on
To the higher calling of my Lord.

# In the Garden

When they came for Him in the garden, did they know?
When they came for Him in the garden, did they know?
Did they know He was the Son of God, did they know that He
    was Lord?
Did they hear when He told Peter, 'Peter, put up your sword'?
When they came for Him in the garden, did they know?
When they came for Him in the garden, did they know?

When He spoke to them in the city, did they hear?
When He spoke to them in the city, did they hear?
Nicodemus came at night so he wouldn't be seen by men
Saying, 'Master, tell me why a man must be born again.'
When He spoke to them in the city, did they hear?
When He spoke to them in the city, did they hear?

When He healed the blind and crippled, did they see?
When He healed the blind and crippled, did they see?
When He said, 'Pick up your bed and walk, why must you
    criticize?
Same thing My Father do, I can do likewise.'
When He healed the blind and crippled, did they see?
When He healed the blind and crippled, did they see?

Did they speak out against Him, did they dare?
Did they speak out against Him, did they dare?
The multitude wanted to make Him king, put a crown upon His
    head
Why did He slip away to a quiet place instead?
Did they speak out against Him, did they dare?
Did they speak out against Him, did they dare?

When He rose from the dead, did they believe?
When He rose from the dead, did they believe?
He said, 'All power is given to Me in heaven and on earth.'

Did they know right then and there what that power was
   worth?
When He rose from the dead, did they believe?
When He rose from the dead, did they believe?

When He rose from the dead, did they believe?
When He rose from the dead, did they believe?
He said, 'All power is given to Me in heaven and on earth.'
Did they know right then and there what that power was
   worth?
When He rose from the dead, did they believe?
When He rose from the dead, did they believe?

# Saving Grace

If you find it in Your heart, can I be forgiven?
Guess I owe You some kind of apology.
I've escaped death so many times, I know I'm only living
By the saving grace that's over me.

By this time I'd-a thought I would be sleeping
In a pine box for all eternity.
My faith keeps me alive, but I still be weeping
For the saving grace that's over me.

Well, the death of life, then come the resurrection,
Wherever I am welcome is where I'll be.
I put all my confidence in Him, my sole protection
Is the savng grace that's over me.

Well, the devil's shining light, it can be most blinding,
But to search for love, that ain't no more than vanity.
As I look around this world all that I'm finding
Is the saving grace that's over me.

The wicked know no peace and you just can't fake it,
There's only one road and it leads to Calvary.
It gets discouraging at times, but I know I'll make it
By the saving grace that's over me.

# Are You Ready

Are you ready, are you ready?
Are you ready, are you ready?

Are you ready to meet Jesus?
Are you where you ought to be?
Will He know you when He sees you
Or will He say, 'Depart from Me'?

Are you ready, hope you're ready.
Am I ready, am I ready?
Am I ready, am I ready?

Am I ready to lay down my life for the brethren
And to take up my cross?
Have I surrendered to the will of God
Or am I still acting like the boss?

Am I ready, hope I'm ready.

When destruction cometh swiftly
And there's no time to say a fare-thee-well,
Have you decided whether you want to be
In heaven or in hell?

Are you ready, are you ready?

Have you got some unfinished business?
Is there something holding you back?
Are you thinking for yourself
Or are you following the pack?

Are you ready, hope you're ready.
Are you ready?

Are you ready for the judgment?
Are you ready for that terrible swift sword?
Are you ready for Armageddon?
Are you ready for the day of the Lord?

Are you ready, I hope you're ready.

# Shot of Love

**Shot of Love**
**Heart of Mine**
**Lenny Bruce**
**Property of Jesus**
**Watered-Down Love**
**Dead Man, Dead Man**
**In the Summertime**
**Trouble**
**Every Grain of Sand**

Let's Keep It Between Us
The Groom's Still Waiting at the Altar
Caribbean Wind
Need a Woman

# Shot of Love

I need a shot of love, I need a shot of love.

Don't need a shot of heroin to kill my disease,
Don't need a shot of turpentine, only bring me to my knees,
Don't need a shot of codeine to help me to repent
Don't need a shot of whiskey, help me be president.

I need a shot of love, I need a shot of love.

Doctor, can you hear me? I need some Medicaid.
I seen the kingdoms of the world and it's makin' me feel afraid.
What I got ain't painful, it's just bound to kill me dead
Like the men that followed Jesus when they put a price upon
    His head.

I need a shot of love, I need a shot of love.

I don't need no alibi when I'm spending time with you.
I've heard all of them rumors and you have heard 'em too.
Don't show me no picture show or give me no book to read,
It don't satisfy the hurt inside nor the habit that it feeds.

I need a shot of love, I need a shot of love.

Why would I want to take your life?
You've only murdered my father, raped his wife,
Tattooed my babies with a poison pen,
Mocked my God, humiliated my friends.

I need a shot of love, I need a shot of love.

Don't wanna be with nobody tonight
Veronica not around nowhere, Mavis just ain't right.

There's a man that hates me and he's swift, smooth and near,
Am I supposed to set back and wait until he's here?

I need a shot of love, I need a shot of love.

What makes the wind wanna blow tonight?
Don't even feel like crossing the street and my car ain't actin'
  right.
Called home, everybody seemed to have moved away.
My conscience is beginning to bother me today.

I need a shot of love, I need a shot of love.

I need a shot of love, I need a shot of love.
If you're a doctor, I need a shot of love.

# Heart of Mine

Heart of mine be still,
You can play with fire but you'll get the bill.
Don't let her know
Don't let her know that you love her.
Don't be a fool, don't be blind
Heart of mine.

Heart of mine go back home,
You got no reason to wander, you got no reason to roam.
Don't let her see
Don't let her see that you need her.
Don't put yourself over the line
Heart of mine.

Heart of mine go back where you been,
It'll only be trouble for you if you let her in.
Don't let her hear
Don't let her hear you want her.
Don't let her know she's so fine
Heart of mine.

Heart of mine you know that she'll never be true,
She'll only give to others the love that she's gotten from you.
Don't let her know
Don't let her know where you're going.
Don't untie the ties that bind
Heart of mine.

Heart of mine so malicious and so full of guile,
Give you an inch and you'll take a mile.
Don't let yourself fall
Don't let yourself stumble.
If you can't do the time, don't do the crime
Heart of mine.

# Lenny Bruce

Lenny Bruce is dead but his ghost lives on and on
Never did get any Golden Globe award, never made it to
  Synanon.
He was an outlaw, that's for sure,
More of an outlaw than you ever were.
Lenny Bruce is gone but his spirit's livin' on and on.

Maybe he had some problems, maybe some things that he
  couldn't work out
But he sure was funny and he sure told the truth and he knew
  what he was talkin' about.
Never robbed any churches nor cut off any babies' heads,
He just took the folks in high places and he shined a light in
  their beds.
He's on some other shore, he didn't wanna live anymore.

Lenny Bruce is dead but he didn't commit any crime
He just had the insight to rip off the lid before its time.
I rode with him in a taxi once, only for a mile and a half,
Seemed like it took a couple of months.
Lenny Bruce moved on and like the ones that killed him, gone.

They said that he was sick 'cause he didn't play by the rules
He just showed the wise men of his day to be nothing more
  than fools.
They stamped him and they labeled him like they do with pants
  and shirts,
He fought a war on a battlefield where every victory hurts.
Lenny Bruce was bad, he was the brother that you never had.

# Property of Jesus

Go ahead and talk about him because he makes you doubt,
Because he has denied himself the things that you can't live
   without.
Laugh at him behind his back just like the others do,
Remind him of what he used to be when he comes walkin'
   through.

He's the property of Jesus
Resent him to the bone
You got something better
You've got a heart of stone

Stop your conversation when he passes on the street,
Hope he falls upon himself, oh, won't that be sweet
Because he can't be exploited by superstition anymore
Because he can't be bribed or bought by the things that you
   adore.

He's the property of Jesus
Resent him to the bone
You got something better
You've got a heart of stone

When the whip that's keeping you in line doesn't make him
   jump,
Say he's hard-of-hearin', say that he's a chump.
Say he's out of step with reality as you try to test his nerve
Because he doesn't pay no tribute to the king that you serve.

He's the property of Jesus
Resent him to the bone
You got something better
You've got a heart of stone

Say that he's a loser 'cause he got no common sense
Because he don't increase his worth at someone else's
   expense.
Because he's not afraid of trying, 'cause he don't look at you
   and smile,
'Cause he doesn't tell you jokes or fairy tales, say he's got no
   style.

He's the property of Jesus
Resent him to the bone
You got something better
You've got a heart of stone

You can laugh at salvation, you can play Olympic games,
You think that when you rest at last you'll go back from where
   you came.
But you've picked up quite a story and you've changed since
   the womb.
What happened to the real you, you've been captured but by
   whom?

He's the property of Jesus
Resent him to the bone
You got something better
You've got a heart of stone

# Watered-Down Love

Love that's pure hopes all things,
Believes all things, won't pull no strings,
Won't sneak up into your room, tall, dark and handsome,
Capture your heart and hold it for ransom.

You don't want a love that's pure
You wanna drown love
You want a watered-down love

Love that's pure, it don't make no claims,
Intercedes for you 'stead of casting you blame,
Will not deceive you or lead you to transgression,
Won't write it up and make you sign a false confession.

You don't want a love that's pure
You wanna drown love
You want a watered-down love

Love that's pure won't lead you astray,
Won't hold you back, won't mess up your day,
Won't pervert you, corrupt you with stupid wishes,
It don't make you envious, it don't make you suspicious.

You don't want a love that's pure
You wanna drown love
You want a watered-down love

Love that's pure ain't no accident,
Always on time, is always content,
An eternal flame, quietly burning,
Never needs to be proud, restlessly yearning.

You don't want a love that's pure
You wanna drown love
You want a watered-down love

# Dead Man, Dead Man

Uttering idle words from a reprobate mind,
Clinging to strange promises, dying on the vine,
Never bein' able to separate the good from the bad,
Ooh, I can't stand it, I can't stand it,
It's makin' me feel so sad.

Dead man, dead man
When will you arise?
Cobwebs in your mind,
Dust upon your eyes.

Satan got you by the heel, there's a bird's nest in your hair.
Do you have any faith at all? Do you have any love to share?
The way that you hold your head, cursin' God with every
    move,
Ooh, I can't stand it, I can't stand it,
What are you tryin' to prove?

Dead man, dead man
When will you arise?
Cobwebs in your mind,
Dust upon your eyes.

The glamour and the bright lights and the politics of sin,
The ghetto that you build for me is the one you end up in,
The race of the engine that overrules your heart,
Ooh, I can't stand it, I can't stand it,
Pretending that you're so smart.

Dead man, dead man
When will you arise?
Cobwebs in your mind,
Dust upon your eyes.

What are you tryin' to overpower me with, the doctrine or the
    gun?
My back is already to the wall, where can I run?
The tuxedo that you're wearin', the flower in your lapel,
Ooh, I can't stand it, I can't stand it,
You wanna take me down to hell.


Dead man, dead man
When will you arise?
Cobwebs in your mind,
Dust upon your eyes.

# In the Summertime

I was in your presence for an hour or so
Or was it a day? I truly don't know.
Where the sun never set, where the trees hung low
By that soft and shining sea.
Did you respect me for what I did
Or for what I didn't do, or for keeping it hid?
Did I lose my mind when I tried to get rid
Of everything you see?


In the summertime, ah in the summertime,
In the summertime when you were with me.


I got the heart and you got the blood,
We cut through iron and we cut through mud.
Then came the warnin' that was before the flood
That set everybody free.
Fools they made a mock of sin,
Our loyalty they tried to win
But you were closer to me than my next of kin
When they didn't want to know or see.


In the summertime, ah in the summertime,
In the summertime when you were with me.


Strangers, they meddled in our affairs,
Poverty and shame was theirs.
But all that sufferin' was not to be compared
With the glory that is to be.
And I'm still carrying the gift you gave,
It's a part of me now, it's been cherished and saved,

It'll be with me unto the grave
And then unto eternity.

In the summertime, ah in the summertime,
In the summertime when you were with me.

# Trouble

Trouble in the city, trouble in the farm,
You got your rabbit's foot, you got your good-luck charm.
But they can't help you none when there's trouble.

Trouble,
Trouble, trouble, trouble,
Nothin' but trouble.

Trouble in the water, trouble in the air,
Go all the way to the other side of the world, you'll find trouble
    there.
Revolution even ain't no solution for trouble.

Trouble,
Trouble, trouble, trouble,
Nothin' but trouble.

Drought and starvation, packaging of the soul,
Persecution, execution, governments out of control.
You can see the writing on the wall inviting trouble.

Trouble,
Trouble, trouble, trouble,
Nothin' but trouble.

Put your ear to the train tracks, put your ear to the ground,
You ever feel like you're never alone even when there's
    nobody else around?
Since the beginning of the universe man's been cursed by
    trouble.

Trouble,
Trouble, trouble, trouble,
Nothin' but trouble.

Nightclubs of the broken-hearted, stadiums of the damned,
Legislature, perverted nature, doors that are rudely slammed.
Look into infinity, all you see is trouble.

Trouble,
Trouble, trouble, trouble,
Nothin' but trouble.

# Every Grain of Sand

In the time of my confession, in the hour of my deepest need
When the pool of tears beneath my feet flood every newborn
   seed
There's a dyin' voice within me reaching out somewhere,
Toiling in the danger and in the morals of despair.

Don't have the inclination to look back on any mistake,
Like Cain, I now behold this chain of events that I must break.
In the fury of the moment I can see the Master's hand
In every leaf that trembles, in every grain of sand.

Oh, the flowers of indulgence and the weeds of yesteryear,
Like criminals, they have choked the breath of conscience and
   good cheer.
The sun beat down upon the steps of time to light the way
To ease the pain of idleness and the memory of decay.

I gaze into the doorway of temptation's angry flame
And every time I pass that way I always hear my name.
Then onward in my journey I come to understand
That every hair is numbered like every grain of sand.

I have gone from rags to riches in the sorrow of the night
In the violence of a summer's dream, in the chill of a wintry
   light,
In the bitter dance of loneliness fading into space,
In the broken mirror of innocence on each forgotten face.

I hear the ancient footsteps like the motion of the sea
Sometimes I turn, there's someone there, other times it's only
   me.
I am hanging in the balance of the reality of man
Like every sparrow falling, like every grain of sand.

# Let's Keep It Between Us

Let's keep it between us.
These people meddlin' in our affairs, they're not our friends.
Let's keep it between us
Before doors close and our togetherness comes to an end.
They'll turn you against me and me against you 'til we don't
    know who to trust.
Oh, darlin', can we keep it between us?

Let's keep it between us.
We've been through too much tough times that they never
    shared.
They've had nothing to say to us before,
Now all of a sudden it's as if they've always cared.
All we need is honesty, a little humility and trust.
Oh, darlin', can we keep it between us?

I know we're not perfect
Then again, neither are they
They act like we got to live for them as if there just ain't no
    other way
And it's makin' me kind of tired.

Can we just lay back for a moment
Before we wake up and find ourselves in a daze that's got us
    out of our minds?
There must be something we're overlooking here,
We better drop down now and get back behind the lines.
There's some things not fit for human ears, some things don't
    need to be discussed.
Oh, darlin', can we keep it between us?

They'll tell you one thing and me another
'Til we don't know who to trust.
Oh, darlin', can we keep it between us?

Let's keep it between us
Before it all snaps and goes too far.
If we can't deal with this by ourselves,
Tell me we ain't worse off than they think we are.
Backseat drivers don't know the feel of the wheel, but they sure
   know how to make a fuss.
Oh, darlin', can we keep it between us?
Can we keep it between us?

# The Groom's
# Still Waiting at the Altar

Prayed in the ghetto with my face in the cement,
Heard the last moan of a boxer, seen the massacre of the
    innocent,
Felt around for the light switch, became nauseated.
She was walking down the hallway while the walls deteriorated.

East of the Jordan, hard as the Rock of Gibraltar,
I see the burning of the page,
Curtain risin' on a new age,
See the groom still waitin' at the altar.

Try to be pure at heart, they arrest you for robbery,
Mistake your shyness for aloofness, your shyness for snobbery,
Got the message this morning, the one that was sent to me
About the madness of becomin' what one was never meant to
    be.

West of the Jordon, east of the Rock of Gibraltar,
I see the burning of the stage,
Curtain risin' on a new age,
See the groom still waitin' at the altar.

Don't know what I can say about Claudette that wouldn't come
    back to haunt me,
Finally had to give her up 'bout the time she began to want me.
But I know God has mercy on them who are slandered and
    humiliated.
I'd a-done anything for that woman if she didn't make me feel
    so obligated.

West of the Jordan, west of the Rock of Gibraltar,
I see the burning of the cage,
Curtain risin' on a new stage,
See the groom still waitin' at the altar.

Put your hand on my head, baby, do I have a temperature?
I see people who are supposed to know better standin' around
   like furniture.
There's a wall between you and what you want and you got to
   leap it,
Tonight you got the power to take it, tomorrow you won't have
   the power to keep it.

West of the Jordan, east of the Rock of Gibraltar,
I see the burning of the stage,
Curtain risin' on a new age,
See the groom still waitin' at the altar.

Cities on fire, phones out of order,
They're killing nuns and soldiers, there's fighting on the border.
What can I say about Claudette? Ain't seen her since January,
She could be respectably married or running a whorehouse in
   Buenos Aires.

West of the Jordan, west of the Rock of Gibraltar,
I see the burning of the stage,
Curtain risin' on a new age,
See the groom still waitin' at the altar.

# Caribbean Wind

She was the rose of Sharon from paradise lost
From the city of seven hills near the place of the cross.
I was playing a show in Miami in the theater of divine comedy.
Told about Jesus, told about the rain,
She told me about the jungle where her brothers were slain
By the man who invented iron and disappeared so
    mysteriously.

Was she a child or an angel? Did we go too far?
Did we snap at the bait, did we follow a star
Through the hole in the wall to where the long arm of the law
    cannot reach?
Could I been used and played as a pawn?
It certainly was possible as the gay night wore on
When men bathed in perfume and practiced the hoax of free
    speech.

And them Caribbean winds still blow from Nassau to Mexico
Fanning the flames in the furnace of desire
And them distant ships of liberty on them iron waves so bold
    and free,
Bringing everything that's near to me nearer to the fire.

Sea breeze blowin', there's a hellhound loose,
Arabian men who have escaped from the noose,
Preaching faith and salvation, waiting for the night to arise.
He was well connected but her heart was a snare
And she had left him to die in there,
He was goin' down slow, just barely staying alive.

The cry of the peacock, flies buzz my head,
Ceiling fan broken, there's a heat in my bed,
Street band playing 'Nearer My God to Thee.'
We met at the steeple where the mission bells ring,

She said, 'I know what you're thinking, but there ain't a thing
You can do about it, so let us just agree to agree.'

And them Caribbean winds still blow from Nassau to Mexico
Fanning the flames in the furnace of desire
And them distant ships of liberty on them iron waves so bold
    and free,
Bringing everything that's near to me nearer to the fire.

Atlantic City by the cold gray sea
I hear a voice crying 'Daddy,' I always think it's for me,
But it's only the silence in the buttermilk hills that call.
Every new messenger brings evil report
'Bout armies on the march and time that is short
And famines and earthquakes and train wrecks and the tearin'
    down of the walls.
Did you ever have a dream that you couldn't explain?
Did you ever meet your accusers face to face in the rain?
She had lone brown eyes that I won't forget as long as she's
    gone.
I see the screws breaking loose, see the devil pounding on tin,
I see a house in the country being torn from within.
I can hear my ancestors calling from the land far beyond.

And them Caribbean winds still blow from Nassau to Mexico
Fanning the flames in the furnace of desire
And them distant ships of liberty on them iron waves so bold
    and free,
Bringing everything that's near to me nearer to the fire.

# Need a Woman

It's been raining in the trenches all day long, dripping down to
    my clothes,
My patience is wearing thin, got a fire inside my nose.
Searching for the truth the way God designed it,
The truth is I might drown before I find it.

Well I need a woman, yes I do
Need a woman, yes I do.
Someone who can see me as I am,
Sombody who just don't give a damn.
And I want you to be that woman every night,
Be that woman.

I've had my eyes on you baby for about five long years,
You probably don't know me at all, but I have seen your
    laughter and tears.
Now you don't frighten me, my heart is jumping
And you look like it wouldn't hurt you none to have a man who
    could give ya something.

Well I need a woman, oh don't I
Need a woman, bring it home safe at last.
Seen you turn the corner, seen your bootheels spark,
Seen you in the daylight, and watched you in the dark.
And I want you to be that woman, all right
Be that woman every night.

Well, if you believe in something long enough you just naturally
    come to think it's true.
There ain't no wall you can't cross over, ain't no fire you can't
    walk through.
Well, believing is all right, just don't let the wrong people know
    what it's all about.

They might put the evil eye on you, use their hidden powers to
   try to turn you out.

Well I need a woman, just to be my queen.
Need a woman, know what I mean?

# Infidels

**Jokerman**
**License to Kill**
**Sweetheart Like You**
**Neighborhood Bully**
**Union Sundown**
**I and I**
**Man of Peace**
**Don't Fall Apart on Me Tonight**

# Jokerman

Standing on the waters casting your bread
While the eyes of the idol with the iron head are glowing.
Distant ships sailing into the mist,
You were born with a snake in both of your fists while a
  hurricane was blowing.
Freedom just around the corner for you
But with the trust so far off, what good will it do?

Jokerman dance to the nightingale tune,
Bird fly high by the light of the moon,
Oh, oh, oh, Jokerman.

So swiftly the sun sets in the sky,
You rise up and say goodbye to no one.
Fools rush in where angels fear to tread,
Both of their futures, so full of dread, you don't show one.
Shedding off one more layer of skin,
Keeping one step ahead of the persecutor within.

Jokerman dance to the nightingale tune,
Bird fly high by the light of the moon,
Oh, oh, oh, Jokerman.

You're a man of the mountains, you can walk on the clouds,
Manipulator of crowds, you're a dream twister.
You're going to Sodom and Gomorrah
But what do you care? Ain't nobody there would want to marry
  your sister.
Friend to the martyr, a friend to the woman of shame,
You look into the fiery furnace, see the rich man without any
  name.

Jokerman dance to the nightingale tune,
Bird fly high by the light of the moon,
Oh, oh, oh, Jokerman.

Well, the Book of Leviticus and Deuteronomy,
The law of the jungle and the sea are your only teachers.
In the smoke of the twilight on a milk-white steed,
Michelangelo indeed could've carved out your features.
Resting in the fields, far from the turbulent space,
Half asleep near the stars with a small dog licking your face.

Jokerman dance to the nightingale tune,
Bird fly high by the light of the moon,
Oh, oh, oh, Jokerman.

Well, the rifleman's stalking the sick and the lame,
Preacherman seeks the same, who'll get there first is uncertain.
Nightsticks and water cannons, tear gas, padlocks,
Molotov cocktails and rocks behind every curtain,
False-hearted judges dying in the webs that they spin,
Only a matter of time 'til night comes steppin' in.

Jokerman dance to the nightingale tune,
Bird fly high by the light of the moon,
Oh, oh, oh, Jokerman.

It's a shadowy world, skies are slippery gray,
A woman just gave birth to a prince today and dressed him in
    scarlet.
He'll put the priest in his pocket, put the blade to the heat,
Take the motherless children off the street
And place them at the feet of a harlot.
Oh, Jokerman, you know what he wants,
Oh, Jokerman, you don't show any response.

Jokerman dance to the nightingale tune,
Bird fly high by the light of the moon,
Oh, oh, oh, Jokerman.

# License to Kill

Man thinks 'cause he rules the earth he can do with it as he
    please
And if things don't change soon, he will.
Oh, man has invented his doom,
First step was touching the moon.

Now, there's a woman on my block,
She just sit there as the night grows still.
She say who gonna take away his license to kill?

Now, they take him and they teach him and they groom him for
    life
And they set him on a path where he's bound to get ill,
Then they bury him with stars,
Sell his body like they do used cars.

Now, there's a woman on my block,
She just sit there facin' the hill.
She say who gonna take away his license to kill?

Now, he's hell-bent for destruction, he's afraid and confused,
And his brain has been mismanaged with great skill.
All he believes are his eyes
And his eyes, they just tell him lies.

But there's a woman on my block,
Sitting there in a cold chill.
She say who gonna take away his license to kill?

Ya may be a noisemaker, spirit maker,
Heartbreaker, backbreaker,
Leave no stone unturned.
May be an actor in a plot,

That might be all that you got
'Til your error you clearly learn.

Now he worships at an altar of a stagnant pool
And when he sees his reflection, he's fulfilled.
Oh, man is opposed to fair play,
He wants it all and he wants it his way.

Now, there's a woman on my block,
She just sit there as the night grows still.
She say who gonna take away his license to kill?

# Sweetheart Like You

Well, the pressure's down, the boss ain't here,
He gone North, he ain't around,
They say that vanity got the best of him
But he sure left here after sundown.
By the way, that's a cute hat,
And that smile's so hard to resist
But what's a sweetheart like you doin' in a dump like this?

You know, I once knew a woman who looked like you,
She wanted a whole man, not just a half,
She used to call me sweet daddy when I was only a child,
You kind of remind me of her when you laugh.
In order to deal in this game, got to make the queen disappear,
It's done with a flick of the wrist.
What's a sweetheart like you doin' in a dump like this?

You know, a woman like you should be at home,
That's where you belong,
Watching out for someone who loves you true
Who would never do you wrong.
Just how much abuse will you be able to take?
Well, there's no way to tell by that first kiss.
What's a sweetheart like you doin' in a dump like this?

You know you can make a name for yourself,
You can hear them tires squeal,
You can be known as the most beautiful woman
Who ever crawled across cut glass to make a deal.

You know, news of you has come down the line
Even before ya came in the door.
They say in your father's house, there's many mansions
Each one of them got a fireproof floor.
Snap out of it, baby, people are jealous of you,

They smile to your face, but behind your back they hiss.
What's a sweetheart like you doin' in a dump like this?

Got to be an important person to be in here, honey,
Got to have done some evil deed,
Got to have your own harem when you come in the door,
Got to play your harp until your lips bleed.

They say that patriotism is the last refuge
To which a scoundrel clings.
Steal a little and they throw you in jail,
Steal a lot and they make you king.
There's only one step down from here, baby,
It's called the land of permanent bliss.
What's a sweetheart like you doin' in a dump like this?

# Neighborhood Bully

Well, the neighborhood bully, he's just one man,
His enemies say he's on their land.
They got him outnumbered about a million to one,
He got no place to escape to, no place to run.
He's the neighborhood bully.

The neighborhood bully just lives to survive,
He's criticized and condemned for being alive.
He's not supposed to fight back, he's supposed to have thick
   skin,
He's supposed to lay down and die when his door is kicked in.
He's the neighborhood bully.

The neighborhood bully been driven out of every land,
He's wandered the earth an exiled man.
Seen his family scattered, his people hounded and torn,
He's always on trial for just being born.
He's the neighborhood bully.

Well, he knocked out a lynch mob, he was criticized,
Old women condemned him, said he should apologize.
Then he destroyed a bomb factory, nobody was glad.
The bombs were meant for him. He was supposed to feel bad.
He's the neighborhood bully.

Well, the chances are against it and the odds are slim
That he'll live by the rules that the world makes for him,
'Cause there's a noose at his neck and a gun at his back
And a license to kill him is given out to every maniac.
He's the neighborhood bully.

He got no allies to really speak of.
What he gets he must pay for, he don't get it out of love.
He buys obsolete weapons and he won't be denied

But no one sends flesh and blood to fight by his side.
He's the neighborhood bully.

Well, he's surrounded by pacifists who all want peace,
They pray for it nightly that the bloodshed must cease.
Now, they wouldn't hurt a fly. To hurt one they would weep.
They lay and they wait for this bully to fall asleep.
He's the neighborhood bully.

Every empire that's enslaved him is gone,
Egypt and Rome, even the great Babylon.
He's made a garden of paradise in the desert sand,
In bed with nobody, under no one's command.
He's the neighborhood bully.

Now his holiest books have been trampled upon,
No contract he signed was worth what it was written on.
He took the crumbs of the world and he turned it into wealth,
Took sickness and disease and he turned it into health.
He's the neighborhood bully.

What's anybody indebted to him for?
Nothin', they say. He just likes to cause war.
Pride and prejudice and superstition indeed,
They wait for this bully like a dog waits to feed.
He's the neighborhood bully.

What has he done to wear so many scars?
Does he change the course of rivers? Does he pollute the moon
   and stars?
Neighborhood bully, standing on the hill,
Running out the clock, time standing still,
Neighborhood bully.

# Union Sundown

Well, my shoes, they come from Singapore,
My flashlight's from Taiwan,
My tablecloth's from Malaysia,
My belt buckle's from the Amazon.
You know, this shirt I wear comes from the Philippines
And the car I drive is a Chevrolet,
It was put together down in Argentina
By a guy makin' thirty cents a day.

Well, it's sundown on the union
And what's made in the USA
Sure was a good idea
'Til greed got in the way.

Well, this silk dress is from Hong Kong
And the pearls are from Japan.
Well, the dog collar's from India
And the flower pot's from Pakistan.
All the furniture, it says 'Made in Brazil'
Where a woman, she slaved for sure
Bringin' home thirty cents a day to a family of twelve,
You know, that's a lot of money to her.

Well, it's sundown on the union
And what's made in the USA
Sure was a good idea
'Til greed got in the way.

Well, you know, lots of people complainin' that there is no
    work.
I say, 'Why you say that for
When nothin' you got is US-made?'
They don't make nothin' here no more,
You know, capitalism is above the law.

It say, 'It don't count 'less it sells.'
When it costs too much to build it at home
You just build it cheaper someplace else.

Well, it's sundown on the union
And what's made in the USA
Sure was a good idea
'Til greed got in the way.

Well, the job that you used to have,
They gave it to somebody down in El Salvador.
The unions are big business, friend,
And they're goin' out like a dinosaur.
They used to grow food in Kansas
Now they want to grow it on the moon and eat it raw.
I can see the day coming when even your garden
Is gonna be against the law.

Well, it's sundown on the union
And what's made in the USA
Sure was a good idea
'Til greed got in the way.

Democracy don't rule the world,
You'd better get that in your head.
This world is ruled by violence
But I guess that's better left unsaid.
From Broadway to the Milky Way,
That's a lot of territory indeed
And a man's gonna do what he has to do
When he's got a hungry mouth to feed.

Well, it's sundown on the union
And what's made in the USA

Sure was a good idea
'Til greed got in the way.

# I and I

Been so long since a strange woman has slept in my bed.
Look how sweet she sleeps, how free must be her dreams.
In another lifetime she must have owned the world, or been
  faithfully wed
To some righteous king who wrote psalms beside moonlit
  streams.

I and I
In creation where one's nature neither honors nor forgives.
I and I
One says to the other, no man sees my face and lives.

Think I'll go out and go for a walk,
Not much happenin' here, nothin' ever does.
Besides, if she wakes up now, she'll just want me to talk
I got nothin' to say, 'specially about whatever was.

I and I
In creation where one's nature neither honors nor forgives.
I and I
One says to the other, no man sees my face and lives.

Took an untrodden path once, where the swift don't win the
  race,
It goes to the worthy, who can divide the word of truth.
Took a stranger to teach me, to look into justice's beautiful face
And to see an eye for an eye and a tooth for a tooth.

I and I
In creation where one's nature neither honors nor forgives.
I and I
One says to the other, no man sees my face and lives.

Outside of two men on a train platform there's nobody in sight,
They're waiting for spring to come, smoking down the track.
The world could come to an end tonight, but that's all right.
She should still be there sleepin' when I get back.


I and I
In creation where one's nature neither honors nor forgives.
I and I
One says to the other, no man sees my face and lives.


Noontime, and I'm still pushin' myself along the road, the
    darkest part,
Into the narrow lanes, I can't stumble or stay put.
Someone else is speakin' with my mouth, but I'm listening only
    to my heart.
I've made shoes for everyone, even you, while I still go
    barefoot.


I and I
In creation where one's nature neither honors nor forgives.
I and I
One says to the other, no man sees my face and lives.

# Man of Peace

Look out your window, baby, there's a scene you'd like to
  catch,
The band is playing 'Dixie,' a man got his hand outstretched.
Could be the Führer
Could be the local priest.
You know sometimes Satan comes as a man of peace.

He got a sweet gift of gab, he got a harmonious tongue,
He knows every song of love that ever has been sung.
Good intentions can be evil,
Both hands can be full of grease.
You know that sometimes Satan comes as a man of a peace.

Well, first he's in the background, then he's in the front,
Both eyes are looking like they're on a rabbit hunt.
Nobody can see through him,
No, not even the Chief of Police.
You know that sometimes Satan comes as a man of peace.

Well, he catch you when you're hoping for a glimpse of the
  sun,
Catch you when your troubles feel like they weigh a ton.
He could be standing next to you,
The person that you'd notice least.
I hear that sometimes Satan comes as a man of peace.

Well, he can be fascinating, he can be dull,
He can ride down Niagara Falls in the barrels of your skull.
I can smell something cooking,
I can tell there's going to be a feast.
You know that sometimes Satan comes as a man of peace.

He's a great humanitarian, he's a great philanthropist,
He knows just where to touch you, honey, and how you like to
  be kissed.

He'll put both his arms around you,
You can feel the tender touch of the beast.
You know that sometimes Satan comes as a man of peace.

Well, the howling wolf will howl tonight, the king snake will
   crawl,
Trees that've stood for a thousand years suddenly will fall.
Wanna get married? Do it now,
Tomorrow all activity will cease.
You know that sometimes Satan comes as a man of peace.

Somewhere Mama's weeping for her blue-eyed boy,
She's holding them little white shoes and that little broken toy
And he's following a star,
The same one them three men followed from the East.
I hear that sometimes Satan comes as a man of peace.

# Don't Fall Apart on Me Tonight

Just a minute before you leave, girl,
Just a minute before you touch the door.
What is it that you're trying to achieve, girl?
Do you think we can talk about it some more?
You know, the streets are filled with vipers
Who've lost all ray of hope,
You know, it ain't even safe no more
In the palace of the Pope.

Don't fall apart on me tonight,
I just don't think that I could handle it.
Don't fall apart on me tonight,
Yesterday's just a memory,
Tomorrow is never what it's supposed to be
And I need you, yeah.

Come over here from over there, girl,
Sit down here. You can have my chair.
I can't see us goin' anywhere, girl.
The only place open is a thousand miles away and I can't take
    you there.
I wish I'd have been a doctor,
Maybe I'd have saved some life that had been lost,
Maybe I'd have done some good in the world
'Stead of burning every bridge I crossed.

Don't fall apart on me tonight,
I just don't think that I could handle it.
Don't fall apart on me tonight,
Yesterday's just a memory,
Tomorrow is never what it's supposed to be
And I need you, oh, yeah.

I ain't too good at conversation, girl,
So you might not know exactly how I feel,
But if I could, I'd bring you to the mountaintop, girl,
And build you a house made out of stainless steel.
But it's like I'm stuck inside a painting
That's hanging in the Louvre,
My throat start to tickle and my nose itches
But I know that I can't move.

Don't fall apart on me tonight,
I just don't think that I could handle it.
Don't fall apart on me tonight,
Yesterday's gone but the past lives on,
Tomorrow's just one step beyond
And I need you, oh, yeah.

Who are these people who are walking towards you?
Do you know them or will there be a fight?
With their humorless smiles so easy to see through,
Can they tell you what's wrong from what's right?

Do you remember St James Street
Where you blew Jackie P.'s mind?
You were so fine, Clark Gable would have fell at your feet
And laid his life on the line.

Let's try to get beneath the surface waste, girl,
No more booby traps and bombs,
No more decadence and charm,
N more affection that's misplaced, girl,
No more mudcake creatures lying in your arms.
What about that millionaire with the drumsticks in his pants?
He looked so baffled and so bewildered
When he played and we didn't dance.

Don't fall apart on me tonight,
I just don't think that I could handle it.
Don't fall apart on me tonight,
Yesterday's just a memory,
Tomorrow is never what it's supposed to be
And I need you, yeah.

# Empire Burlesque

**Tight Connection to My Heart**
**(Has Anybody Seen My Love)**
**I'll Remember You**
**Seeing the Real You at Last**
**Clean-Cut Kid**
**Never Gonna Be the Same Again**
**Trust Yourself**
**When the Night Comes Falling from the Sky**
**Emotionally Yours**
**Something's Burning, Baby**
**Dark Eyes**

# Tight Connection to My Heart
# (Has Anybody Seen My Love)


Well, I had to move fast
And I couldn't with you around my neck.
I said I'd send for you and I did
What did you expect?
My hands are sweating
And we haven't even started yet.
I'll go along with the charade
Until I can think my way out.
I know it was all a big joke
Whatever it was about.
Someday maybe
I'll remember to forget.


I'm gonna get my coat,
I feel the breath of a storm.
There's something I've got to do tonight,
You go inside and stay warm.


Has anybody seen my love,
Has anybody seen my love,
Has anybody seen my love.
I don't know,
Has anybody seen my love?


You want to talk to me,
Go ahead and talk.
Whatever you got to say to me
Won't come as any shock.
I must be guilty of something,
You just whisper it into my ear.
Madame Butterfly
She lulled me to sleep,
In a town without pity

Where the water runs deep.
She said, 'Be easy, baby,
There ain't nothin' worth stealin' in here.'

You're the one I've been looking for,
You're the one that's got the key,
But I can't figure out whether I'm too good for you
Or you're too good for me.

Has anybody seen my love,
Has anybody seen my love,
Has anybody seen my love.
I don't know,
Has anybody seen my love?

Well, they're not showing any lights tonight
And there's no moon.
There's just a hot-blooded singer
Singing 'Memphis in June,'
While they're beatin' the devil out of a guy
Who's wearing a powder-blue wig.
Later he'll be shot
For resisting arrest,
I can still hear his voice crying
In the wilderness.
What looks large from a distance,
Close up ain't never that big.

Never could learn to drink that blood
And call it wine,
Never could learn to hold you, love,
And call you mine.

# I'll Remember You

I'll remember you
When I've forgotten all the rest,
You to me were true,
You to me were the best.
When there is no more,
You cut to the core
Quicker than anyone I knew.
When I'm all alone
In the great unknown,
I'll remember you.

I'll remember you
At the end of the trail,
I had so much left to do,
I had so little time to fail.
There's some people that
You don't forget,
Even though you've only seen'm
One time or two.
When the roses fade
And I'm in the shade,
I'll remember you.

Didn't I, didn't I try to love you?
Didn't I, didn't I try to care?
Didn't I sleep, didn't I weep beside you
With the rain blowing in your hair?

I'll remember you
When the wind blows through the piney wood.
It was you who came right through,
It was you who understood.
Though I'd never say
That I done it the way

That you'd have liked me to.
In the end,
My dear sweet friend,
I'll remember you.

# Seeing the Real You at Last

Well, I thought that the rain would cool things down
But it looks like it don't.
I'd like to get you to change your mind
But it looks like you won't.

From now on I'll be busy,
Ain't goin' nowhere fast.
I'm just glad it's over
And I'm seeing the real you at last.

Well, didn't I risk my neck for you,
Didn't I take chances?
Didn't I rise above it all for you,
The most unfortunate circumstances?

Well, I have had some rotten nights,
Didn't think that they would pass.
I'm just thankful and grateful
To be seeing the real you at last.

I'm hungry and I'm irritable
And I'm tired of this bag of tricks.
At one time there was nothing wrong with me
That you could not fix.

Well, I sailed through the storm
Strapped to the mast,
But the time has come
And I'm seeing the real you at last.

When I met you, baby,
You didn't show no visible scars.
You could ride like Annie Oakley,
You could shoot like Belle Starr.

Well, I don't mind a reasonable amount of trouble,
Trouble always comes to pass
But all I care about now
Is that I'm seeing the real you at last.

Well, I'm gonna quit this baby talk now,
I guess I should have known.
I got troubles, I think maybe you got troubles,
I think maybe we'd better leave each other alone.

Whatever you gonna do,
Please do it fast.
I'm still trying to get used to
Seeing the real you at last.

# Clean-Cut Kid

Everybody wants to know why he couldn't adjust
Adjust to what, a dream that bust?

He was a clean-cut kid
But they made a killer out of him,
That's what they did

They said what's up is down, they said what isn't is
They put ideas in his head he thought were his

He was a clean-cut kid
But they made a killer out of him,
That's what they did

He was on the baseball team, he was in the marching band
When he was ten years old he had a watermelon stand

He was a clean-cut kid
But they made a killer out of him,
That's what they did

He went to church on Sunday, he was a Boy Scout
For his friends he would turn his pockets inside out

He was a clean-cut kid
But they made a killer out of him,
That's what they did

They said, 'Listen boy, you're just a pup'
They sent him to a napalm health spa to shape up

They gave him dope to smoke, drinks and pills,
A jeep to drive, blood to spill

They said 'Congratulations, you got what it takes'
They sent him back into the rat race without any brakes

He was a clean-cut kid
But they made a killer out of him,
That's what they did

He bought the American dream but it put him in debt
The only game he could play was Russian roulette

He drank Coca-Cola, he was eating Wonder Bread,
Ate Burger Kings, he was well fed

He went to Hollywood to see Peter O'Toole
He stole a Rolls Royce and drove it in a swimming pool

They took a clean-cut kid
And they made a killer out of him,
That's what they did

He could've sold insurance, owned a restaurant or bar
Could've been an accountant or a tennis star

He was wearing boxing gloves, took a dive one day
Off the Golden Gate Bridge into China Bay

His mama walks the floor, his daddy weeps and moans
They gotta sleep together in a home they don't own

They took a clean-cut kid
And they made a killer out of him,
That's what they did

Well, everybody's asking why he couldn't adjust
All he ever wanted was somebody to trust

They took his head and turned it inside out
He never did know what it was all about

He had a steady job, he joined the choir
He never did plan to walk the high wire

They took a clean-cut kid
And they made a killer out of him,
That's what they did

# Never Gonna Be
# the Same Again

Now you're here beside me, baby,
You're a living dream.
And every time you get this close
It makes me want to scream.
You touched me and you knew
That I was warm for you and then,
I ain't never gonna be the same again.

Sorry if I hurt you, baby,
Sorry if I did.
Sorry if I touched the place
Where your secrets are hid.
But you meant more than everything,
And I could not pretend,
I ain't never gonna be the same again.

You give me something to think about, baby,
Every time I see ya.
Don't worry, baby, I don't mind leaving,
I'd just like it to be my idea.

You taught me how to love you, baby,
You taught me, oh, so well.
Now, I can't go back to what was, baby,
I can't unring the bell.
You took my reality
And cast it to the wind
And I ain't never gonna be the same again.

# Trust Yourself

Trust yourself,
Trust yourself to do the things that only you know best.
Trust yourself,
Trust yourself to do what's right and not be second-guessed.
Don't trust me to show you beauty
When beauty may only turn to rust.
If you need somebody you can trust, trust yourself.

Trust yourself,
Trust yourself to know the way that will prove true in the end.
Trust yourself,
Trust yourself to find the path where there is no if and when.
Don't trust me to show you the truth
When the truth may only be ashes and dust.
If you want somebody you can trust, trust yourself.

Well, you're on your own, you always were,
In a land of wolves and thieves.
Don't put your hope in ungodly man
Or be a slave to what somebody else believes.

Trust yourself
And you won't be disappointed when vain people let you
   down.
Trust yourself
And look not for answers where no answers can be found.
Don't trust me to show you love
When my love may be only lust.
If you want somebody you can trust, trust yourself.

# When the Night
# Comes Falling from the Sky

Look out across the fields, see me returning,
Smoke is in your eye, you draw a smile.
From the fireplace where my letters to you are burning,
You've had time to think about it for a while.

Well, I've walked two hundred miles, now look me over,
It's the end of the chase and the moon is high.
It won't matter who loves who,
You'll love me or I'll love you
When the night comes falling from the sky.

I can see through your walls and I know you're hurting,
Sorrow covers you up like a cape.
Only yesterday I know that you've been flirting
With disaster that you managed to escape.

I can't provide for you no easy answers,
Who are you that I should have to lie?
You'll know all about it, love,
It'll fit you like a glove
When the night comes falling from the sky.

I can hear your trembling heart beat like a river,
You must have been protecting someone last time I called.
I've never asked you for nothing you couldn't deliver,
I've never asked you to set yourself up for a fall.

I saw thousands who could have overcome the darkness,
For the love of a lousy buck, I've watched them die.
Stick around, baby, we're not through,
Don't look for me, I'll see you
When the night comes falling from the sky.

In your teardrops, I can see my own reflection,
It was on the northern border of Texas where I crossed the line.
I don't want to be a fool starving for affection,
I don't want to drown in someone else's wine.

For all eternity I think I will remember
That icy wind that's howling in your eye.
You will seek me and you'll find me
In the wasteland of your mind
When the night comes falling from the sky.

Well, I sent you my feelings in a letter
But you were gambling for support.
This time tomorrow I'll know you better
When my memory is not so short.

This time I'm asking for freedom,
Freedom from a world which you deny.
And you'll give it to me now,
I'll take it anyhow
When the night comes falling from the sky.

# Emotionally Yours

Come baby, find me, come baby, remind me of where I once
    begun.
Come baby, show me, show me you know me, tell me you're
    the one.
I could be learning, you could be yearning to see behind closed
    doors.
But I will always be emotionally yours.

Come baby, rock me, come baby, lock me into the shadows of
    your heart.
Come baby, teach me, come baby, reach me, let the music
    start.
I could be dreaming but I keep believing you're the one I'm
    livin' for.
And I will always be emotionally yours.

It's like my whole life never happened,
When I see you, it's as if I never had a thought.
I know this dream, it might be crazy,
But it's only one I've got.

Come baby, shake me, come baby, take me, I would be
    satisfied.
Come baby, hold me, come baby, help me, my arms are open
    wide.
I could be unraveling wherever I'm traveling, even to foreign
    shores.
But I will always be emotionally yours.

# Something's Burning, Baby

Something is burning, baby, are you aware?
Something is the matter, baby, there's smoke in your hair
Are you still my friend, baby, show me a sign
Is the love in your heart for me turning blind?

You've been avoiding the main streets for a long, long while
The truth that I'm seeking is in your missing file
What's your position, baby, what's going on?
Why is the light in your eyes nearly gone?

I know everything about this place, or so it seems
Am I no longer a part of your plans or your dreams?
Well, it is so obvious that something has changed
What's happening, baby, to make you act so strange?

Something is burning, baby, here's what I say
Even the bloodhounds of London couldn't find you today
I see the shadow of a man, baby, makin' you blue
Who is he, baby, and what's he to you?

We've reached the edge of the road, baby, where the pasture
    begins
Where charity is supposed to cover up a multitude of sins
But where do you live, baby, and where is the light?
Why are your eyes just staring off in the night?

I can feel it in the night when I think of you
I can feel it in the light and it's got to be true
You can't live by bread alone, you won't be satisfied
You can't roll away the stone if your hands are tied

Got to start someplace, baby, can you explain?
Please don't fade away on me, baby, like the midnight train

Answer me, baby, a casual look will do
Just what in the world has come over you?

I can feel it in the wind and it's upside down
I can feel it in the dust as I get off the bus on the outskirts of
  town
I've had the Mexico City blues since the last hairpin curve
I don't wanna see you bleed, I know what you need but it ain't
  what you deserve

Something is burning, baby, something's in flames
There's a man going 'round calling names
Ring down when you're ready, baby, I'm waiting for you
I believe in the impossible, you know that I do

# Dark Eyes

Oh, the gentlemen are talking and the midnight moon is on the
   riverside,
They're drinking up and walking and it is time for me to slide.
I live in another world where life and death are memorized,
Where the earth is strung with lovers' pearls and all I see are
   dark eyes.

A cock is crowing far away and another soldier's deep in
   prayer,
Some mother's child has gone astray, she can't find him
   anywhere.
But I can hear another drum beating for the dead that rise,
Whom nature's beast fears as they come and all I see are dark
   eyes.

They tell me to be discreet for all intended purposes,
They tell me revenge is sweet and from where they stand, I'm
   sure it is.
But I feel nothing for their game where beauty goes
   unrecognized,
All I feel is heat and flame and all I see are dark eyes.

Oh, the French girl, she's in paradise and a drunken man is at
   the wheel,
Hunger pays a heavy price to the falling gods of speed and
   steel.
Oh, time is short and the days are sweet and passion rules the
   arrow that flies,
A million faces at my feet but all I see are dark eyes.

Morris Zollar wants to No HOO-HOO-WOO
  Barry Goldsmith is and How far is
 it to the nearest tatoo parlour! (jump)

OK. Tell Morris Zollar that HE CAN'T
HAVE No "Potato house" but if he
wantza pancake ... (yeah)
   But
   ~~~~ what if he does want a pancake?

OK, so tell Morris Zollar that the service is out
  and the Nicks are OVER THE Limit/
        (wraaa a)

     WALL WALL, see how smaLL
     The (WOILD) is (AFTAH) ALL
     is SAID And done, it tiz —

              M

            (This makes/sense,
                  perfet
               Morris

# Index

The song or poem titles appear in capital letters;
first lines or key lines in upper and lower case letters.

709

712

714

716

718